BEDOUIN OF THE NEGEV

TO

DALIA

BEDOUIN OF THE NEGEV

by

EMANUEL MARX

FREDERICK A. PRAEGER, *Publishers*
New York · Washington

BOOKS THAT MATTER

Published in the United States of America in 1967
by Frederick A. Praeger, Inc., Publishers
111 Fourth Avenue, New York, N.Y. 10003

Library of Congress Catalog Card Number: 67-19214

Printed in Great Britain

Contents

Illustrations

PLATES

MAPS

DIAGRAMS

TABLES

TABULAR APPENDICES

ABBREVIATIONS

AA	*American Anthropologist*
IAE	*International Archives of Ethnography*
IMJ	*Israel Medical Journal*
JRAI	*Journal of the Royal Anthropological Institute*
New East	*Hamizraḥ Heḥadash: The New East. Quarterly of the Israel Oriental Society*
New Outlook	*New Outlook: Middle East Monthly*
SWJA	*South Western Journal of Anthropology*

Preface

BEDOUIN life has fascinated me for many years; perhaps I am a romantic at heart. My first chance to become acquainted with it came in 1955, when a grant from the Israeli Prime Minister's Office enabled me to spend three months in the Negev, to collect material for an M.A. thesis at the Hebrew University, Jerusalem, on Bedouin social structure. Parts of the thesis were published, in Hebrew, in the *Journal of the Israel Oriental Society* (*The New East*, vol. 7, no. 2, 1956 and vol. 8, no. 1, 1957). I felt, at the time, that a longer period of field work among the Bedouin was needed, but saw little hope of carrying out this project.

Then in 1959 a British Council scholarship gave me a year of post-graduate study in Social Anthropology at the University of Manchester. I was greatly gratified when, at the end of my stay, the University offered to finance field work among the Bedouin. I spent fifteen months in the Negev, from October 1960 to December the following year, for the greater part of which I worked with the Abu Gweʿid tribe east of Beersheba. For most of the two years that followed, I wrote up the material as a Ph.D. thesis at Manchester.

The argument presented in this book is essentially that of the thesis and thus reflects Bedouin society as it was in 1960–1, but I have been able to sharpen it a little by using additional material collected in 1963, when a grant from Hayter funds and a loan from the Israeli Centre for Anthropological Research permitted me to spend three more months among the Bedouin, from August to October. I wish to express my thanks to all the institutions that have helped to finance this work, and in particular to the University of Manchester, which provided the major part.

I would like here to express thanks to my teachers at the Hebrew University, who helped to shape my interests and thinking. Professor S. N. Eisenstadt and Dr Y. Garber-Talmon, of the Department of Sociology, have always been helpful and kind, besides introducing me to sociology. Professors D. Ayalon and U. Heyd turned my general interests in Middle Eastern studies into a permanent fascination with the subject. I am also very grateful to the Adviser on Arab Affairs in the Israeli Prime Minister's Office, and to my former colleagues there, for the many ways in which they have helped me in my work. The British Council not only granted me a scholarship, but its officers have also been helpful in a most considerate and thoughtful manner. Mr R. A. C. Duvivier and Miss O. A. Henry of the Manchester Area Office have been most kind, and were never too busy to tender advice and assistance.

The Department of Social Anthropology at Manchester University under Professor Gluckman has for the last four years been more than a place of study and work for me; it was rather like home. Here I and others were subtly weaned of our sociological theories; and a desire for independent thought about society was inculcated in us. We learned to delight in detailed facts and figures not for their own sake but because only they can provide a sound basis for theory. Dr Emrys Peters, who supervised the preparation of my Ph.D. thesis, has been a great teacher and friend, and always gave unstintingly of his time and thought. I feel that he pushed, rather than led, me on to many of the ideas expressed here, and not only those explicitly acknowledged in footnotes. I am deeply grateful for his help. I also owe much to many heated discussions with my friend Richard Werbner; I sincerely hope we shall continue them.

From among my friends in the Negev I would like to single out two who have been unfailingly helpful: Sasson Bar-Zvi, who became Military Governor of the Negev in 1961, knows more about Bedouin culture than I can ever aspire to, and has always been ready to share his wide knowledge; and Ḥmēd Muḥēsin Abu Gweʿid, who has been a good friend and has taught me much about his society. I have also been treated kindly and hospitably by many members of Abu Gweʿid tribe and by other Bedouin. I am indebted to the writings of ʿĀref al-ʿĀref, formerly a District Officer in Beersheba, who collected customs and historical traditions with meticulous regard to detail. The Military Governor of the Negev and his staff took an interest in my work, assisted me in every way, and permitted me to use their archives. Government and Trade Union officials have been invariably helpful in supplying information on their activities among the Bedouin.

Professor E. E. Evans-Pritchard of Oxford University examined my Ph.D. thesis and let me have a list of corrections. Dr

I. M. Lewis, who read the manuscript for the Press, kindly made a number of valuable suggestions. I have also incorporated corrections suggested by Mr Y. Orev of Beersheba and Mr A. Efrat of Kibuts Doroth, who both read the chapters on environment. Professor M. Gluckman kindly offered to edit the book, and his detailed advice guided me in preparing the final revision. I am grateful to Mrs J. M. Sutcliffe of the University Press, for the efficient manner in which she dealt with the manuscript, and to Mr W. J. Smith for redrawing the maps and diagrams.

Above all, I wish to acknowledge my greatest debts: to our parents who, if they did not approve of our nomadic way of life, never said so; and to my wife, Dalia, the main sufferer of my anthropological interests, to whom I wish, therefore, to dedicate this book.

* * * *

Adopting Professor M. Gluckman's maxim: 'follow your material, wherever it may lead you', I have tried neither to put the material into ready-made sociological moulds, nor to construct sociological models, those short-cuts to reality. Both these procedures would force me to disregard part of the evidence. By doing this, not only would much of the wealth of evidence be suppressed, but usually fundamental facts which might lead to different interpretations would also go overboard. For who is competent to judge whether one set of facts represents reality better than another? In practice, facts which fit a scheme of analysis once adopted, are included; those that do not are often discarded.

My account begins with the environmental factors affecting the lives of the Negev Bedouin. I then move on to the political organization of a single tribe, and from there I discuss small-scale groups and relations. This does not imply that the analysis is mainly concerned with groups and institutions, and the manner in which they affect the lives of people. The converse is true: this analysis deals only with people. It observes individuals, tries to learn about their needs (or interests), and finds out how they are able to implement some of them by interacting with other people. It also deals with the complications that arise when, as so frequently happens, interests come into conflict. And, a most crucial point, the analysis shows how people adapt their relationships to suit rapidly changing conditions.

The aim of my analysis throughout is to present a picture of

Bedouin life that approximates to reality as much as possible, yet that treats the facts systematically. I try to bring out, rather than to obscure, the complexities of social life. This treatment shows that the people constituting a single tribe occupy a great variety of interlinked and interdependent positions. Only by considering how all the positions are related to one another, can one gain insight, on the one hand, into a specific social situation and, on the other hand, chart interrelations between different aspects of the social framework. Such connections are found to exist between the administrative order, land ownership, the composition of camps and movement cycles, political organization and leadership, and patterns of marriage.

The analysis includes only as much of the ethnological material as I considered absolutely necessary, although the temptation to describe Bedouin life and events more fully and to draw biblical comparisons, was hard to resist. A whole area of social life, that of competition for status, has not been covered in the analysis. Originally I had planned to concentrate on this aspect, and hope I shall at a later stage have leisure to work out my material about it.

* * * *

Transliteration of spoken Arabic is risky, for however one goes about it, some demands remain unsatisfied. I have tried to effect a compromise solution by transliterating the Arabic consonants according to literary usage, and the vowels as pronounced by the Bedouin. The consonants are transliterated as follows:

Arabic	*Transliterated*	*Arabic*	*Transliterated*
ا	'	ض	ḍ
ب	b	ط	ṭ
ت	t	ظ	ẓ
ث	th	ع	ʻ
ج	g	غ	gh
ح	ḥ	ف	f
خ	kh	ق	q
د	d	ك	k
ذ	dh	ل	l
ر	r	م	m
ز	z	ن	n
س	s	ه	h
ش	sh	و	w
ص	ṣ	ي	i or y

The consonants in Bedouin dialect are pronounced roughly as in literary Arabic, except for the 'q', which is pronounced as 'g' in gale. The consonants are stated even where they are muted. On the other hand, vowels have been put down as pronounced. They are transliterated as pronounced in Italian; thus 'ā' is pronounced as in part, 'ū' as in moot, etc. There was no need, of course, exactly to transliterate Arabic words commonly used in English, such as Sheikh.

E. M.

1966

PART ONE

Environment

B

CHAPTER 1

Ecology

AMONG Israel's inhabitants in 1960, about 230,000 were officially described as 'non-Jewish', practically all of whom remained from the indigenous Arab population of former Palestine. The census classified 22,700 of the non-Jews as Bedouin. The Arabic term *badawi*, from which 'Bedouin' is derived, denotes a nomadic inhabitant of the desert (*bādiah*) who depends for his livelihood on herds of camels and sheep. The word conjures up pictures of camel-herds moving over the vast expanse of the Arabian desert, of billowing black tents, of fierce bearded Arabs in flowing robes, and of daring raiders on swift horses. The Bedouin in Israel today do not entirely conform to this romantic image, but they do retain much of the traditional way of life of Bedouin. Most of them are primarily farmers, who also rear camels and sheep and earn part of their income from wage labour. Raiding ceased long ago, and continued contacts with the settled Arab population have had a considerable impact on their way of life. In Galilee, in the north of Israel, where about 7,000 Bedouin remain, they have for several generations lived interspersed with the peasant population, and assimilation to the peasants has gone so far that many Bedouin have abandoned their tents for stone houses and thus shed the last outward sign of their nomadic origin. Their houses, however, are not arranged in tight clusters as are those of villagers, but are usually scattered over an extensive area. The census describes these people as Bedouin mainly on their own definition.

The remaining 16,000 Bedouin are all concentrated in the Negev, the southern half of Israel. Although they come closer to the 'ideal type' Bedouin, they are a far cry from the North Arabian nomads so well described by Burckhardt, Doughty and others.[1] There is a large element of peasant newcomers among the Bedouin, but the old-established herdsmen are politically the dominent element. They are organized on a tribal basis, and

[1] J. L. Burckhardt, *Notes on the Bedouins and Wahábys* (London 1830); C. M. Doughty, *Travels in Arabia Deserta* (London 1921).

pastoralism is one of their major sources of income, second only to farming. Nearly all the Negev Bedouin, including those of peasant origin, still live under black goat-hair tents. They consider themselves, and are considered by the settled population, to be true Bedouin.

Bedouin life in the Negev has been, and is being, shaped by complex environmental factors. These can be grouped under four headings: there are, firstly, the ecological factors, such as the land, the water, the climate of the area at present occupied by the Bedouin. Secondly, there is the political impact of the Israeli Administration, with its bureaucratic machinery, and the special Military Administration for the Bedouin of the Negev. Thirdly, there is the gradually increasing impact of the dynamic Israeli economy on Bedouin life, involving wage labour, taxes, and so forth. And lastly, there is the cultural background of the Bedouin: Islamic religion, Arab language, historical heritage, and the other cultural strands connecting them to Middle Eastern society, not to mention their own particular history.

Each of these factors impinges on Bedouin society in many ways, and one cannot always gauge the specific effects of a single factor. This is particularly true of the cultural factors. So inextricably are these cultural factors bound up with the organizational aspects of Bedouin society, which will be our central interest in this book, that it would be futile to treat them separately. But it is feasible to present the ecological data and to analyse the administrative framework as it affects the Bedouin. The ecology and the administrative framework combine to form the environment within which the Bedouin lives; they act in many ways as delimiting, boundary-setting factors to his range of action. This does not imply that one may set out this background material without ever referring to it in the main body of the study. Indeed, we shall have to use it again and again, in order to explain many aspects of Bedouin society.

* * * *

From the viewpoint of Bedouin history, the Negev forms an extension of the Sinai peninsula. For many generations Sinai has been the main source of influx of Bedouin into the Negev; only a few tribes appear to have entered the area directly from their former pastures on the Red Sea littoral. Of the three great tribal confederations which inhabited the Negev till the establishment of Israel, the Tarabīn, Tiāha and ʿAzāzmah confederations, some parts never left Sinai, while others rejoined them after 1948. When discussing the Bedouin of the Negev, one must always bear in mind the geographical contiguity of the Negev and Sinai. Movement between these areas was in the past little hampered by the international boundaries between Egyptian Sinai and the Palestinian Negev. A very large part of the cultural heritage of the Negev Bedouin must have been formed during the sojourn in Sinai. They still look there for advice on customary law, although for many generations the Bedouin population of the Negev was larger than that of Sinai. They feel that their brothers in Sinai have remained closer to the ideal way of life of nomadic herdsmen, are more militant and independent, and have preserved intact their traditional culture.

The peninsula of Sinai covers an area of approximately 60,000 sq km (over 23,000 sq miles), but the larger part of this immense area consists of rugged, inhospitable mountains. It provides only a meagre livelihood for a handful of camel- and goat-raising Bedouin. Of the 33,000 Bedouin now living in the Sinai peninsula, about 26,000[1] live in the northern half, from the Tīh Plateau to the shores of the Mediterranean Sea. Among these there are members of the tribal confederations which are still represented in the Negev. There are about 2,500 to 3,000 Tiāha tribesmen, as against 14,000 now living in the Negev; between 5,000 to 7,000 Tarabīn, compared to 880 remaining in the Negev; and 2,000 to 2,500 ʿAzāzmah, compared to 1,000 in the Negev. All these Bedouin lead a nomadic way of life and cultivate only isolated patches of land in valleys. Permanent settlements are found only along the coast, among which the little port of al-Ṭūr is the largest. The population density seems to be less than two persons to a square kilometre (or five to a square mile) for the whole of the peninsula.

The Hebrew word *Negev* is usually rendered in English as South or Southland. The geographical region of Israel bearing that name, occupies the southern half of the country, which until the establishment of Israel was solely inhabited by Bedouin. But *Negev* also means dry land, desert, and although the geographical boundaries of the Negev remained unchanged throughout the

[1] The data apply to 1961: those for the Sinai Bedouin are estimates, those for the Negev are based on statistics of the Public Registration Office.

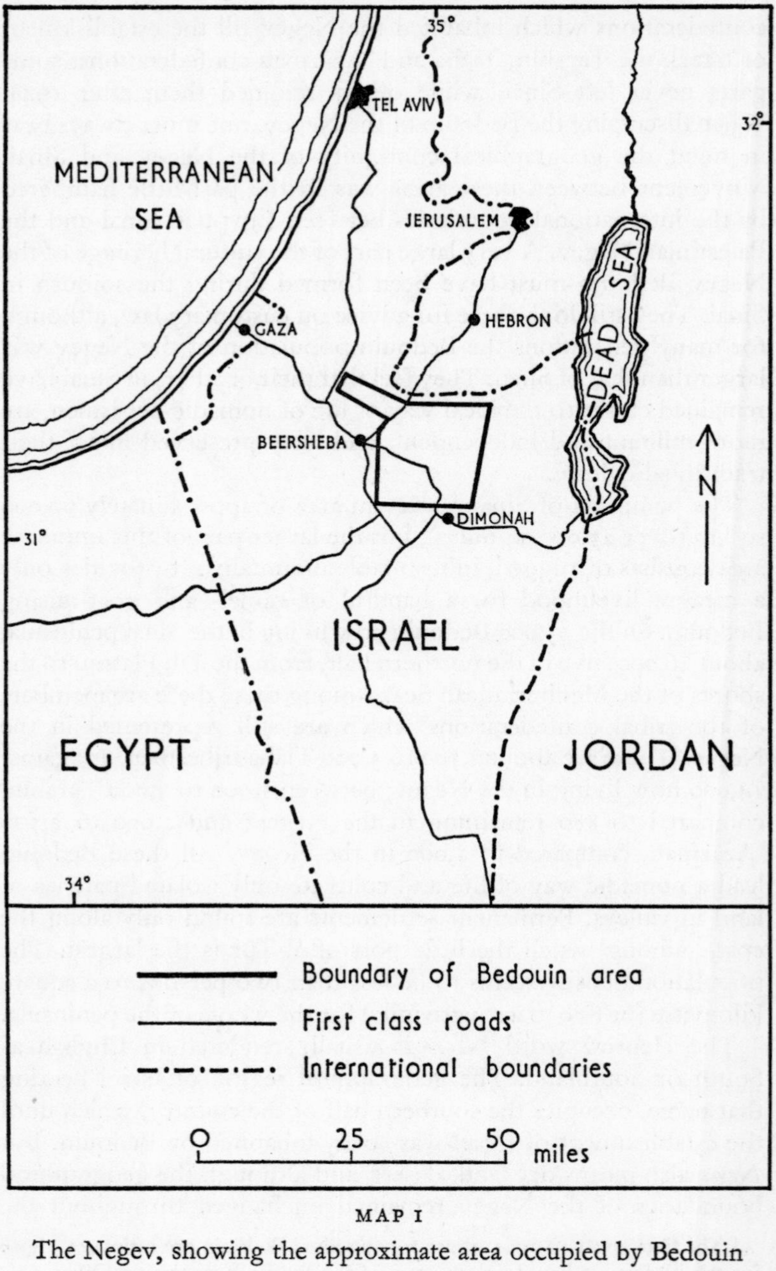

MAP I

The Negev, showing the approximate area occupied by Bedouin

generations, not all parts of it were barren at all times. The limits of the desert seem to have fluctuated considerably during the 4,000 years of the Negev's history. Whenever the country was ruled by a strong hand, the sown land advanced from the north and pushed back the desert, while during periods of turmoil the farmers who remained without military protection would be exposed to the depredations of the nomads from the south. At such times the desert would penetrate deep into cultivated territory and lay everything waste.

Geographically the Negev may be defined as the area lying to the south of the Judean mountains and west of the Dead Sea and the ʿArabah, that part of the Great Rift extending from the Dead Sea to Elath (Aqabah) on the Red Sea coast. On the western side, the border runs along the international boundaries between Egypt and Israel, from the vicinity of Rafiaḥ (Rafah) to Elath. The Negev thus forms a large triangle, whose area extends over 12,500 sq km, out of the 20,700 sq km, total area of Israel. This region is roughly co-extensive with the administrative district of Beersheba during the British Mandatory period, but it also includes a small enclave of the former Hebron sub-district (Jerusalem district). These administrative boundaries were instituted during Turkish rule, and designed roughly to fit the areas predominantly occupied by semi-nomadic Bedouin. Up to the establishment of the State of Israel, the Bedouin took little heed of either the district or the international boundaries. They used to move freely into the Transjordanian part (now Jordan) of the ʿArabah to the east, and south-west into the northern and central regions of Sinai. The movements across the latter frontier were especially extensive, so much so that one dealt with a single Bedouin population ranging over Sinai and the Negev. Only through political events of the last decades have Bedouin of Sinai and the Negev gradually grown apart.

Large tracts of the Negev, in particular its central and southern parts, have been so niggardly endowed by nature that they have always been populated very sparsely, and mostly during the short weeks of spring, when Bedouin herds would graze off the patches of short-lived verdure. Generally speaking, ecological conditions in the Negev improve as one advances from the south-east northwards and westwards. The ground becomes more even, the soil more fertile, and rainfall increases. Therefore, it was quite natural that the greater part of the Negev's population concentrated in the northern end, pressing mainly on the relatively fertile Beersheba Plain. Before the pacification of the Negev, in the latter part of the 19th century, tribes used to contest each other's rights in the land of this region. In effect the Bedouin hardly ever enjoyed periods of peace and security, and engaged in farming only on a very limited scale. But not only Bedouin fought each other in this area; this was the ground too, on which the battles between 'the desert and the sown' raged. Fighting was a permanent feature in the life of both the Bedouin and the peasants converging on the area from north and west, although, judging by numbers, the pressure of population on the land generally could not have been very great. At the beginning of the 20th century, Southern Palestine was inhabited by less than 400,000 people, of whom over 150,000 were peasants and an estimated 55,000 Bedouin.[1] The ecological conditions of the Beersheba Plain often made it a centre of turbulence.

There were times when the Negev supported a fully settled population, and settlements were established even in the more inhospitable parts. These were periods in which peace reigned in the countries bordering on the Negev, and it served as a major highway connecting the lands of the Fertile Crescent with Egypt. At such times military posts would spring up along the trade routes, which then attracted a civilian population. The settlers were little concerned with the harsh environment: they derived their income mainly from services supplied to passing caravans. As the settlements increased in size and in wealth, and were

[1] A. Ruppin, *Syrien als Wirtschaftsgebiet* (Berlin 1917) p. 356, relying on a semi-official Turkish source, states the area of the administrative district of Jerusalem, which then included both the Negev and the settled areas north of it to beyond Jaffa, as 23,144,580 dunams (as the Turkish dunam measured 919 sq metres, this area would amount to almost 21,270 sq km). The cultivated area is stated at 1,223,188 dunams (1,124 sq km), a mere 5·28 per cent of the total area. According to Government of Palestine, *A Survey of Palestine* (Jerusalem 1946) p. 370, the cultivable area of the Negev alone is 1,640 sq km, i.e. larger than the area said to have been cultivated in the whole of the Jerusalem district in late Ottoman times.

Ruppin obtained the following population figures for 1915 from Turkish official sources: In Jerusalem district there were 398,362 inhabitants, of whom an estimated 55,000 were Bedouin living in the Beersheba sub-district (ibid., p. 7). 187,000 people lived in the larger towns of the district (ibid., p. 10), so that the remaining 156,000 inhabitants could be considered peasants.

generally protected and subsidized by governments, their inhabitants took to the construction of ingenious engineering works, calculated to conserve the scanty rainfall for agricultural purposes. This was the situation, for instance, in early times, as during the heyday of the kingdom of Judea (10th century B.C.), during the Nabatean period (approximately 100 B.C. to A.D. 100), and during the period of Byzantine rule (mainly the 4th and 5th centuries A.D.). Evidently the Negev flourished during these periods, because it was economically integrated into large and prosperous polities. The population in the fortified cities of the Negev during the Byzantine period is estimated at times to have been as high as 52,000 to 71,000.[1]

When the Negev was thrown back onto its own resources it could only sustain a small nomadic population at subsistence level. This general condition persisted, apparently, from the time of the Arab conquest of Palestine in A.D. 636: the vicissitudes of life in the Negev brought no radical change. During almost thirteen centuries of Muslim rule no permanent settlements were established in the Negev. Only in the year 1900 was such a settlement founded once more, when the Ottoman authorities established an administrative centre at Beersheba.

In the 1870's the Ottoman government began to pacify the Negev Bedouin tribes, which had until then been left to their own devices, except for occasional raids by government troops. At that time the Government became increasingly apprehensive about the future of Egypt, where in 1869 the Suez Canal had been opened. Tribal warfare was suppressed by drastic methods and tribal chiefs were held personally responsible for the good behaviour of their tribes.

The authorities fixed the formerly fluid tribal boundaries, and these remained unchanged until 1949. Each tribe was allowed to retain the territory it held at the time, so that the powerful tribes came off best. A map prepared by the authorities in 1917, the last year of Ottoman rule, shows that the two largest tribal confederations, the Tarabīn and the Tiāha, had secured the best land in the northern Negev, and had relegated the weaker ʿAzāzmah to the arid mountains of the central Negev and to sandy desert tracts around Ruḥēbah (Reḥovot). The formerly powerful tribes of the Gubarāt and Ḥanāgrah confederations had been pushed out of the

[1] S. Ambramski, *Parashash be-toldot ha-Negev* (Jerusalem 1953) p. 10.

purely Bedouin occupied area and now lived side by side with the fully settled peasants of the coastal strip. Supervision over the tribes was exercised through chiefs, whose election by their tribesmen had to be confirmed by the authorities. By refusing to acknowledge new chiefs of dissident groups the Ottoman authorities kept in check the splitting up of tribes.

During the period of British rule, from 1917 to 1948, the authorities effectively maintained law and order in the Negev and, for the rest, intervened as little as they could in Bedouin affairs. Many Bedouin look back to those times with profound nostalgia, which one man explained thus:

> The British were good to us, they are the best government in the world. They were always true to their word, and we were at liberty to do as we liked, except fight one another. The whole country was ours then, and nobody bothered about permits for work, for weapons, or even for the sale of animals.

The peaceful conditions affected the land situation in two ways. Firstly, Bedouin could now devote themselves more than before to farming, and land values rose accordingly. Secondly, they were no longer so keen to maintain the tribal boundaries. This enabled the wealthy families of Gaza, such as the al-Shāwa, Bsēso and Shhēbar, some of which had established strong commercial links with the Negev Bedouin in Turkish times, to acquire tracts of farm land in the western and central parts of the Beersheba Plain. Landless peasants from the coastal area also found opportunities to acquire land, often settling permanently in the tribal area. Many of the tribal chiefs, too, bought up land and began to live off the income derived from tribesmen whom they engaged as sharecroppers. Some of the chiefs left the tribe at times to live in their town houses at Beersheba and Gaza. The tribes living east of Beersheba, though, were affected to a lesser extent, as their inferior land did not attract many buyers.

Towards the end of the period of British rule there were approximately 55,000–65,000 Bedouin in the Negev,[1] divided into 95 tribes. 'Tribes' were territorial and administrative units led by elected chiefs whom the authorities recognized as official representatives of their followers. Tribes combined into Confederations,

[1] See Y. Shimoni, *'Arvei Erets-Israel* (Tel-Aviv 1947) pp. 148-50.

which were mainly larger territorial divisions whose contiguity was expressed in terms of common descent. There were eight such tribal confederations (*qabīlah*, pl. *qabā'il*), of which seven were located in Beersheba sub-district, where usually an Arab was appointed as District Officer to attend to Bedouin affairs. The Gahalīn confederation was administratively affiliated to the Hebron sub-district. Table 1 provides some data on the tribal confederations of the Negev prior to 1948.

TABLE 1

Bedouin tribes of the Negev prior to 1948

Confederation	*No. of tribes*	*Persons*	*Area*
Tarabīn	25	21,000	Western Beersheba Plain
Tiāha	28	18,000	Central and Eastern Beersheba Plain
ʿAzāzmah	12	12,000	Central Negev
Ḥanāgrah	4	7,000	South of Gaza
Gubarāt	14	5,000	North of Gaza
Saʿidīn	6	1,000	South of Dead Sea
Aḥēwāt	3	1,000	Near Gulf of Elath
Gahalīn	3	750	Hebron Mountains
Total	95	65,750	

All the figures are maximum estimates, following Shimoni. Official censuses of the Negev Bedouin were held in 1931 and 1946, with either inconclusive or partial results.

Most of the tribes of the two largest confederations also formed smaller territorial combinations, for which I shall use the term 'group of tribes'. There exists no Arabic term for such associations. A tribe is referred to as *ʿashīrah* (pl. *ʿashā'ir*), and also sometimes as *badīdah*. The group of tribes is conceptualized as descended from a common named ancestor, of whom the ancestors of the tribes are sons. In some cases, though, the connection is recognized as one of political alliance. The tribal groups are referred to by name. Thus the Tiāha confederation is sub-divided into the following groups of tribes:

1. Ḥkūk	6 tribes
2. ʿAlamāt	4 tribes
3. Ramaḍīn	4 tribes
4. Qderāt	5 tribes
5. Ẓullām	4 tribes
6. ʿEyāl ʿOmri	2 tribes
7. Bdenāt	1 tribe
8. Qalazīn	1 tribe
9. Qaṭāṭwah	1 tribe, and another was officially recognized towards the end of the period

As the coalitions of tribes into groups followed the changing territorial and political alignments, they were very fluid. There were no formal arrangements to facilitate political co-operation between the tribes of a group, nor was there a paramount chief around whom they could rally.

When the Israeli Army occupied the Negev at the end of 1948, the Bedouin were afraid of the new rulers. Many of them fled, particularly those who had taken an active part in the fighting. Thus about half of the Tiāha Bedouin are said to have left the country for the Hebron mountains or the Dead Sea area,[1] while the remaining groups sought refuge in the hilly parts of the Negev. The situation in the Negev remained unsettled for several years. While some tribes filtered back into their former areas, others were moved about or expelled by the military authorities. Tribes re-formed around their former chiefs, or around men who wielded influence with the Israeli authorities, though always along the lines of the traditional tribal groups. In 1953, when the dust had finally settled, about 11,000 Bedouin remained in the Negev. They had clustered around 19 men whom the Israeli Military Administration recognized as chiefs.[2] Over 90 per cent of the Bedouin were of the Tiāha confederation, while only a few hundred ʿAzāzmah and even fewer Tarabīn remained. The other confederations were represented by a handful of individuals each. The only tribal group to come out almost unscathed were the Ẓullām, who left only a few members in Jordanian territory.

Since then the Bedouin population in the Negev has increased to 16,000 and its tribal composition is shown in Table 2.

[1] S. Ben-Elkanah, *ʿArab al-Tiāha* (unpublished).
[2] Israeli Army, *Beduei ha-Negev bi-Medinat Israel* (Tel-Aviv 1954) p. 32.

TABLE 2

Bedouin tribes of the Negev, 1960

Confederation and Tribal Group	*Tribe*	*Tribal chief*	*Population*
Tiāha			
Ḥkūk	Hazail	Salmān ʿAli Hazail	2,116
,,	Abu al-Qiʿān	Farhūd Gabr al-Qawaʿīn	189
,,	al-Asad	Farāg Salīm al-Asad	259
,,	Abu ʿAbdūn	Ḥassan ʿĪd Abu ʿAbdūn	198
Ntūsh	ʿAṭaunah	Mūsa Ḥassan al-ʿAṭaunah	528
Qderāt	Abu Rqaiq	ʿAwaḍ Ibrāhīm Abu Rqaiq	3,067
,,	al-Aʿsam	Salmān Muḥammad al-Aʿsam	961
,,	al-Ṣaneʿ	Manṣūr Muḥammad al-Ṣāneʿ	1,193
—	al-ʿOqbi	Sālem Muḥammad al-ʿOqbi	543
—	Afēnish	Muḥammad Sālem al-Afēnish	315
Ẓullām	Abu Rbēʿah	Ḥamād Sālem Abu Rbēʿah	2,079
,,	Abu Qrenāt	ʿAli Salmān Abu Qrenāt	1,452
,,	Abu Gweʿid	Mḥemmed Muḥesin Abu Gweʿid	1,148
,,	al-Kashkhar	Sālem Sulimān al-Kashkhar	150 *
			14,198
Tarabīn			
Garawīn	Abu Sriḥān	Gabr Musallam Abu Sriḥān	118
Ghawāli	Abu ʿAmrah	Halail ʿĀsi Abu ʿAmrah	83
Nigmāt	al-Ṣāneʿ	Muḥammad Sulimān Abu Ṣhibān	322
			783
ʿAzāzmah			
—	Masʿudīn	ʿAudah Manṣūr Abu Muʿammar	1,023
		Total Population	16,004

* This figure is approximate, as the Kashkhar tribe is not included in official statistics.

The foregoing figures for the Bedouin population are correct for September 1960.[1]

All the Bedouin remaining in the Northern Negev were placed under Military Administration and were concentrated in the

[1] The figures were obtained from the Public Registration Office, Beersheba. There is a small number of unregistered ʿAzāzmah Bedouin, besides the Masʿudīn.

north-eastern corner of the Negev. The account of ecological conditions will therefore be focussed on this area. Its geographical boundaries lie roughly between 34° 45′ and 35° 05′ east and between 31° 05′ and 31° 25′ north, and it comprises about 1,100 sq km of the former Beersheba sub-district, or about 5½ per cent of Israel's total area. It constitutes, in size, only about 10 per cent of the area formerly occupied exclusively by Bedouin. In value it includes a considerable proportion of the best farm land in the Negev. Legally, the whole Negev falls under military jurisdiction. In practice the Military exercise jurisdiction mainly over the part reserved for the Bedouin, and pronounced a 'Closed Area'. The boundary of this part runs along the Beersheba–Hebron road in a north-easterly direction almost up to the Jordanian frontier, there turning east, running parallel to the present international boundary for about 30 km until it reaches Wadi Ṭayib, along which it curves southward. The boundary continues south along the ridge of the Diyah hills, which constitute the watershed between the Mediterranean and the Dead Sea, down to Kurnub (Mampsis), though the ruins of this ancient town lie outside the reservation. From Kurnub the boundary line runs almost due west, across rolling stony ground, until it reaches the main Beersheba–Elath highway, along which it continues due north almost to Beersheba, the capital of the Negev, which again has been left outside the area under Military Administration. From the Beersheba–Hebron road, also, a separate Bedouin enclave extends in a north-westerly direction, an elongated strip of land whose width nowhere exceeds 5 km. This strip touches the Beersheba–Tel-Aviv highway opposite the communal settlement of Shuval.[1] This enclave is, in military language, called the B1 zone, while the main Bedouin reservation to the east is called the B2 zone. Anyone wishing to enter the zones, to leave them for any purpose, or only to pass from one to the other, has first to obtain a permit from the Military Administration. In the following chapter we shall discuss how the permit system, the most important power of the Military Administration, affects the Bedouin.

Population density in the area under Military Administration is about 15 persons to the square kilometre. This compares with a density of two to the square kilometre in Sinai, on one hand, and about 220 in the settled half of Israel on the other. The Bedouin

[1] See Map 1 for the approximate boundaries of the closed areas.

cultivate practically all the arable land found in the reservation, up to 400 sq km of it, sowing chiefly barley, while the remaining land provides part of the pasture for their livestock, about 70,000 sheep and goats and around 10,000 camels.[1]

From a glance at the map one learns that the Bedouin straddle all the trunk roads radiating out from Beersheba, in the direction of Tel-Aviv, Hebron, the Dead Sea and Elath. This makes it easy for them to reach Beersheba on the two days in every week in which the town is open to them. In addition, their reservation and the adjacent areas are criss-crossed by dirt tracks, many of which can be negotiated by ordinary lorries. There are also innumerable animal trails. All these roads do not end at the limits set by the Military Administration. As in former days, they join the Bedouin with other parts of the country, and do not even cease at international boundaries. In particular this applies to the little-guarded Jordanian frontier. The Bedouin are thus to some extent able to circumvent the formally very strict surveillance of the Military Administration.

Some of the tracks are highways of great antiquity. One of them is the Way of Shur (Darb al-Sūr), leading from Jerusalem to Hebron and Beersheba, and from there on to Khalasa (Khalutsa) and across the Egyptian border.[2] Through Khalasa also passes another ancient road, leading from Gaza through the Wilderness of Zin to the Wadi ʿArabah. There it parts, one branch leading to Petra and Maʿān in Jordan, and the other to the Red Sea coast of Aqaba (Elath). This is called the Darb al-Sulṭāneh (King's Highway ?). Another road also leads from Gaza into Transjordan, but passes further north through Beersheba and Sodom to Kerak and Amman. This used to be called by Bedouin Darb al-Salīṭi (Way of the man from al-Salṭ),[3] and is now metalled as far as Sodom. For the time being, these international highways are only used as smuggling tracks. But the easiest and shortest smuggling route for the Bedouin is across the nearby Jordanian frontier into the Hebron mountains. The smuggling tracks into Gaza and into Sinai have almost fallen into disuse since the Suez campaign at the

[1] Estimates of the Military Administration.

[2] See *Genesis*, 16: 7 and 20: 1.

[3] Al-Salṭ used to be the administrative centre of the Belqa district before the rise of Amman. See F. G. Peake, *History of Jordan and its Tribes* (Coral Gables 1952) p. 92.

end of 1956. The tracks into the Hebron mountains run parallel to the river beds going from north to south, and some of them are even suited to motor vehicles. Bedouin cross the frontier not only for smuggling purposes but also to visit kinsmen living across the border, or often only to buy provisions for their own use. There exist no permanent settlements or frontier posts on the Israeli side of the border, while the Jordanians man only two military posts on a wide-open frontier extending over more than 30 km. Neither are there any permanent settlements, Jewish or Arab, within the Bedouin reservation, which thus comprises only one element of the population, semi-nomadic Bedouin. These nomads are not too susceptible to government interference. They are able to do much as they please inside their reservation, and even cross the international frontier unimpeded. As part of a plan to introduce Jewish settlers into a solely Bedouin-occupied area, in 1961 the authorities founded the town of ʿArad, in the hilly area to the east of the Beersheba Plain. The town is situated outside the Bedouin reservation but on land which was till then exploited exclusively by Bedouin as pasture.

The Bedouin reservation is not physically a uniform area. In its northern part it includes the foothills of the Hebron mountains, which rise to a height of up to 700 metres. Here, in the north-eastern corner of the Negev, 'the hills end very suddenly and the boundary is thus sharply defined between the lands of the settled population and the district of the Bedouin'.[1] In the north-western parts of the Negev, though, there is no such sharp transition from the settled to the pastoral land. The distinction between peasants and Bedouin is sharper in the north-east, today's Bedouin reservation, than in the north-west, for here the clear-cut geographical boundary accentuates differences in the styles of life which in themselves are too slight to provide a precise occupational barrier. To the south of the Hebron foothills lies the eastern part of the Beersheba Plain, whose eastern limits are the Diyah hills, which form the main watershed in this part of the country. Standing on the ridge of the Diyah hills, which attain a height of up to 660 metres, one can on clear days see the Mediterranean to the west near Gaza, about 75 km away, while to the east one looks down to the Dead Sea, about 30 km distant, and to the mountains of Moab beyond. The southern, south-eastern and eastern parts of

[1] C. R. Conder, *Tent Work in Palestine* (London 1887) p. 246.

PLATE I

Above: Landscape in the Hilly Area: Wadi Dabdab

Below: Preparations for ploughing in the Plain, near Tel ʿArad: the land is marked by parallel furrows

Photo: Dov Barnea

PLATE II

Above: A girl ploughing, using the ancient wooden plough
Below: Most of the ploughing is now mechanized

the reservation are in the main gently undulating hills, which gradually descend westwards and northwards into flat country, frequently intersected by tributaries of Wadi Beersheba. The south-eastern parts of the area consist of rock-strewn desert (*ḥamād*), but on the lower hills only the crests are stony and the lower slopes covered by light soils. The Plain itself is covered, often to a considerable depth, by light loess or loess-like soils, which give it the characteristic yellowish appearance.

In addition to the Diyah hills, there are two more chains of hills further west, which almost transect the Beersheba Plain. The Gharrah hills, outrunners of the Hebron mountains, reach down in a south-westerly direction almost to the Wadi Beersheba near the perennial wells at Bir Mshāsh. The hills serve as boundary between the cultivated land of two tribal groups of the Tiāha confederation, the Ẓullām to the east and the Qderāt to the west, but they provide common pasture to both groups. The other chain of hills, the Laqīah hills, also reach out from the Hebron mountains. They lie west of the Hebron–Beersheba road and run parallel to the Gharrah hills in a south-westerly direction right down to the outskirts of Beersheba. Before 1948 they constituted a general dividing line between the land cultivated by the Ramaḍīn group of tribes to the east and the Ḥkūk to the west, while providing some pasture to both groups of tribes and to others besides them. The natural boundary of the Laqīah hills appears now to affect relationships between the tribes which were resettled in the early fifties. The formerly numerous relations between the Hazail tribe, now living west of it, and the two other tribes of the Ḥkūk group which are now camped east, have contracted considerably.

The region now under Military Administration is almost co-extensive with the drainage area of the upper reaches of Wadi Beersheba. The Wadi starts in the Diyah hills and runs almost dead west through the Beersheba Plain. Its main tributaries from the North are Wadis Qiriatēn (Qerioth), Ghuwēnah (ʿAnim), ʿAṭīr (Yatir) and Khalīl (Hebron), which together supply the larger part of the Wadi's water flow. They originate in the Hebron mountains, which receive an annual precipitation of 500–600 mm (approximately 20–24 in.), as compared with only 200 mm (8 in.) at Beersheba. But the southern affluents of Wadi Beersheba, Wadis Musīk (ʿAdarim), ʿArʿarah (ʿAroʿer), Abu Tlūl (Nevatim) and Shqēb

(Tson) also supply large quantities of water, as they drain off water not absorbed into the ground after the cloudbursts occurring in the area in winter. Government experts estimate the annual quantity of water borne down Wadi Beersheba at 18 million cubic metres at Beersheba.[1] Only a minute proportion of this water is used for irrigation. Instead, the floods are allowed to carry away the light loess soil, so that the area is a veritable network of gullies, to which each cloudburst adds several new ones. Frequently the water has gnawed deep into the soft soil, and produced steep perpendicular banks.

The fertile loess or loess-like soils which cover the larger part of the Beersheba Plain conserve water very well and make a high proportion of the water available to the plants. But they often form a dense crust on the surface, which is almost impervious to water, and thus causes the rainbursts to run off into the gullies without moistening the ground to any depth.[2] Soil scientists consider this type of soil as 'suitable for growing many kinds of irrigated crops. Under arid conditions,[it] can be made to produce good yields of winter crops, by augmenting the scant rainfall through supplementary irrigation. In years of high rainfall, these soils produce good crops of cereals, legumes and vegetables.'[3] For at least two reasons the basically fertile land of the Beersheba Plain often produces small crops or remains entirely barren: sufficient water is available only occasionally, and the Bedouin make little effort to conserve the run-off water.

The slopes of the calcareous hills in the southern part of the Bedouin reservation are also largely covered by loess. The valley floors, too, show extensive pockets of shallow, but cultivable, loess soil. Near the eastern boundary the land becomes more rugged and barren and can be exploited mainly as pasture. Only small patches are cultivated, generally in, and along, watercourses. Still further east and south, towards the Dead Sea and the Wadi ʿArabah, the land becomes almost inaccessible. Grotesquely eroded rock formations are intersected by spectacular gorges. There is

[1] This figure has been compiled by G. Shelef, a soil conservation engineer, from records of the Public Works Department.

[2] Y. Orev, a soil conservation engineer, found that part of every rain exceeding an intensity of 3–4 mm ($1\frac{1}{8}$–$1\frac{1}{2}$ in.) per hour runs off.

[3] S. Ravikovitch, 'The Aeolian Soils of the Northern Negev', 1953, p. 428. *Desert Research: Proceedings, International Symposium.*

very little rain, and even the spring vegetation is so sparse that in many years these parts provide no grazing even for the hardy camels and goats.

Bedouin are well aware of the great potentialities of the loess soils. In good years they produce excellent crops of barley and wheat, despite the little effort exerted, and the simple techniques used by the Bedouin. The rare bumper crops induce the Bedouin every year to gamble on their luck and to cultivate extensive areas of their land. Their diet is based on cereals and they attempt to produce the grain required for their own consumption. In order to achieve this self-sufficiency Bedouin must, in an average year, sow about 100 dunams (about 25 acres) of cereals in the western reservation, and in the eastern reaches of the Beersheba Plain up to 150 dunams (about 37 acres) per family. The total arable area in the reservation is, according to maximum estimates, 400,000 dunams.[1] If the 3,300 Bedouin families are to draw their requirements of cereals out of this land, they must keep the whole area permanently under cultivation. The population has been growing rapidly and pressure on farm land has been mounting, so that during recent years some Bedouin have had to seek alternative sources of income.

It is thus inevitable that year by year all the arable land is cultivated, allowing neither for rotation of crops nor for fallows. But as, on an average, only one year in four produces a good crop, this procedure in itself does not impair the fertility of the soil. On the other hand, the too frequent ploughing up of the land, the plucking out of the whole stalk when reaping, and the thoughtless overgrazing of the harvested land, destroy the protective plant cover and precipitate processes of erosion. Bedouin are quite familiar with the dangers of erosion, but consider it an unavoidable evil. One man put it like this:

Loess (*trāb*) is very good agricultural land. The Buḥērah area [in the eastern Beersheba Plain] is of this kind, and all of it is cultivated annually, either with barley or with wheat. But when it is cultivated for four to five years it deteriorates, erodes away (*al-matar binshafhā*, the rain dries it out) and it becomes rocky. When this kind of land is not

---

[1] Information supplied by Ministry of Agriculture, Beersheba. (1 dunam = 1,000 sq m = 0·247 acres.)

cultivated (and denuded by camels and goats), it becomes rocky (*galād*) very fast. When you cultivate it, it also turns into rocky land, but somewhat more slowly. In the end you just have to stop cultivating it, because it has no more power to produce crops. Then it deteriorates even faster, and there is nothing you can do about it. There is no way to improve deteriorating land.

Bedouin farming techniques are very simple and do not require men to stay close to their land for long periods. During the sowing, which generally begins after the first heavy rains have fallen around November or December, the Bedouin pitch their tents near the land. Then they have to return only for the harvest in May or June. For the rest of the year they are not bound to remain on their land and part of the Bedouin move into other areas, following the dictates of pasture and water. But by no means all the inhabitants of the Negev keep up a nomadic routine: we shall examine their problem in a later chapter.

While the potential fertility of the land exercises a pull on Bedouin towards a settled way of life, the peculiarities of the rainfall keep them on the move. The rain falls mainly between November and March, with slight showers also occurring in October, April and May. The period from June to September is hot and dry. The most trying characteristics of the rainfall are its annual fluctuations, the unequal distribution of the rains within the rainy season, the geographical scatter of the rain, and above all, the general scarcity of water. Broadly speaking, rainfall decreases from North to South and from West to East, but within this general trend it is somewhat higher in elevated areas. In the climate prevailing in Israel, a rainfall of 200 mm (about 8 in.) is considered the margin for agricultural exploitation even where hardy winter cereals are concerned.[1] The 200 mm rainfall line runs from Rafah (Rafiaḥ) on the Mediterranean coast through Beersheba and further eastward to Tel al-Milḥ (Malḥeta) in the Bedouin reservation. There it curves sharply north into the Judaean mountains, leaving the greater part of the reservation with a lower rainfall.[2] The annual average rainfall for Beersheba is 200 mm (about 8 in.), while at the south-eastern corner of the area cultivated by the Bedouin, at Kurnub, only 35 km's distance, it falls to 120 mm

[1] Some farming experts now consider the 250 mm (about 10 in.) rainfall line the boundary for grain-growing.

[2] D. Ashbel, *Aklim Erets-Israel le-ezoreha* (Jerusalem 1951) p. 106.

(about 4¾ in.), as Table 3 shows. The averages for the other parts of the reservation fall between the two figures.

TABLE 3

Multi-annual averages of precipitation, by months*

	Beersheba		*Kurnub*	
Latitude	N31.14		N31.01	
Longitude	E34.47		E35.04	
Elevation	270 m.		450 m.	
Period covered	1921–50		1933–48	
	mm.	*Rain days*	*mm.*	*Rain days*
September	0·3	0·1	0·3	0
October	4·0	0·9	1·0	0
November	25·2	3·4	13·0	2
December	39·6	4·4	20·4	3
January	47·9	5·6	34·1	5
February	40·8	5·1	25·4	4
March	30·5	6·2	15·6	4
April	7·4	1·3	5·3	1
May	4·3	0·8	4·9	1
Totals	200·0	27·8	120·0	20

* Israel Meteorological Service, *Climatological Norms*, (Tel-Aviv 1958) pt. 1: Rainfall, and information supplied by H. Roznan, Meteorological Service, Tel-Aviv.

The data suggest that the greater part of the Eastern Beersheba Plain should be considered as marginal for agricultural purposes. But the extreme variations in rainfall from one year to another make farming an even more risky proposition. Thus the maximum rainfall recorded for Beersheba was 336 mm (about 13¼ in.), in 1933–4, while the minimum came as low as 40 mm (about 1½ in.), in 1962–3. Kurnub had a maximum rainfall of 162 mm (about 6½ in.), in 1944–5, while its lowest recorded precipitation was 44 mm (1¾ in.), in 1935–6. There exists no clear pattern or cycle of rainfall, and several good years are often followed by a series of bad ones, although Bedouin wishfully claim that one dry year is often followed by one blessed with rain. An excellent harvest in 1956–7 was followed by six consecutive lean years, four of which were extremely bad droughts.[1]

The distribution of rains in a season is of immense importance to the success of crops. The Bedouin are made cautious by experience. Most of them sow and plough (in that sequence) only after there have been rains which they consider sufficient to germinate the seeds and to supply them with moisture for a reasonable time. They consider that crops are safe when the moisture has penetrated the ground to the depth of an arm's length. But the plentiful rains are sometimes so late that the ripening corn is hit by a scorching heatwave in spring; this withers the crop and sometimes the parched ears produce no grains at all. Even if a Bedouin sows in time, he still runs the risk that a long dry spell will destroy the germinated seeds. This is what happened to Bedouin farmers in 1960–1, a year which, to all appearances, had close to average rainfall of 185 mm (about 7¼ in.). After a good start in November there were six weeks with only a few drops of rain, which killed off the seeds of those farmers who had relied on the first showers. Then in January and February there were heavy showers in which 125 mm (about 5 in.) of rain fell. Some of this came in cloudbursts which the soil was unable to absorb, and most of the water ran off to waste. Still many Bedouin sowed or re-sowed their land. Then in March there followed a spell of scorching easterly winds which parched the late corn; many Bedouin cut it only for straw.

Rains often descend over small areas, sometimes of only a few square kilometres. In the cultivated areas these patchy rains will usually not change much in the overall situation of the crops. In the pasture areas which are generally the parts with lower rainfall, a generous isolated shower may sometimes fill up the cisterns and produce good spring herbage in a small area while leaving dry land lying only a few miles away. A man wishing to assure a regular water supply for his herds in the eastern pasture areas will either have to construct a number of cisterns in different parts, or will have to reach agreement with the owners of such cisterns. A drought often spells for the farmer the difference between getting some crop or none. The shortage of water and pasture will affect

[1] The severest droughts occurred in 1957–8, 1959–60, 1962–3. 1961–2 was bad in some areas.

the herdsman too, but he will not feel the drought to such an extent as the farmer. In particular, the spacing of rains and their location will make less difference to the herdsman, for he can adapt his movements to them. It is known that droughts do not necessarily coincide in all parts of the country. Thus Ashbel reports that although the years 1926–7 and 1928–9 were dry in the Negev, with rainfalls of 131·7 and 129·8 mm at Beersheba, the rest of the country had more than the average quantity of rain.[1] These peculiarities of the rainfall will tend to draw away the Bedouin from farming and towards animal husbandry, particularly after a series of bad harvests. But herding too has its risks; epidemics may cause havoc in herds, or a widespread drought may kill off animals. Bedouin claim that during the first two years of the recent drought they lost half of their newborn lambs. Therefore a Bedouin can entirely rely for a living neither on herding nor on farming. Most men regard farming as their economic mainstay. In the eastern part of the Beersheba Plain many men also maintain herds as an important economic reserve on which they can fall back should their crops fail. A few individuals depend more on herds than on land. These are all men who also own large areas of farm land, for a man who owns no land or has no access to the cultivated land of others, is in no position to keep herds. For while the access to spring pasture in the hilly area to the east of the reservation is open to all, around harvest time one depends on the stubble left in the fields in the cultivated areas. At that time herds are not permitted to move out of the Bedouin area, so as not to endanger fields which have not yet been harvested. In the interim period it is essential to have access to stubble fields in the reservation.

The balance between the two branches of the economy varies from family to family and from area to area. The general trend is for animal raising gradually to increase as one moves eastward and southward into the more marginal agricultural areas. But at no point does cultivation cease completely, even the few Bedouin staying in the ʿAbdeh (Ovdat) area maintain small patches of cultivation along the dry river-beds, where the soil receives more moisture than elsewhere.

In all parts of the Negev the Bedouin make some use of a technique of water conservation developed by the ancient Nabateans

[1] D. Ashbel, op. cit., p. 108.

and settlers of the Byzantine period.[1] They construct series of low dams of compressed earth across slopes having a very gradual incline. Behind these the rainwater flowing off the surrounding hillsides collects and gradually seeps into the ground. Some Bedouin still make use of the original installations of the Nabatean and Byzantine periods: these dams are firmly constructed of layered stones. Other Bedouin build their own dams on their land. If the structure is not swept away by the force of sudden floods, as frequently happens, one can grow in these gardens vegetables, such as tomatoes and cucurbits and even plant fruit trees, such as olives, almonds, pomegranates, figs and vines.

Water is frequently in scarce supply. Throughout the Negev there are no perennial watercourses. In the rainy season water can be obtained without much difficulty from rock pools and puddles. But in the dry season Bedouin may encounter real trouble in watering their animals, for water may only be available at a great distance from their grazing areas. There is only a small number of perennial wells in the Bedouin reservation, and even in most of these the water level falls dangerously towards the end of summer. Bedouin claim that there are only five wells which never dry up, even in bad droughts. These are Bīr al-Skāti, Bīr Abu Manṣūr, Bīr al-Milḥ, Bīr Mshāsh and Bīr ʿArʿarah. The last three are all situated in the territory of the Ẓullām group of tribes in the Eastern Beersheba Plain. This claim of inexhaustibility should not mean that the water supply in these wells is unlimited, but that it flows abundantly and waters large herds. As there is little pasture in the reservation towards the critical period at the end of the dry season, the herds are moved north and westwards, so that the wells are never put to the crucial test. Most of the copious wells are found on the banks of Wadi Beersheba and its tributaries. Such wells feed on the ground water retained after the swift winter floods have rushed through the river-beds. The flow of water in the Wadis often lasts only for a few hours, at the most several days, then only isolated pools are left and even these dry up after a while. The small proportion of water which has not flowed down to the sea and has not evaporated in the heat, is absorbed in the ground. This water is tapped by the wells, some of which are sunk to a considerable depth.

The direct dependence of the chief water supply on the floods

[1] N. Glueck, *Rivers in the Desert* (London 1959) pp. 201 ff. and 253.

running through a particular river-bed is an additional source of uncertainty in Bedouin economy. Therefore the cisterns which dot the whole area not only provide water to areas too distant from the wells, but also constitute an independent supply of water. The cisterns are filled up by the rains falling locally, while the wadis depend on rain falling higher up along their course. Thus one often finds cisterns which have been constructed quite close to wells, although Bedouin do not think much of making daily journeys of up to 10 km to the wells. Cisterns are relatively easy to excavate and present no serious obstacle to the simple tools of the Bedouin. They do represent a considerable investment of labour, initially in excavation, and constantly in maintenance. For a cistern which is not cleaned out year after year soon silts up. As Bedouin seldom take the trouble to reinforce the sides of the cisterns dug into the soft loess soil many cisterns have to be abandoned after some years. A considerable number of well-built cisterns, lined with stone and often covered with water-resistant layers of plaster, date back to the Nabatean and Byzantine periods; some even go as far back as Jewish times.[1] Bedouin give the ancients full credit for their useful works, but do not emulate them, as they cannot be tied to one place and invest such great efforts in any one cistern.

Cisterns are always owned by individual men whose kinsmen have claims to their use. Most wells are uncontested public property. In practice wells are exploited mainly by members of the tribal group in whose territory they are situated. The Mandatory authorities repaired the most important wells at public expense, and they seem to have reasserted public ownership so that now all tribes should have free access to wells. Normally this causes no difficulties. But at one time in 1961 water in one of the large wells ran low. Members of the tribal group in whose territory it lay then attempted to enforce priority of access.

In the central and southern parts of the Negev water is so scarce that it becomes the most important economic asset. Here pressure on the few wells is so great that in the last century the tribes fought regular battles over their possession. These struggles usually ended by all the contenders gaining access to the water. Therefore the few springs and wells became common boundaries between groups of tribes.

[1] Glueck, op. cit., pp. 222 ff.

After the establishment of Israel several water pipes were laid in the Bedouin reservation. Those laid on especially for Bedouin remained almost unused. No sooner had the water started to flow than the Bedouin began to squabble about rights of use and payments. In the end the water bills remained unpaid, the supply was shut off and the installations neglected. But there were also pipes which provided water to Jewish settlements, and where these ran through Bedouin territory the authorities provided outlets. In these cases the authorities could not just shut off the supply whenever they ran into difficulties with their Bedouin customers, but instead had to persuade them to come to an arrangement. These outlets have, in recent years, begun to assume increasing importance for the water supply in some areas, and the authorities have found it useful to sign agreements with individuals, mainly tribal chiefs, who were to be held responsible for payments. Some men then monopolized the use of their water taps and gave access to others only against payment. Groups which gained access to such a permanent water supply tend to establish camps in its proximity for some of their members. The Ẓullām tribes first obtained access to a permanent water supply in November 1961 towards the end of my field work. The pipe had been laid for the new town of ʿArad and ran right through the farming area in the Plain. The first men to apply for outlets were the chiefs of Abu Gweʿid and Abu Rbēʿah tribes.

The seasonal shortages of food, the frequent years of drought, the difficulties which a semi-nomadic way of life poses to the storage and transportation of food reserves, all these factors may have contributed to the Bedouin's frugal eating habits. Bedouin make a virtue of frugality, and it is considered good manners to eat only a few morsels when in company. When at a feast huge platters of steaming meat in gravy are set in front of the guests, the honoured men among them daintily pick a scrap of meat and chew it thoughtfully, so as to allow the other men around the platter to eat their fill; for when one of the diners rises the others should soon follow suit. On a working day a Bedouin will generally only have one meal, usually a dish of *fatt*, a porridge made of bread soaked in liquid fat and water. This meal is called the dinner (*ghada*), and might be served at any time between say, 8 a.m. and 5 p.m., according to the wishes of the master of the house on that day. After rising in the morning Bedouin usually have only a cup of coffee or tea and a piece of dry bread left over from the preceding day. Meat is reserved only for festive occasions, and the staple food is cereals. These are the only foodstuffs for which Bedouin have evolved methods of long-term storage. They maintain centrally situated storage areas (*manṭarah*) in which each family keeps its heaps of grain (*muṭmārah*) or straw (*kimr*). These are covered by a layer of compressed earth, which is removed gradually as the stored food is required. In spring, the monotonous diet is relieved by milk and by some wild-growing vegetables, such as *khubēzah* (mallow) and *kima* (truffle-like mushrooms). For the rest of the year fruits and vegetables used to be out of the question, and are only now gradually included in the diet, though by no means of all Bedouin.

Many Bedouin, including wealthy people, suffer from nutritional deficiencies caused by their unbalanced diet. This results in anything from a general state of physical weakness to tuberculosis, to which Bedouin are more prone than any other section of the population.[1] The havoc that can be wrought by this disease can be seen from the case of one family in which, within the span of ten years, the husband, wife and two of their three children died of tuberculosis. The diseases are made the more contagious by the closeness of living in a small tent.

Temperatures in the Negev undergo quite extreme, and at times rapid, changes. Although the winter months are often rather cold, and temperatures as low as −5 °C (23 °F) have been recorded, there also occur in the same months days in which the temperature rises to over 30 °C (86 °F). There is rarely a year in which the temperature does not fall below freezing for at least a day or two. The cool days fall within the main rainy season, between December and March. Snow falls very rarely. Indeed, even old men recall only one or two such occasions in their lifetime. At the beginning of summer, in March and April, and again in October to November, a transitional climate is often experienced, with average temperatures of between 25–30 °C. This is a far cry from a mild spring and autumn type of weather, because it is almost regularly punctuated by spells of hot, dry weather, accompanied by strong gusts of south-easterly winds, carrying fine particles of sand from the

[1] B. J. Ben Assa, 'Vital Statistics Concerning Tuberculosis Among Bedouin Tribes in Southern Israel' (*IMJ* 1960). The mortality rate per 10,000 was 29·3 in 1958, 17·6 in 1957.

Arabian desert. The scorching breath of these winds frequently wilts the spring vegetation in a short time.

Throughout summer the temperatures are consistently high, but as the air is relatively dry, the weather is generally not too oppressive. Only on a few days do temperatures rise into the forties. On the hottest day I experienced, 7 June 1961, the temperature reached 45°C (113°F) in the shade. On that day Bedouin remained as far as possible under the cover of their tents, trying either to get some sleep or to sip some water, and they even went as far as to shed their upper clothing. Shepherds caught out in the open sheltered in the scant shade of overhanging rocks or shrubs, cowering low with their cloaks wrapped round their heads.

The intense heat of the day is generally relieved during the last hours of the night, when one often wakes up shivering. The daily fluctuation averages even in winter 10–12°C, and in summer 15–17°C. Sometimes, especially on days concluding a hot spell, the difference in temperature can amount to 25°C.[1] Table 4 gives an impression of the daily and seasonal variations of temperatures.[2]

TABLE 4

Temperatures in Beersheba, by months, 1921–48 (in °C)

	Jan.	*Feb.*	*Mar.*	*Apr.*	*May*	*June*
Mean max. temp.	18·5	19·1	23·6	28·1	32·3	33·9
Mean min. temp.	5·4	6·1	7·4	8·7	13·1	15·8
Absolute max. temp.	28·2	32·0	36·5	43·6	44·7	43·1
Absolute min. temp.	−5·0	−1·0	−1·0	2·3	4·5	8·0
	July	*Aug.*	*Sept.*	*Oct.*	*Nov.*	*Dec.*
Mean max. temp.	34·7	34·8	33·6	31·6	26·5	20·7
Mean min. temp.	17·6	17·8	16·5	14·2	10·9	7·4
Absolute max. temp.	42·0	41·5	43·8	39·6	35·6	30·2
Absolute min. temp.	12·0	12·0	9·4	6·0	4·0	−1·0

[1] D. Ashbel, op. cit., p. 117. [2] Ibid., p. 122.

The specific blend of rains and temperatures found in the Negev has its effects on plant life there. When and where the rains have been sufficient, a varied succulent spring vegetation (*rabīʿ*) shoots up, covering the land, and particularly the pastures, with a many-coloured plant carpet. To exploit this vegetation fully, Bedouin permit it to grow to a certain height before they let loose their herds. At this time camels can go without watering, while sheep and goats have to be watered only at infrequent intervals, once in about every ten days when conditions are favourable. This permits Bedouin at this time to make use of pastures in the most easterly parts, where almost no water is available, and from there to work their way gradually westwards. The spring vegetation wilts at the first spell of the dry hot easterly winds (*shird* or *khamsīn*), and even in the best conditions lasts only to May. After that the camels and goats have to feed off the prickly drought-resistant perennials, whereas sheep require at least hay or stubble pasture. The Bedouin cannot provide much of the latter type of pasture on their own land because they reap the grain by tearing out stalks from the ground in order to produce the maximum of straw for the most critical period in autumn. Therefore, the larger flocks of sheep soon have to be taken outside the Bedouin area to farm land which has been harvested mechanically, leaving long stubbles. At this time, Bedouin flocks of sheep, to which for economy's sake the goats are attached, press westward and northward in search of suitable pasture, each man negotiating arrangements for his herd. In years of drought, when the available pasture is limited, this turns into a competitive scramble for grazing land, especially as the Military Administration used to open up new areas in a piecemeal fashion, and only under considerable pressure from Bedouin herd owners. In bad years there is altogether not enough pasture for all the Bedouin herds; each man attempts to increase his herd to the utmost limits, as he is quite unable to gauge the overall pasture available. Thus many herd owners are hard hit in years of drought, and they have the difficult choice between buying expensive fodder for their animals, letting them die off, or selling them at a loss. Even in a prosperous year this is a hard time for the Bedouin. The most critical period, however, comes at the end of summer, and is anticipated by Bedouin with great misgivings: soon after the first showers have fallen, the remains of the withered vegetation begin to rot and the animals refuse to eat it, while the new 'spring' pasture (*rabīʿ*) will have attained sufficient growth only four to six weeks later. The *rabīʿ* will spring up best in the uncultivated eastern parts, whereas the herds are at that time at the most westerly point of their annual cycle of movement. Therefore, even if the rain falls in its time, the enfeebled animals, the ewes in the last stages of pregnancy, have to be driven a distance of at least 40 km (about 25 miles) to reach the new pastures, and inevitably some fall by the wayside. If the rains arrive late, their lot may be even worse, because then the hunger period may coincide with the lambing season in October to November, and cause great losses among the newborn lambs. It is for such emergencies that Bedouin store their straw, although they have to supplement it frequently by straw bought from farms. When they manage to struggle through these hard times, they can enjoy the spring, the best season of the year.

CHAPTER 2

The Administrative Environment

THE Ottoman administration ruled the Bedouin in a haphazard fashion, by a combination of stratagem and force. Mr Finn, British consul in Jerusalem, thus sums up his impressions of these methods of tribal administration (in 1853):

When two chiefs, or tribes . . . were too nearly equal in strength and had therefore become troublesome, they were set to fighting each other till one had obtained the upper hand. Both were weakened in the process, and ambiguities were ended by the results. Thereafter one could be held responsible for whatever might occur.[1]

The cruel internecine struggles of the Tiāha tribal confederation, remembered by Bedouin to this day as the 'War of ʿAudah and ʿĀmer',[2] provide a good example. The Hazail tribe tried to wrest the hegemony over the Tiāha from the ʿAṭauneh, and for a long time the Turks looked on passively. Only when the Hazail had come out victors in 1856 did the Turks intervene, break their power and execute their chief, Salmān al-Hazail.[3]

The opening of the Suez Canal in 1869 brought home to the Ottoman authorities the extent of European penetration into this corner of their empire, and they began thenceforth to pay greater attention to the Negev and to intervene more directly, and in more sustained fashion, in Bedouin affairs.

With a sudden spurt of energy, they first attempted to solve the Bedouin problem radically. In 1870 Rāshid Pasha, the Ottoman governor of the Syrian province,

sent word down to Gaza that the Bedawin of those parts must for the future live in huts instead of tents; our friends [the Bedouin] were

---

[1] J. Finn, *Stirring Times* (London 1878) vol. 1, p. 219.

[2] ʿĀref al-ʿĀref, *Ta'arīkh Bīr al-Sabaʿ wa-qabā'ilha* (= *Ta'arīkh*) (Jerusalem 1934) pp. 175 ff., gives detailed accounts of the struggle, collected from descendants of the chief participants.

[3] ʿĀref, *Ta'arīkh*, p. 107, gives the chief's name incorrectly as Sulimān al-Hazail.

acute enough to see that this was a deadly blow aimed at their very existence, and the first fifteen Turkish soldiers who appeared amongst the Teyāhah were killed. A detachment of troops was sent down, and all the herds were confiscated, brought to Jerusalem and sold for a nominal value to the Fellahīn.[1]

The strong-arm approach was bound to fail, and no further attempts were made to settle Bedouin. Government supervision over them, however, became increasingly effective. Intertribal fighting and raiding were gradually suppressed, though not completely eradicated.[2] Instead of collecting tribute through the tribal chiefs, the authorities now sent army detachments to collect the annual tax payments. Elected tribal chiefs had to be confirmed in office by the authorities. In 1894 the first permanent gendarmerie post was established in the area, at Khirbet Ftēs, followed in 1900 by the founding of an administrative centre at Beersheba.[3]

The British administration, which took over from the Turks in 1917, pursued only limited objectives in the Negev. It did not seek to improve the Bedouin's way of life but effectively maintained peace and security. Bedouin were no longer permitted to resort to self-help or fight out their disputes. The carrying of firearms was made conditional on a licence, except in the sparsely populated interior of the Negev.[4] In addition to the regular law courts, whose jurisdiction extended to the Negev, special tribal courts were established to deal with litigation arising out of the Bedouin way of life, such as payment of blood-money for a murder, or compensation to a man, the sanctity of whose tent had been violated. Although Bedouin were appointed as judges, the judgments of these courts bore only formal resemblance to customary

[1] E. H. Palmer, *The Desert of the Exodus* (Cambridge 1871) vol. 2, p. 298. This incident is not mentioned in other sources, but is in line with similar attempts to settle Bedouin made in other parts of the empire at about the same time. See E. Sachau, *Reise in Syrien und Mesopotamien* (Leipzig 1883) p. 264.

[2] ʿĀref, *Taʾarīkh*, cf. pp. 188 and 192. In 1875, intertribal fighting still had to be suppressed by a punitive expedition, while by 1890 matters had improved to the extent that when fighting broke out, the Pasha ordered the Bedouin chiefs concerned to appear before him in Gaza, and inflicted on them the punishment he saw fit.

[3] ʿĀref, *Taʾarīkh*, p. 244.

[4] Y. Shimoni, *ʿArvei Erets-Israel* (Tel-Aviv 1947) p. 144 and map on p. 149.

PLATE III

Above: Grain storage plot in Abu Gweʿid tribe. Some of the grain mounds already covered with earth

Below: Goats are slaughtered for a festive meal

PLATE IV

Above: Watering herds at the wells of Bīr Mshāsh

Below: Bedouin examining their flock in the summer pasture west of Beersheba. The shepherd stands back

Bedouin justice, for while there the judge's task had been to mediate between and conciliate the parties, now sentences became enforceable by the administration[1] and the judges were not concerned to see that all the disputants were satisfied.

Bedouin were also drafted into a camel-mounted police unit whose task was to patrol the Negev and keep an eye on its population. This mobile force established nine permanent police posts in various parts of the Negev, three of which were situated close to the present reservation, though outside its boundaries: these three were the headquarters at Beersheba, and the posts of Kurnub and Ras Zuwērah, the latter not far from the site of the new town of ʿArad.[2] The authorities preferred to enlist members of the more powerful 'true' Bedouin groups to this force: 'We were allowed to join up after being questioned about our genealogies (*silsilah*)', reminisced one former trooper. A list of policemen compiled in 1933 includes the names of three men of the Ẓullām group of tribes; all three were members of powerful groups, just those groups which often also supplied the tribal chiefs: Abu Rbēʿah, Abu Gweʿid and Qabūʿah.[3] Men like these not only represented the authority of the State but also the influence of their groups. In this manner the administration exploited the Bedouin political organization in maintaining public security. It also promulgated a law specifically for the Negev, which permitted the District Commissioner to anticipate and prevent fighting if he considered that

> reasonable grounds exist for supposing that a raid or other breach of the peace is intended by any tribesman or tribesmen . . . [to] seize so much of the movable property of such tribesman or tribesmen and of his or their relatives to the fifth degree . . . as he may consider necessary.[4]

Thus it was made quite clear to the Bedouin that, in spite of the

[1] ʿĀref al-ʿĀref, *Al-qaḍā bain al badu* (= *Qaḍā*) (Jerusalem 1933) pp. 62–9.

[2] ʿĀref, *Taʾarīkh*, p. 43, states that there had been a post at Tel al-Milḥ, i.e. in the heart of the reservation, which was in 1933 transferred to Ras Zuwērah.

[3] ʿĀref, *Taʾarīkh*, p. 281.

[4] Government of Palestine. Ordinances, Regulations, Rules, Orders and Notices. Jerusalem, vols. 1942 and 1945: *Beduin Control Ordinance*, No. 18 of 1942; *Beduin Control* (*Amendment*) *Ordinance*, No. 38 of 1945. See particularly paragraph 4(c).

special conditions prevailing in the Negev, fighting, feuding and raiding would not be tolerated, and that their areas were to become as tranquil as the settled parts of the country.

During most of the thirty years of British administration, Arabs were appointed as District Officers in Beersheba to facilitate relations with the Bedouin population.[1] Though no Bedouin were ever appointed to this position, all its incumbents were in sympathy with their needs and problems and maintained personal contacts with the tribal chiefs. The District Officer not only met the chiefs when they visited Beersheba on business, to attend to tribal affairs, or to take part in the sessions of the tribal court, but also used to make the round of the chiefs' guest tents, so as to enhance their prestige in the eyes of their tribe. Sheikhs were given small salaries to compensate them for services rendered to the authorities. A boarding school for Bedouin was established at Beersheba, and it was attended almost exclusively by the sons of chiefs. It was hoped thus to provide the future tribal leaders with the skills necessary for maintaining relations with government officials.

The Bedouin had definitely come under the rule of the state, but in most other respects they were still generally left to their own devices. Only when an emergency arose did the Administration extend generous assistance to the Bedouin; thus during the serious drought of 1927 it transported a large number of Bedouin and their herds to the Beth Shean Plain in the north of the country.[2] For the rest it took no positive action to help Bedouin adapt their economy to new conditions. As a result, it seems that during this period their standard of living sank considerably, because of the declining demand for their main products, camels and barley.[3]

Around 1942, for the first time a considerable number of Bedouin sought employment outside their tribes, on the construction of camps, airfields and roads for the allied armies stationed in the Negev. Three years later this source of income dried up, and for several years the Bedouin had again to rely solely on the meagre income from their traditional occupations.

The Bedouin participated only to a limited extent in the Israeli-Arab fighting in 1948–9. They neither formed military units of

[1] ʿĀref al-ʿĀref, author of two books on the Negev Bedouin frequently quoted on these pages, served two extended terms in this position.

[2] ʿAref, *Qaḍā*, p. 220.

[3] Ibid., pp. 225, 228.

their own, nor joined the regular Arab armies, but they engaged in some guerilla fighting and occasional attacks on Jewish settlements and patrols. Some groups, however, stood on the side lines and a few individuals actively co-operated with the Jews. When the Egyptian army occupied the Negev after the British withdrew in May 1948, it considered the Bedouin unreliable and made little effort to enlist their services. Between October and December of that year Israeli forces wrested most of the Negev from the Egyptians. The Bedouin feared their new rulers would treat them as enemies. Many fled, particularly those who had been involved in fighting. Thus about half the members of the Tiāha confederation are said to have left the country for the Hebron mountains or the Gaza area,[1] while the remaining groups took to the hilly and less accessible parts of the Negev.

For some years the situation in the Negev remained unsettled. Some Bedouin left the country, some were moved from one part of the Negev into another, while others filtered back into the Negev. The dust finally settled in 1953; people registered in the census of the Bedouin population undertaken in the following year were thenceforth regarded as Israeli citizens; later arrivals had to apply individually for citizenship. All these Bedouin now lived in a reservation under military rule in the eastern Beersheba Plain.

The reservation had been established in an area which prior to 1948 had been largely occupied by the Tiāha. Members of this confederation who had formerly lived on this land, and who had stayed on under Israeli rule, have retained their land. These were the three large tribes of the Ẓullām group (Abu Rbēʿah, Abu Qrenāt and Abu Gweʿid), the al-Aʿsam and al-Asad tribes, and parts of the Abu Rqaiq and Hazail tribes. The remaining eleven tribes had held land only in other areas and were moved into parts of the reservation which had been vacated by Bedouin who had left the country, and which had not already been occupied by the local tribes. These tribes now own no land in the reservation except for a few isolated parcels, and they cannot gain access to areas where they had formerly ranged. They now live on State land, which they are given in annually renewable leases. The total arable area is limited, and the authorities have tried to make the little go a long way, to ensure each family in these tribes a fair minimal quota of 100 dunams (nearly 25 acres) of farm land.

[1] S. Ben-Elkanah, *ʿArab al-Tiāha* (unpublished paper).

When in 1948 the State of Israel was established in war-torn Palestine, all areas in which fighting went on were proclaimed Military Zones. At the time, the greater part of the country came under that definition. When hostilities ceased, military administration was gradually abolished and remained in force only in three parts of the country: in Galilee, in the border areas in the Sharon (the so-called little Triangle), and in the Negev. These are predominantly Arab areas with relatively few Jewish inhabitants. About 84 per cent of the Arab population of 230,000[1] live in these areas.

Although fighting between Israel and the neighbouring Arab states had formally ceased with the signing of the several Armistice Agreements in 1949, this was not considered by the Arab states to end the war. Arab leaders repeatedly announced their determination to wipe Israel off the map and to restore the Palestine refugees to their homes. They enforced an economic boycott against Israel and conducted endemic guerilla activities along Israel's borders. They also incessantly waged a psychological campaign, one of whose main objectives was to incite the Arabs of Israel, who constitute an important minority within the state,[2] to civil disobedience and sabotage. On the whole, the Arabs remained law-abiding, if not enthusiastic, citizens of Israel, in spite of being exposed to a constant stream of hostile propaganda, in particular from Cairo radio. There occurred few cases of espionage and no serious acts of sabotage, but people hesitated to co-operate with the authorities and only rarely identified themselves publicly with the State. The authorities considered the Arab areas as specially vulnerable from a security point of view and maintained the Military Administration so as to keep a constant eye on their inhabitants. The Military Administration was to concern itself solely with military security, while the civilian branches of the administration were to exercise their functions in full, as in the rest of the country.

The Military Administration had, however, for a long time an important voice in all civilian affairs too, for it had been vested with considerable powers, due to the precarious military situation. For some years the military authorities could overrule the administrative decisions of their civilian counterparts. Only when

[1] Information supplied by an official source, correct for the end of 1959.

[2] Arabs constitute 11 per cent of Israel's population.

the security situation improved after the Suez campaign at the end of 1956, were the powers of the Military Administration gradually curtailed.

In the Basic Principles of Policy approved by the Knesset (the Israeli Parliament) on 17 December 1959, the intention to scale down security regulations was clearly stated:

> Security measures in border areas, which are inevitable in view of the refusal of the neighbouring Arab states to make peace with Israel, will be limited to actual and vital security requirements.[1]

All the political parties in Israel have been agreed on this point, and the sometimes quite acrimonious differences of opinion range on the question how secure the state was and to what extent the Arab population could endanger its chances of survival. The governments headed by D. Ben-Gurion (from the founding of the state in 1948, with a short interval, until 1963) were wary about relaxing military government.

The Military Administration derives its legal powers from the Defence (Emergency) Regulations 1945, originally issued by the Mandatory authorities of the day to combat the Jewish underground. The Israeli administration took these regulations as a legal basis for military rule, and as it viewed this as a temporary measure never replaced them by specific legislation. In their 150 sections these drastic regulations legalize almost any arbitrary administrative act. The Israeli authorities, however, have gradually circumscribed their application, through self-imposed restraints, stated in the Knesset on repeated occasions when the annual renewal of the regulations was discussed. By 1961 only six sections were employed, among them, however, perhaps the most important, section 125, which permits a military commander to designate 'Closed Areas', which may be entered or left only with his written authorization. On this basis a system of movement permits was evolved and the military governors were able to enforce their policies by issuing permits judiciously. On 21 October 1963 the Prime Minister announced in the Knesset that most of the Arab inhabitants of Galilee and the central areas

[1] The full text of those parts of the Basic Principles having special reference to the Arab population is found in Israel, Ministry of Foreign Affairs, *The Arabs of Israel* (Jerusalem 1961) p. 10.

would henceforth be able to move without restriction, implying that movement permits would still be required in the Negev.[1]

The improving security situation not only resulted in curtailment of the Military Administration's powers; it also brought about a shift in its activities from the military to the civilian plane. As long as a bureaucratic body retains powers—and in this case these are still quite formidable—it will tend to exercise them to their limits. With fewer primary security problems to occupy them, the military administrators paid increasing attention to civilian affairs which, under certain conditions, could become relevant to security.[2]

The Military Administration has been able to exercise its powers more extensively in the Negev than in the other military zones. In the latter the local Arab population was articulate, could exert political pressure on the authorities, and could defend itself through legal action. The illiterate Bedouin of the Negev are not versed in these ways, and moreover had for many years been under government tutelage. Thus they were less able to restrain the Military Administration. Up to about 1958, movement permits were issued in limited number and usually for short periods. Later control was slightly relaxed, and policy was as far as possible not to deny anyone a movement permit, but if necessary to apply various limiting conditions. The most stringent of these can affect the period of validity of the permit and the localities the bearer is permitted to visit. When the validity is limited to a shorter period than the customary 30 days, and a man is directed to visit only certain places the value of the permit can become negligible. Other conditions can direct him to proceed by a predefined route, to perform only a specific activity while outside the reservation, or to check in at regular intervals at Military Administration or Police posts. Permits are usually issued only to personal applicants at their local Military Administration post, so that men working outside the reservation must return for each renewal of their permit.

Conversely, the Military Governor can also supervise entry into the closed area. While no check is kept on people entering other

[1] *Haarets* (daily newspaper), Tel-Aviv, 22 October 1963.

[2] Z. Schiff, 'The Pros and Cons of the Military Government', *New Outlook*, vol. 5, no. 3 (1962), examines the actual administration of the Defence Regulations in 1961. Here we shall discuss only the Negev.

zones of Military Administration, in the Negev only a few persons gain access to the reservation, unless the Military Administration approves of their purpose.

The Military Administration has established posts in various parts of the reservation, to facilitate contacts with its inhabitants: at Shuval, Umm Baṭīn, Shqēb, Abu Tlūl, Tel al-Milḥ and ʿArʿarah. Each post caters for the tribes camping in its vicinity, and the army officer responsible for these tribes has fixed times of attendance, usually once or twice weekly. The post at Tel al-Milḥ, for instance, was according to the schedule of attendance in force from November 1961, to open on Monday and Wednesday for members of two of the Ẓullām tribes, Abu Rbēʿah and Abu Gweʿid, and of the Qderāt al-Ṣāneʿ tribe.[1] The three tribes numbered together in 1961 about 4,500 persons, for whom one army officer assisted by one military clerk, was responsible. Most of the current business, namely the issue of movement permits, is not handled by the area officer, but by the clerk, usually a young national serviceman. The clerks are supposed to deal only with straightforward cases and to refer any intricate matter to the officer, but in time they become acquainted with numerous tribesmen and their problems. After a year or two in service, though, they are released, and the information accumulated by them is lost. Area officers usually serve for longer terms, yet obtain only a limited insight into tribal affairs, for their contacts with Bedouin are restricted to a small number of notables, who provide them with carefully sifted bits of information. Relationships even with tribal chiefs remain on a formal level. Officers occasionally visit tribal chiefs in their tents and take meals with them in order to demonstrate support for them: these visits, however, are not reciprocated, for officers do not ask Bedouin to their homes. The officers do not adhere closely to the routine of attendance at their post. Sometimes they are late and at others prevented altogether from attending. Average attendance of the officers at Tel al-Milḥ was less than once a week, instead of the twice laid down by rule. The Military Administration's officers, then, meet regularly only a small number of Bedouin, mainly tribal chiefs with whom they conduct tribal business. With most other Bedouin they have only slight acquaintance.

[1] The third Ẓullām tribe, Abu Qrenāt, was served by another post, ʿArʿarah, on Wednesdays only.

The concentration of the Negev Bedouin in the compact and easily accessible reservation in the eastern Beersheba Plain in the first years of Israeli rule, facilitated the policing of these unsettled people. Here the Bedouin reconstituted tribes around men recognized as chiefs by the authorities. This was no new departure, for previous administrations had ruled in the same manner for many years. Both the tribal and the administrative organization fell into a well-tried customary pattern. This arrangement had considerable advantages from the administrative point of view. Not only were the Bedouin accustomed to it, but it was also economical, at least at first sight, because the officers did not have to treat with individuals, and obtained the virtually unpaid services of chiefs for this purpose. It was not as rigidly bound by irksome legal restrictions and by specialization of activities as a bureaucratic administration: the officers could give the chiefs instructions by word of mouth, which they then carried out to the best of their understanding. If later it should turn out that the law had been infringed, no blame could attach to the administrators.

The tribesmen were also keen to join tribes, for thus they became part of a recognized political framework, and this gave them some sense of security. In most cases they rejoined the tribe they had belonged to before the turbulent events of 1948–9 had scattered the tribes and broken them up. In their eagerness to 'belong', many Bedouin registered during the first partial census held in 1949, and during the complete registration in 1954, under assumed names. They took the patronymic of large politically active groups in the tribes they had joined, in the hope that this would give them a better chance to be allowed to remain in the country. Thus in one extreme case, the 200 or so members of the ʿAwāwdeh of Abu Rbēʿah tribe registered in 1949 under five different names, not one of them the group's own patronymic. Bedouin often paid a chief varying amounts for consenting to have them registered in his tribe. And indeed, the tribal registration was taken as the basis of all subsequent administrative activity. Every Bedouin had to have a tribal affiliation, which was entered on his identity card, that vitally important document which confirmed his legal domicile in Israel. The tribal affiliation could be altered only by consent of the Military Administration, which was rarely forthcoming in the early years.

The military administrators were generally interested in strong chiefs, able to keep their tribesmen firmly in hand, for such men could be relied on to carry out its instructions. On the other hand, they did not lightly intervene in the election of new chiefs, because they believed that a free play of the internal forces of the tribe would throw up a man acceptable to most members. Thus when the chieftaincy of al-Aʿsam tribe became vacant in 1958, the Military Administration left the members to make their own choice, although they had a favoured candidate. In the event the late chief's younger son was elected, and confirmed by the Administration, in spite of serious misgivings. The Tarabīn al-Ṣāneʿ, whose chief had died in 1957, could not agree on a successor for three years. Only then did the Administration appoint its own nominee, whom it had sponsored all this time. For a tribe without a chief was even less manageable than a tribe with a weak chief. Even chiefs whose political attitudes were uncongenial to the Administration were tolerated, for they could always be brought into line, at least temporarily. Only chiefs convicted of crimes had to be deposed. One such man had been the sheikh ʿĀmer Ṭalālqah, who in 1956 had been caught smuggling narcotics.[1] Officers of the Military Administration, talking about this man several years later, still thought that he had the making of a successful chief; 'He had personality and strength of character. He ruled his small tribe with an iron hand, and attained for himself a position quite incommensurate with its size.' Strong chiefs could be more useful to the administrator, and therefore he approved of them.

The Administration, on its side, helped to strengthen the chief's position. Thus, when in the early fifties the Bedouin were supplied with rationed foodstuffs, such as sugar, flour and edible oil, at subsidized prices, these were distributed through tribal stores (*ḥanūt*). The licensees of these stores were the chiefs or their representatives, and their tribesmen were their linked customers. The chiefs would levy prices slightly above the fixed official ones, and thus obtained a steady and lucrative source of income. Only in the largest tribe, Abu Rqaiq, were there stores in addition to the chief's. As late as 1958 the Abu Rqaiq chief wrote to the Military Governor about this: '. . . In all other tribes there exists only one store, but in my tribe there is one to each sub-tribe (*rubaʿ*) . . . the other stores ought to be closed.' A peasant shopkeeper in Abu

[1] This man died a year later. His tribe was subsequently incorporated in the ʿAṭauneh tribe.

Rbēʿah tribe voluntarily gave up his store in 1952, so that the whole tribe could thenceforth buy its rations from the shop maintained by the chief's family. The Administration did not accede to requests by tribesmen other than chiefs to establish stores until about 1957–8. By that time rationing had been discontinued and stores were no longer such good business.

The tendency to strengthen chiefs was even clearer in the allocation of State lands. Here one has to distinguish between tribes that own land and those that obtain theirs from the authorities in annual leases. The former dispose freely of their land, and the authorities neither interfere in its distribution among the tribesmen, nor allocate to them additional State land. An official committee, on which the Military Administration is represented, allocates to each of the landless tribes a tract, within which members can lease a limited area, as long as land is available. A man cannot obtain land in another tribe's tract, unless he is permitted to transfer his registration, or the Military Administration makes an exception on other grounds. The tribal blocks of land are annually revised so as to compensate for changes in membership. As the total available State land in the reservation is not enough to satisfy the Bedouin requirements, these adjustments can be only slight, but their effect is considerable.

Since 1955 most of the State land in the reservation has been leased to the landless tribesmen through their tribal chiefs, though from 1956 onwards chiefs were required to produce authorizations signed by the heads of groups and families. The government department dealing with land leases tended increasingly to lease land directly to groups smaller than tribes, and first applied this policy to the Hazail and Abu Rqaiq tribes. This was partly due to their being the two largest tribes, so that chiefs could not easily cope with all the complex details of land allocation, and partly, perhaps, to the fact that in these tribes there were groups which still owned some land, and which had to be dealt with separately and were not to be given State land. During succeeding years leases were also made with individual farmers and groups in other tribes, but the process is still far from complete, and the chief still often has a say in the allocation of land to his tribesmen. The Military Administration realized that the individualization of land leases was an inevitable development, although it lessened its hold over the tribes.

The allocation of land through chiefs enabled these men not only to decide how and where each group of tribesmen was to get land, but also to retain large slices of land, which they then let out in sharecropping agreements to members of their own or even of other tribes. Chiefs were allowed to retain double the average quota of land for their own uses; in practice they could often handle the distribution of much of the tribe's land in accordance with their economic and political interests. In one large tribe, the chief had leased all the land on behalf of his tribesmen. Instead of passing it on to them he engaged them as sharecroppers against a third of the harvest. Chiefs went so far as to withhold land from tribesmen with whom they had quarrelled. Thus the chief of the Masʿudīn tribe refused to allocate land to the Ḥamāmdah group of his tribe after a dispute in 1959, and in the end the Lands Department leased land directly to this group. When tribesmen complained about such cases of discrimination and exploitation, the Military Administration warned and exhorted the chiefs, but it did not institute legal proceedings against them.

Members of landowning tribes are not normally given leases on scarce State land. Yet the chiefs of the Ẓullām tribes, whose personal holdings are relatively large, are each year allowed to lease additional farm land. 'Their leases are renewed almost automatically year after year', stated one official. Thus in the year 1958–9[1] the chiefs of three Ẓullām tribes obtained the following areas of arable State land: Abu Rbēʿah 9,500 dunams, Abu Qrenāt 3,250 dunams, and Abu Gweʿid 3,000 dunams. Viewed in relation to the efforts being made to provide each Bedouin family with 100–150 dunams (about 25–37 acres) of arable State land, these were very large areas. In succeeding years the quotas of the Abu Qrenāt and Abu Gweʿid chiefs were officially eliminated, but they still dispose of even larger areas of land to which the State lays claim, without signing lease contracts.

In the years 1953–6, tractors could be obtained only with official buying permits. The few permits issued to Bedouin all went to chiefs. Later, other Bedouin were able to acquire tractors and to break the chief's monopoly on the ploughing of his tribe's land. To this day, however, the majority of tractor-owners are chiefs. Thus all three Ẓullām chiefs own tractors: the Abu Rbēʿah

[1] Lease contracts are made out for eleven months, from 1 October to 31 August. The gap is designed to prevent continuity of lease.

chiefs had as many as five in 1960. In November of that year Abu Rbēʿah's tractors, together with a few machines owned by other tribesmen, could not cope with the ploughing, and some tribesmen hired a tractor from outside the reservation. The Abu Rbēʿah chiefs tried to persuade the Military Administration first to refuse an entry permit to the tractor-driver, and then when he entered the area in spite of this, to have him ejected. This man had committed an additional offence: he had undercut the chiefs by charging IL. 0.80 for disc-ploughing a dunam of land, against their charge of IL. 1.–.

The Military Administration has, at various times, augmented the chief's authority in numerous other ways, though not always intentionally. One of the most effective means was the channelling of many of the contacts between Bedouin and government departments through the chiefs. Thus 15 out of the 18 tribal chiefs have also been appointed as salaried village headmen (*mukhtār*) by the Ministry of the Interior.[1] As such they register births and deaths of tribesmen and occasionally provide them with affidavits and other references, for which they are entitled to charge a stipulated fee. As the legal status of a person in Israel, including citizenship, is ultimately founded on these documents, it can well be imagined that these duties give chiefs considerable influence.

Eight out of nine Bedouin schools have been built near the encampments of tribal chiefs, thus giving children of their groups a higher than average chance to acquire literacy.[2] Chiefs headed the tribal education committees which were to raise funds for the

[1] Initially the chiefs of all 18 tribes were, between 1950–2, appointed as village headmen. The decrease to 15 is due to the accession of new chiefs, not all of whom were recognized by the Ministry. The quarterly emoluments of headmen ranged from IL. 66 to IL. 105 in 1960, according to the size of tribe. (Information supplied by the Military Administration.)

[2] In 1960–1 only seven of the schools were open: those of Abu Rqaiq, Abu Rbēʿah, Hazail, al-Asad (and neighbouring tribes), ʿAṭauneh, and Masʿudīn tribes, and one in the al-Sayid group of Abu Rqaiq tribe. There were 556 registered pupils, out of an estimated 4,000 children of school age. (Information supplied by Arab Education Department, Ministry of Education.)

In the tribe studied, the Abu Gweʿid, there was no school and only three of the tribe's children attended the school of the neighbouring Abu Rbēʿah tribe at Ksēfeh. They were two sons of the tribal chief, and a brother's son. Some of the tribe's peasant children attended, and paid for, a private class maintained by a young tribesman. State elementary schooling is given free.

construction of school buildings, and thus could influence decisions on siting.

When the Ministry of Agriculture decided to assist farmers who had suffered losses through drought, from 1955 to 1956 onwards, the Bedouin at first received loans according to lists drawn up by the tribal chief, stating the loss sustained by each farmer. The chief also signed for receipt of the loans, or their equivalent in seeds or agricultural services, on behalf of his tribesmen. After the very serious drought year of 1957–8, Bedouin farmers received compensation in the form of cash grants, at the rate of IL. 3.– for the first 100 dunams cultivated. The grants were calculated according to data on cultivated areas presented by the chiefs, who thus had some influence on the amounts paid. Another drought year followed, and this time the cash grants were not based on chiefs' assessments. Instead, each family head filled in a form in which he declared the area cultivated by him. This form was then scrutinized by a committee of notables from the tribe, headed by the chief, which sat together with the officials of the Ministry. Even though the new procedure diminished the influence of chiefs on the allocation of payments, it did not completely eliminate it. This was especially the case in the big landowning tribes, where there was no way to collate the compensation claims with the area owned, or held in sharecropping agreements, by each cultivator.

Lastly, whenever the issue of movement permits for work outside the reservation was restricted, chiefs would intercede with the authorities on behalf of their tribesmen, with varying degrees of success. Conversely, when government departments required a number of labourers, the officers of the Military Administration usually asked one or other of the chiefs to send along his tribesmen. In the early years of the State of Israel there were few jobs, and Bedouin often paid their chiefs for arranging work. Gradually more permits were issued, and tribesmen could usually obtain them directly from the Military Administration. They, then, requested chiefs to intervene only when their applications had been refused.

By strengthening the chiefs, the Military Administration sought to augment its rule over the tribes. A chief who had access to the Military Administration could gain many advantages for his tribesmen and, therefore, greatly increase their dependence on him. This put him in a position effectively to carry out the Administration's instructions in the tribe. A chief, then, had to be influential in the tribe in order to become valuable to the Military Administration, and had to wield influence with the authorities to become useful to his tribesmen.

This aspect of chiefship is most pronounced among the landless tribes where, on one hand, the chief and his co-liable group do not exercise direct control over a considerable part of the land and, on the other, some members of the tribe have to make a living outside the tribe. We shall see later on that in the landowning tribes the position of chiefs is to a large extent also affected by internal Bedouin politics.

During the first years after the establishment of Israel, there was an immense influx of immigrants which, in under four years, from mid-1948 to the end of 1951, added over 700,000 immigrants to the country's Jewish population of 655,000, thus more than doubling it. In succeeding years immigration slowed down, but until 1961, when the one millionth immigrant arrived, it continued to bring in, on an average, around 33,000 people per year. Economic development could not keep pace with the rapidly expanding population, so that there was serious unemployment. In the desperate efforts to integrate the new immigrants economically each job counted, and the authorities feared that Bedouin would take on work which could be given to the immigrants. The Bedouin were making a living out of their traditional pursuits and were accustomed to low standards of living, so that when entering the labour market in the towns they were satisfied with low wages and could easily dislodge the immigrants from hard-won jobs. There was also some apprehension that new immigrants settled in the Western Negev would yield to the temptation to let low-paid Bedouin do their farming for them, and sit back to enjoy the fruits of their labour. This would have vitiated the painstaking efforts made to turn the settlers into earthbound farmers. It was felt that the Bedouin were already self-supporting and should stay at their traditional pursuits.

The Military Administration strictly delimited the number of movement permits issued to Bedouin, and acceded to requests for such permits only for purposes it considered reasonable. Thus when a man applied for a permit to work outside the reservation, the officers knew how scarce jobs were and would refuse unless he could produce a written offer of employment. Even where a Bedouin succeeded in obtaining a permit on other grounds, it was still difficult for him to locate, and even more, to hold, a job, for permits were issued for very short terms. The maximal period was one month, and Bedouin found outside the reservation were frequently checked by the police. Only where employers were unable to procure their labour from other sources, would they approach the Military Administration, which then asked a tribal chief to supply the required gang. Bedouin thus found employment in road construction in the Negev, as on the Beersheba–Sodom and the Beersheba–Elat roads, in quarries, in phosphate mining and in farm work. A few persons were employed in semi-skilled work, among them several tractor-drivers, joiners and mechanics. No labour statistics are available, but it is estimated that in a male working population of approximately 2,850,[1] the average number of Bedouin employed outside the reservation was, up to 1958, well under 100,[2] or about 3·5 per cent.

The employment situation in the country gradually improved. By 1959 the balance had tipped the other way: there occurred shortages of seasonal agricultural labour. These were chiefly felt in the citrus harvest of the Shefelah (Reḥovoth–Rishon le-Zion area) and in the Negev itself, where, in that year, cotton had been grown on a larger scale than before. Cotton picking is concentrated in September and October, and the orange season runs at its height from January to mid-April. Both peak seasons fall conveniently in slack periods of the Bedouin's agricultural year. Many of the younger men are then free to go out on wage labour.

Most Bedouin flocks are so small that they can be tended by women and children. Male labour is required only to herd camels and the relatively few large flocks exceeding a hundred head of sheep or goats. Table 5 shows how the seasonal outside employment fits in neatly with the seasonally tied farming activities of

[1] The male population between the ages of 14 to 45 is here taken as the working population. For all Muslims in Israel, 38·6 per cent fell in this category in 1960 (*Statistical Abstract of Israel*, vol. 12, 1961). Applied to half the 1958 Bedouin population of 14,724, so as to include only the male labour force, this gives 2,841·7 men.

[2] Field data collected in 1955, and personal communication from A. Efrat, representative of the Trade Union (*Histadruth*) for the Negev Bedouin. Mr Efrat began in 1959 unofficially to mediate employment for Bedouin. A regular Labour Exchange for Bedouin was set up in 1962, and has been functioning only in a small way.

men in the reservation. Therefore there were generally more men prepared to take on seasonal employment than there were jobs available.

TABLE 5

Calendar of working Bedouin men, 1960–2

Month	*Activity* — *In Reservation*	*Activity* — *Outside Reservation*	*No. of Men on outside work**
January		Orange picking	600
February			
March			
April			100
May	Harvesting and threshing; maintenance of dams and cisterns		
June			400
July			
August			600
September		Cotton picking	
October			
November	Sowing and ploughing		100
December			

* The estimates of men employed outside the reservation at various times are based on information of A. Efrat and the Military Administration. No records of employment were kept or of movement permits issued for work. Some Bedouin took jobs without having recourse to mediation and without obtaining permits.

Some 400 Bedouin undertook outside employment for the greater part of the year, except for periods they had to devote to their own farming. During the cotton and citrus seasons, an average of 600 Bedouin were employed. These 600 included many of the men working outside the reservation for long periods throughout the year, for at such times they drifted into the relatively well-paid seasonal jobs, where they could also meet their relatives and friends. The maximum number of employed at a time occasionally rose to over 1,000.[1] At their own harvesting and sowing

[1] A figure of 1,000 Bedouin employed outside the reservation sometimes quoted (as in a pamphlet issued by the Prime Minister's Office in September 1960, or *Haarets* of 9 September 1961), can only refer to the seasonal peaks.

times, the number of Bedouin working outside the reservation dropped considerably. At these times they had to attend also to the seasonal change from summer to winter camps at home.[1] On a very rough calculation it would appear that in the years 1960–2 an average of about 400 men, constituting about 13 per cent of the male working population, were employed outside the reservation.[2]

This is still a far cry from an African migrant labour situation.[3] In the Negev, men did not enter into extended labour contracts. They were given only short-term movement permits, and in the off-season these were often suspended. They applied for work permits when they required cash, and left work when they were needed at home or when relations with the employers became unsatisfactory. Distances are small in Israel: the citrus belt is located about 90 km (about 55 miles) from Beersheba, and most men returned to their families at least once in a fortnight, besides having to renew their monthly movement permits at their area officer's post. The cotton fields in the western Negev were even closer to home, and the employers arranged for many Bedouin to return home every evening. Many men went away for short periods, in order to earn some ready cash, or to taste life in towns, but they were not under heavy economic or moral pressure to do so. There was almost no emigration of Bedouin from the reservation.

Men who spent longer periods away from home were usually those who had no other sources of income, such as land and herds. Arable land was distributed unevenly among the various tribes.[4] Some tribes thus took a much greater share of long-term employment than others. As the authorities leased land only to married men, as heads of families, bachelors constituted a high proportion of the long-term migrant labourers in the landless tribes. In the

[1] See Chapter 4.

[2] See Appendix 1. In the 1962 cotton season fewer Bedouin were employed, for by then 80 per cent of the work had become mechanized (*Israel, Government Yearbook* 1962, p. 109.)

[3] See, for instance, Schapera, *Migrant Labour and Tribal Life* (Oxford 1945) p. 39. In Bechuanaland, in 1943, an estimated 45·7 per cent of the male population between the ages of 15–44 were labour migrants. At the time, men spent an average period of approximately eight years abroad (p. 54), and about six out of every hundred were said to have gone away permanently (p. 61).

[4] See below, and Appendix 2.

land-owning tribes one could expect to find among them many men from landless families. When one looks more closely at these general categories of potential migrant labourers, one finds that familial status frequently plays a great part in the decision to seek work. A Bedouin from Abu Gweʿid, a tribe which, it will be recalled, has kept its land, explained the considerations thus: 'All the young men go out to work, those who have not yet married, and all those married men who do not have nubile girls at home, and those who have kinsmen to whom they can entrust their families.' The last reference is to wives, whom a man fears to leave, unless they are properly supervised by close kin, preferably his or her mother.

Still, even in these times of full employment, the issue of movement permits was kept under control. Thus on a typical day at the Tel al-Milḥ post, at the beginning of the citrus season of 1960–1, an official of the Military Administration dealt with 43 applications for movement permits. Eighteen men had their permits extended, 21 were given new permits, all of them issued only for 'Rishon le-Zion Ness Zionah area', in the orange belt. Four applicants were refused permits on technical grounds, such as their being too young or not in possession of an identity card.[1] About 30 further applicants were unable to obtain movement permits, as the official had exhausted his quota for the day. At times, the Military Administration suspended the issue of new work permits and only renewed lapsed ones. Even in these years of labour shortage, the issue of monthly movement permits was drastically curtailed between the seasons. Men were not permitted to take along their families when going away for work, so as to ensure their return to the reservation. Some Bedouin, independently of the Employment Service, found work with farmers in Ramlah and Reḥovoth areas. Sporadically, officials of the Employment Service ferreted out these and other independently employed Bedouin. The fact that these Bedouin possessed movement permits did not concern the officials. From time to time the Police arrested some Bedouin found without valid movement permits, and a military tribunal in Beersheba then fined them amounts usually ranging from IL. 5 to IL. 30 (approx. 12*s.* 6*d.* to £3 15*s.*). In short, the regulations were neither drastic, nor applied rigorously, but they sufficed to

[1] Every adult Israeli is required by law to carry an identity card on his person.

keep most Bedouin out of permanent employment outside the reservation.

With regard to pasture, the Military Administration permitted Bedouin during the early years to use the spring pastures east of the reservation. The remainder of the Negev was at that time also sparsely settled, so that whenever the summer pasture had been exhausted—usually around June—the closed area was expanded westward, to allow Bedouin herds to move in. These areas were intended as pasture, and the Administration permitted one man only to accompany each herd. One such pasture area west of Beersheba (near Kibutz Ḥazerim), which I saw in June 1955, was thickly dotted with the tents of Bedouin families, as well as their herds. The officials of the Administration did not make any attempts to regulate the size of the herds, which were becoming much too large to be contained in the reservation, yet found it increasingly difficult to locate pasture outside it. The price of meat on the Israeli market was relatively high, so that Bedouin sought to increase their herds by all means, including smuggling in animals from across the Jordanian border. In 1955 Bedouin herds were estimated at 60,000 heads of sheep, goats and camels.[1]

Gradually, the Western Negev was settled and the pasture areas decreased. Bedouin herds did much damage to new plantations and sown fields, and clashes between herders and the settlers occurred frequently. By degrees the Military Administration policy on pastures changed: it had to contend with the settlers' complaints. Instead of actively helping the Bedouin in their search for pasture, the Administration now tried to postpone the inevitable move westward as long as possible, and yielded but slowly to Bedouin pressure. When during the summer months the limited pasture in the reservation became depleted, chiefs, who themselves owned some of the largest herds, asked the Administration with daily increasing urgency to open up new pastures. The officers prevaricated. They postponed decisions as long as possible, and then issued some grazing permits to the areas situated west of

[1] Figures communicated by the Military Administration. The number of camels was at that time estimated at under 10,000. The Bedouin population in 1955 stood at about 13,000. Compare these figures to ʿĀref's (*Qaḍā*, pp. 223–5), according to which in 1932 a Bedouin population of about 60,000 owned between 10,000–14,000 camels and nearly 100,000 sheep and goats. In 1955, then, Bedouin herds were relatively about two and a half times larger than in 1932.

Beersheba, generally, at first as far as Bīr Abu Rqaiq, one of the abundant wells of the Negev. More and more herds thronged into the area until it was overgrazed, or access to the water supply became difficult. Then the process repeated itself: chiefs and notables renewed their pressure and the grazing area was by stages extended further west and then northwards, to the Falūgah (Plugot) and Beth Gubrin areas and sometimes even further north. In 1959 and 1960, the Ministry of Agriculture arranged for pasture areas as part of its drought compensation scheme, which the Military Administration, true to its method, gradually released for Bedouin herds. In the following year Bedouin had to seek their summer pastures almost unaided by the authorities. They were again given access to State land west of Beersheba, but had to reach individual agreements with settlements and individual farmers for late summer pasture in the more northerly parts. The Military Administration issued pasture permits to almost any area south of Ramlah and Reḥovoth which was not considered a security risk, and to some areas even further north. It did its best to help Bedouin herds survive the drought, taking only precautions against tribes moving out of the reservation even temporarily, by forbidding the erection of tents in the pasture area outside the reservation. Herdsmen slept under the open sky, but did not consider this an inconvenience as long as it did not rain.

The policy of the Military Administration, as implemented by the selective issue of movement permits, largely succeeded in segregating the Bedouin from permanent employment outside the reservation. This policy further succeeded in keeping Bedouin organized in tribes in the reservation, where they continued their traditional mixed economy of farming and herding. Within these limits, the Administration was prepared to aid the Bedouin economically, to provide them with farm land—where needed—and seeds, to improve their supply of drinking water, to open up sufficient pastures and to pay them drought compensation.[1]

The account of ecological conditions in the Negev and of the administrative environment has indicated that, although there are regional and seasonal variations, most Bedouin families now

[1] In 1962 the Ministry of Agriculture divided the Negev by a line, to the south of which no drought compensation would be payable. As a result, only 15,000 out of 400,000 dunams of land cultivated by Bedouin remained entitled to compensation (*Haarets*, 9 September 1962).

depend for their living on a combination of three sources of income: land, herds and operations in the wider Israeli economy. Bedouin themselves distinguish between three types of wealth, and employ non-interchangeable terms for them. *Milk* (landed property) denotes arable land which the owner alone is entitled to cultivate.[1] Cash income is termed *māl* (capital), and includes all wealth derived from the sale of goods and labour. The third category is *ḥalāl*, the herds of camels, sheep and goats. Obviously, the three categories are identical with the Bedouin's three main sources of income, and they may indicate that this has been so for many years. Only wage labour is a relatively new aspect of the *māl* category. The category of *ḥalāl* differs from the two others by its emotional overtones: it is applied to things which are considered as permitted, respectable and ritually pure to the Muslim. The use of this term by the Bedouin implies that pastoralism is an honourable and prestigious occupation, so that where ecological conditions are equally favourable to both farming and herding, he will often prefer the latter.

The Lands Department of the Ministry of Agriculture has constantly sought to assert, or reassert, State ownership over the land. Two further objectives qualify this major aim: firstly, always to take account of the economic situation created by the Military Administration's policies, and secondly, to try to achieve an equitable distribution of the available land.[2] Bedouin were only in exceptional cases, with the Military Governor's special permission, leased land outside the reservation. As the holdings of the Lands Department increased year by year, it was able to apply this policy with increasing effect over a larger area. The legal aspects of land ownership in the Negev are still obscure. The State claims the land because legally it is considered as non-cultivable, and as such belongs to the State according to the Ottoman land laws of 1858. The Bedouin claim ownership of part of the land over which, they say, they have longstanding uninterrupted occupancy. They

[1] I have retained the Bedouin pronunciation *milk* (for *mulk*), as the term is used in the Negev in a special sense. The legal category of *mulk*, connotating full ownership over land conferred by the State on persons, does not apply to the Negev, all of which is formally 'State land' (*mīri*). See A. Granott, *The Land System in Palestine* (London 1952) p. 95.

[2] See p. 42 above.

have, however, very little documentary proof of this.[1] The Lands Department seeks to assert the State's rights over the land in the reservation by inducing Bedouin to sign leases on land allocated to them for cultivation, and on some pasture areas. The Department at first charged only a nominal IL. 0.05 per dunam of arable land,[2] or IL. 0.03 for pasture. Bedouin knew that the authorities did not intend to make profits out of the leases. They knew that the authorities wished them to acknowledge the State's ownership, or wished to prevent them from acquiring rights of occupancy on the new areas assigned to them. Therefore Bedouin were often very reluctant to sign leases.

Until the end of 1953, the Negev Bedouin doubted whether they would be permitted to stay on in the country, and the question of what would become of their former land holdings was of relatively little import to them. In 1954 they were provided with Israeli identity cards, which meant that their citizenship had been recognized, and the land problem came to the fore again. The tribes which had been removed from their land entertained some hope of returning to it and viewed their stay in the reservation as a temporary one. Each tribe cultivated, in the meantime, the land which it had been allocated in the reservation, and some tribesmen now assumed that they would be settled there and compensated for their lost land. But from 1955 onwards, the authorities insisted that tribesmen sign leases for land held by, or allocated to, them. Table 6 shows that the authorities succeeded each year in increasing the area the Bedouin acknowledged to be State land. Up to 1960 the authorities had obtained control over 38 per cent of the total arable area in the reservation.[3]

During succeeding years additional land has been brought under government control, but the annual increment tends to become smaller and smaller as this method of securing the State's land-holdings yields its full results.

The Lands Department was not uniformly successful with all tribes. It succeeded in gaining control over land that had been

[1] During the Mandatory period, some Bedouin had paid land tax (*werko*), and their official receipts now constitute their only tenuous proof of ownership. The receipts indicate neither the location of the land nor its real area, as Bedouin regularly understated the area for tax purposes.

[2] This is equivalent to about 10*d*. per acre, at the official rate of exchange then in force (IL. 5 = £1). Later the charges were slightly increased.

[3] Assessing the total arable area at 400,000 dunams.

TABLE 6

Land leases in the Bedouin reservation, 1955–60 (in dunams)*

Season	*Arable*	*Pasture*	*Total*	*Annual Increment*
1955–6	40,960	36,580	77,540	—
1956–7	86,254	157,900	244,154	166,614
1957–8	102,121	182,090	184,211	40,057
1958–9	149,594	193,085	342,679	58,468
1959–60	153,000	214,000	367,000	24,321

* Data for the 1955–6 to 1958–9 seasons are taken from annual reports of the Lands Department, Beersheba, adjusted to include retroactive leases. The figures for 1959–60, which seem to be provisional, are taken from a report by the State Controller on 'Drought Assistance of the Min. of Agriculture to the Bedouin' of July 1960 (1 dunam = 1,000 sq metre = 0·247 acres).

allocated to groups which had not formerly held land in the reservation. These people agreed without giving many objections to sign leases on land which obviously was not theirs: they did not thereby relinquish claims on land formerly held. People who had hoped to be compensated with land in the reservation were disappointed. Some of them held out for a long time before they finally signed leases.

The Hazail and Abu Rqaiq tribes were able to retain the portions of their land which fell within the boundaries of the reservation, and refused to sign leases for these areas. The rest of the territories of the two tribes came under the Lands Department control.

The Department had little, if any, success among the five tribes which had been left on land in the reservation over which they claimed ownership. These people did not acknowledge State ownership over these compact territories. The land vacated by individuals and groups which had left the country could legally be claimed for the State.[1] But the tribesmen either distributed such land among kinsmen of the owners or it was taken over by powerful chiefs. Almost all traces of its real status were thus obliterated. The authorities thus found it very hard to drive a wedge into the tribal territories. Indeed, the Lands Department believes that the

[1] According to the Absentees' Property Law, 1950.

Ẓullām tribes, especially, took over land which had formerly belonged to the Gahalīn confederation, whose members had left *en bloc* for the Hebron mountains. Relatively insignificant tracts of land were surrendered by the Ẓullām chiefs, one suspects, in order to stave off the over-inquisitive authorities, and in recognition of their co-operation they were subsequently granted leases, partly on the same land. The Administration does not even possess an approximate idea about the proportion of State land contained in the territories of the four large landowning tribes. This results in a landholding situation set out in Table 7.

TABLE 7

Areas cultivated by Bedouin tribes, 1958–9 (in dunams)*

Land ownership position	*No. of tribes*	*Persons*	*Cultivated area*	*Arable land held in lease*	*Average area per person*
Living on own land	5	5,567	189,880	16,000	34·1
Owning some land supplemented by leased land	2	4,674	110,695	35,939	23·7
Living on leased land	11	4,483	92,615	97,655	20·7
Totals	18	14,724	393,190	149,594	26·7

* Compiled from figures supplied by the Lands Department and the Department for Agricultural Development. The population figures relate to December 1958. Detailed figures for each tribe are set out in Appendix 2.

As almost all the arable land is normally cultivated year after year, especially with the added insurance of drought compensation, the cultivated area given for each category of tribes will be nearly identical with its total arable land. The figures for the cultivated areas are derived from applications for drought compensation submitted by Bedouin in 1958–9, brought down to realistic proportions by tribal checking committees. The officials of the Department for Agricultural Development also carried out rough ground surveys of the tribal blocks of land, which were used to fix ceilings to a tribe's total claims. While the cultivated areas of landless tribes had to tally with their leases, the areas of the four large landowning tribes, the three Ẓullām tribes and al-Aʿsam, were especially difficult to check, so that their cultivated areas may be slightly exaggerated.

Table 7 shows that the land was not portioned out evenly. The landless tribes were the worst off, with an average area of 20·7 dunams per person. This was the state of things after practically all the available State land had been put under cultivation. Tribes still owning some land were leased an area roughly equivalent to their own land, and achieved an average area of 23·7 dunams per person. They were then slightly better off than the landless tribes: in fact, the difference is somewhat greater than suggested by the bare figures, for this category includes the Hazail tribe, whose land, in the better-watered north-western corner of the reservation, is considered to give at least twice the harvests of other parts.

The tribes living on their own land do not require leased land from the authorities,[1] for they also possess the relatively largest areas of arable, an average of 34·1 dunams per person. In detail, it can be seen that this does not apply to the al-Asad tribe living at Laqīah, which owns only a small area, and has been totally engulfed by State-owned land.[2] But the al-Aʿsam tribe, and even more so the three big Ẓullām tribes, are endowed with more land than any of the other tribes.

The tribesmen act together in order to retain their advantageous land situation. In this the chiefs are supported by their tribesmen, who consider it one of the chief's main duties to keep the authorities out of their internal affairs, some of which offend against the State laws, such as child marriage and polygynous marriage. They are particularly anxious about everything relating to the ownership of land, and their tribal organization maintains a barrier against changes in land tenure.

Though landless tribes are worse off with regard to the average holding per person, they enjoy one advantage over the landowning tribes: the ordinary tribesman has a better chance to obtain a fair quota of land. For the authorities see to it that most of the State land is distributed equitably; even where it has been distributed through chiefs, complaints of deprived tribesmen have usually been investigated and put right. Where the Lands Department

[1] We saw on p. 43 that the land held in lease by the three Ẓullām tribes was in the hands of the chiefs only.

[2] See Appendix 2.

deals directly with families, land is apportioned in fair shares, and chiefs are entitled only to double portions. Even with these well-meant efforts, the average area falls somewhat below the minimum quota of 100 to 150 dunams aimed at.[1] Considering also that the official quota takes no account of droughts, this situation adds to the other pressures on men to seek outside employment.

The landowning tribes, to which the following chapters will be chiefly devoted, have sufficient land for their needs, and also as a rule have less contact with the Israeli public, so that there is little desire and less need for men to go away for long periods of wage labour. But the internal distribution of land among the tribesmen is very uneven; some men have exceedingly large holdings, while a large number are without any land. This situation has far-reaching effects on the social structure of these tribes.

[1] In January 1959 the Minister of Agriculture announced in the Knesset that efforts would be made to supply each landless Bedouin family with between 100–150 dunams of State land, according to region, areas which the Ministry's experts considered as minimum subsistence quotas. The average Bedouin family is composed of between 4–5 persons, so that a family in a landless tribe has a chance of obtaining about 90 dunams.

PART TWO

Kinship and Corporate Groups

CHAPTER 3

Composition of a Tribe

THE Administration deals with tribes mainly through their chiefs, and is concerned only to a small extent with their internal politics. Within the limits set by the administrative framework, Bedouin tribes can still deal with some of their problems autonomously, and maintain a political organization. In this chapter I shall try to outline the political organization of one of the large Ẓullām tribes.[1]

When in 1856 the Turks acceded to the Ẓullām's request to pay taxes to the authorities directly, and no longer through the Tiāha chiefs,[2] this step turned the Ẓullām into a practically separate group of tribes. Since then three of the four tribes, the Abu Rbēʿah, Abu Gweʿid and Abu Qrenāt, have remained secure in occupancy of most of their territory. Bedouin define its boundaries thus:

> The territory covered the eastern Beersheba Plain from the wells of Bir Mshāsh and Bir Abu Ghānem in the west to the shores of the Dead Sea in the east. The northern boundary was at Tel ʿArād. To the south lived the small Kashkhar tribe, and the boundary ran through Wadi Khatīrah (Makhtesh Qaṭan), Harab al-Qaṭar (ʿEin Neṭafim), ʿAbdeh (Ovdat) and Maṭradah (Ramat Maṭred).

Under Israeli Military Administration the small Kashkhar tribe was left outside the reservation, though part of it was later resettled in the reservation. The three large Ẓullām tribes lost much of their eastern pasture, but were left in possession of their former land in the Beersheba Plain, and thus retained practically all their farm land and, no less important, all three large watering places, at ʿArʿarah (ʿAroʿer), Tel al-Milḥ (Malḥeta) and Mshāsh.

According to all accounts, the four tribes of today[3] were at that

[1] For the early history of these tribes, see pp. 123ff.

[2] See detailed accounts in ʿĀref, *Taʾarīkh* (1934) pp. 175 ff.

[3] The earliest printed list of tribes, in Jaussen's *Coutumes des Arabes au pays de Moab* (Paris 1908) p. 410, was compiled only some time between 1900 and 1905. It refers to the same four tribes, but provides no details beyond their names.

time established in their present territories, each tribe's farm land constituting a separate sub-territory. Through sale and transfer of farm land, the tribal boundaries of the three large tribes became somewhat blurred. Our attention will be directed mainly at one of the large tribes, Abu Gweʿid.[1]

The group within which economic activities are carried on is generally the family, either in its nuclear or in its extended form. Land and herds are owned by individual men who can ultimately dispose of their property according to their wishes, although they are under pressure to give priority to potential buyers from among their kin.

Theoretically, a man could decide to specialize in one of the two main branches of the economy, but most men usually engage in both farming and herding, and at the most put more emphasis on one than on the other. As groups of agnates often hold land in the same area, they are at times able to live in close proximity, or even in one camp, and to co-operate in certain economic activities, such as reaping; or several men will take on outside employment together, and leave their families in the care of kin in the joint camp.

The people living in these camps combine for various purposes in territorial[2] and political groups. The widest political associations of Bedouin today are the tribe (*ʿashīrah*, pl. *ʿashāʾir*) and the sub-tribe (*rubaʿ*, pl. *rubūʿ*). The tribes, the groups which formerly waged war, are now administrative units. At the head of such a group stands an elected leader, the *Sheikh* (elder), who, in an officially recognized unit, is confirmed in office by the authorities and is permitted officially to take the title *Sheikh*.[3] Other groups not acknowledged as tribes may not have leaders styled *Sheikh*, and they are kept subjected to the authority of appointed sheikhs. In these cases the group is termed a *rubaʿ*, but it is evident that were the administrative pressure relaxed, many *rubūʿ* would soon become independent tribes. The sheikh is now the main channel through which communications between the tribesmen and the

[1] For the ecology of the eastern Beersheba Plain where the tribe lives, see Chapter 1.

[2] I deal with the territorial organization of the Ẓullām tribes in Chapter 5.

[3] The Israeli Ministry of the Interior considers that the style should properly be *Mukhtār* (village chief), but this has not yet found acceptance in common usage.

authorities flow, and therefore much power is vested in him. But even earlier, before the Negev was pacified, the tribe often became the largest active political group in Bedouin society, for in times of need it had at its command a relatively large number of fighting men who could unite under the leadership of one man. The tribe also had a considerable degree of continuity, which was demonstrated by the fact that it was the minimal group to figure in the commonly accepted genealogies linking up the members of each confederation of tribes.[1] The tribe is not a landholding group and its boundaries are not as clear-cut as those of the confederation, but in general its constituent groups hold farming land in roughly contiguous areas, and exploit the same pastures.

Being a political group, a tribe was interested in augmenting its manpower to the utmost, even to the extent of incorporating groups from outside. Thus one finds that each tribe is now composed of people originating from different stocks, who are traditionally classed into three categories. There is first the dominant Bedouin stock (Bedouin call themselves Arabs (*ʿarab*), in the sense of tribesmen), who do not necessarily make up a majority of the tribe. They claim descent from the ancient Bedouin tribes of Arabia, and ownership of the land by right of conquest. Secondly there are groups of peasants (*fallāḥ*, pl. *fallaḥīn*), originating from the cultivated areas bordering on the desert. Lastly, there are groups of 'slaves' (*ʿabd*, pl. *ʿabīd*), descendants of the Negro slaves formerly kept by the Bedouin. In the sub-tribe, groups of these diverse origins are welded into one unit.

In between the family and the tribe and sub-tribe there exist groups sharing some of the characteristics of both. These I shall call 'co-liable groups', for reasons given shortly.[2] These groups are ideally composed of kinsmen who are able to trace descent in the male line to an ancestor five or more generations removed. A considerable proportion of marriages of members is always

[1] See p. 123 for examples of these genealogies.

[2] I have considered other terms denoting groups sharing in the payment of blood-money currently employed by anthropologists, such as the *ḥamūlah* in A. Cohen, *Arab Border-Villages in Israel* (Manchester 1965) (see, in particular, the footnote on pp. 2–3), or the *diyah-paying group* in I. M. Lewis, *A Pastoral Democracy* (Oxford 1961). The groups described by these authors differ considerably from the Bedouin *khams*, so that the use of a new term may be justified. It will be shown, in Chapter 7, that the co-liable group also engages in activities other than the payment of blood-money.

contracted within the group. Membership is usually acquired by being born into the group, and only rarely are men allowed to join by incorporation. Women who marry away do not sever their connections with the group; their children become full-fledged members of the father's group, but even so the mother's group of origin will often seek to reclaim at least one of the daughters in marriage. Members of the group usually take the name of an ancestor to whom all claim to be connected, but a gradual process of separation may induce some members to adopt the name of a closer ancestor, while yet forming part of the group. As we shall be concerned at length in the following pages with the structure and activities of these co-liable groups, I shall not here try to define them further, and only repeat that most economic, and some political, activities have been pre-empted by the family and the tribe, so that the co-liable groups' activities are related to other areas of social life.

'Co-liable' is here employed in a sense built from its two components as defined in the *Concise Oxford Dictionary*: 'Co- = jointly, together, mutually; liable = legally bound, answerable for, subject or amenable to tax or penalty.' These definitions describe neatly the most important and central tasks of the group, all of whose members are mutually responsible in matters of 'blood', either when a member or members have shed blood, or when one of the members has been killed or wounded. Bedouin employ a host of terms for this group. In conversation it is often referred to as '*ʿēleh*' (for the classical *ʿā'ilah*), the term mostly used for the family, or *ʿashīrah*, the term for the tribe, or *rubaʿ*, the term for the sub-tribe.[1] Then one sometimes hears the term *fakhdh* (thigh), *baṭn* (womb) or *ḥamūlah* (birth group), all of which obviously refer to common descent. But the only term almost exclusively designating a co-liable group, *khams* (five), does not, strictly speaking, apply to the whole group, but only to the men who can trace common descent to an ancestor five generations removed. In Bedouin ideology these are the men who normally make up a 'co-liable group', because men who are further removed can legally exempt themselves from responsibility in certain situations. But the term is definitely also used for a group whose members' common ancestor is more than five generations removed. As long

[1] The term *rubaʿ* will here be reserved for the Bedouin 'core-groups' with their accreted groups, the sub-tribe. See p. 65.

as no part of the group takes active steps towards separation, its members all share full responsibility, as if they were related within the five generations.[1]

Before entering into a detailed discussion of the co-liable group, we shall see how a number of such groups, arranged in a particular pattern, constitutes a tribe. The Abu Gweʿid tribe is one of four tribes of the Ẓullām tribal group. Its farm land lies mainly in the Tel al-Milḥ-ʿArʿarah area, about 30 km east of Beersheba on the Beersheba Plain, while its pastures used to extend eastward down to the shores of the Dead Sea. The tribe numbers 1,150 people and is somewhat smaller and contains fewer groups than the neighbouring tribes of the same tribal group (Abu Rbēʿah 2,080; Abu Qrenāt 1,450). Each of these three large tribes is divided into four sub-tribes. Even though the Arabic term for sub-tribe is *rubaʿ*, meaning a quarter, this division into four sub-tribes is probably pure coincidence, and the number of sub-tribes in other tribes varies. The sub-tribes of the Abu Gweʿid tribe differ considerably in size and importance. The most powerful sub-tribe, which, as in this case, is usually also the largest, provides the 'sheikh', the chief of the tribe. This situation in present-day conditions gives this particular sub-tribe overwhelming influence over its congeners, both in internal politics of the tribe and in its relations with the authorities. Thus the tribal chief's sub-tribe often holds more land and is able to attract more outsiders than the other sub-tribes, and with its accretions can soon outstrip them in size.

The Abu Gweʿid sub-tribe is over three times larger than each of the other sub-tribes. The size of the sub-tribe is not directly relevant to its actual power, for the internal structure varies a great deal. Each sub-tribe has at its centre a comparatively powerful Bedouin core, a group of people who form a co-liable group, and who claim direct descent in the male line from the ancestor of the tribe. The manpower of this Bedouin core is perhaps the main factor determining the power of the *rubaʿ*, not its overall size. The sheikh's group, although even numerically the largest, wields

[1] The difference between the formal and the actual structure of the *khams* can probably account for the many and diverse definitions of the *khams* in the literature on the Bedouin. E. Graef, *Das Rechtswesen der heutigen Beduinen* (Walldorf-Hessen 1952) pp. 34 ff. cites no less than seven explanations, all different, to which an eighth should be added, as set out by G. W. Murray in *Sons of Ishmael* (London 1935) p. 205.

influence out of proportion to its size. Table 8 sets out the figures relating to the sub-tribes of Abu Gweʿid tribe.

TABLE 8

Bedouin core-groups and sub-tribes in Abu Gweʿid tribe

Sub-tribe	*Persons in core-group*	*Persons in sub-tribe*
Abu Gweʿid, the sheikh's sub-tribe	145	639
Ṣarāiʿah	123	199
Maʿābdah	133	190
Abu Msāʿad	37	112
Total (for mid-1961)	438	1,140

Around the core-group there accrete, for diverse reasons, other co-liable groups and individual families. There are firstly smaller independent Bedouin co-liable groups, which have either split off from the main group or used to be large groups themselves, but declined in numbers. All these Bedouin groups claim kinship with their core-group through a common ancestor who is believed to have lived many generations ago, who was 'perhaps a son of the tribe's founding ancestor, and whose name was lost in the passage of time'. This relationship is acknowledged by the core-group, which also intermarries with the attached Bedouin groups, although marriage is not limited to such groups. Then there are a few Bedouin groups originating from outside the tribe, who are considered by the other Bedouin as equal in birth to themselves. They intermarry freely with these small groups. Then one finds attached groups of peasant descent (*fallaḥīn*), who are categorized according to their place or area of origin. All these *fallaḥīn* are organized in co-liable groups, and from a legal viewpoint are the 'juxtaposed' equals of the Bedouin groups. As the diverse peasant groups do not usually feel that they have much in common as 'settled' people as against the 'nomads' they do not easily see their way towards political co-operation, and have not developed a common genealogy which would facilitate their fusion in times of crisis. Each group of peasants states that it will not intermarry with others, whether of Bedouin or of peasant origin. As they put it, 'we neither give them [women], nor take [women] from them'.

In fact, however, a limited number of intermarriages take place between the peasant groups, especially between those originating from the same locality, even when they do not claim a common ancestor. Bedouin put the relationship with the peasant groups as 'we do not give to them, only take from them', meaning that they are willing to take peasant girls in marriage, but will not give their daughters in return. There is no case on record in which a Ẓullām Bedouin gave his daughter to a peasant tribesman, but one in which a man gave his daughter to a townsman of Hebron, with whom he maintained intensive business relations. No exception was taken to this marriage by other Bedouin. In a few cases sheikhs married peasant girls, as additional wives, though in the Ẓullām group of tribes only one such marriage took place during the present generation, and one in the last.

Other attached groups are the so-called 'slaves' (*ʿabīd*), a synonym for the negroes residing in the tribe, who had, it is true, originally been brought in as slaves. The term is still applied today, even by the negroes to themselves, although slave-holding was prohibited by the Ottoman authorities at the turn of the century.[1] The negroes again have the same form of co-liable groups, consider themselves as being more Bedouin than the peasants, and feel a stronger attachment to their tribes than to negroes of other tribes. Their opinions as to intermarriage with other groups are even stricter than those of others; not only do they refuse to intermarry with Bedouin and peasants, but they express such abhorrence to a match of this kind that they claim they would kill the culprits were one to occur. No case of a mixed negro-Bedouin or negro-peasant marriage has been heard of in the Negev. They claim they do not even marry into other negro groups, but in reality have to do so, as their numbers are small.

In addition to these categories, each *rubaʿ* accumulates also a number of individuals and isolated families who may originate from almost anywhere. These are of some importance politically, but will not be referred to in the present context.

A schematized diagram of a *rubaʿ* would look like Diagram 1. The diagram requires some immediate qualifications; others will become evident as we go on. The 'attachment' of the groups to the core-group should not be taken too literally; it is not solid and unchangeable, nor is the attachment equally strong for all

[1] A. Jaussen, *Coutumes des Arabes au pays de Moab* (Paris 1908) p. 125.

groups. Then also, the isolated families often do not become attached to the core-group in a political sense, being too small to be politically significant. Single men and families do not find it difficult to form attachments to other groups, as this can be brought about simply by entering the guest tent of a camp, where they are fed and lodged. After staying for a short spell as guests, they ask for permission to remain in the camp. The attachment

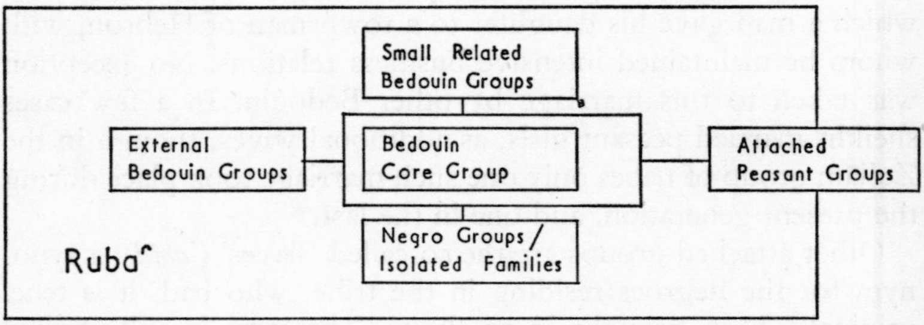

DIAGRAM I

Political structure of a Bedouin *rubaʿ*

of some peasant groups to the sheikh's *rubaʿ* might equally well be considered as attachment to the sheikh's person, in view of his privileged position *vis-à-vis* the authorities.

We shall now examine what an actual tribe looks like, when seen as a congeries of co-liable kin-groups. Diagram 2 gives a detailed picture of the Abu Gweʿid tribe, omitting only some of the individual attached families, to which we shall have occasion to refer in another context. The diagram reflects the political affiliation of co-liable groups to sub-tribes current in 1960, which in some cases is not identical with the affiliation stated during the official registration in the early fifties.

The composition of the several *rubaʿs* of the tribe is only superficially similar, in that each has a core of Bedouin, around which smaller groups of several kinds have aggregated. The political weight of the Abu Gweʿid group is so great, owing to the sheikhship and the large tracts of land at their disposal, that groups amounting to thrice their number are attached to them. The Ṣarāiʿah group, though numbering almost as many men, has fewer attached groups, because from a political point of view it cannot offer the same advantages to its retainers. But the Ṣarāiʿah have still a considerable following of groups and isolated families, to whom they are able to supply farm land. Some of these are people who were dissatisfied with the sheikh's rule or had quarrelled with their own co-liable groups, and have thrown in their lot with the second political caucus, at least for a time, till they

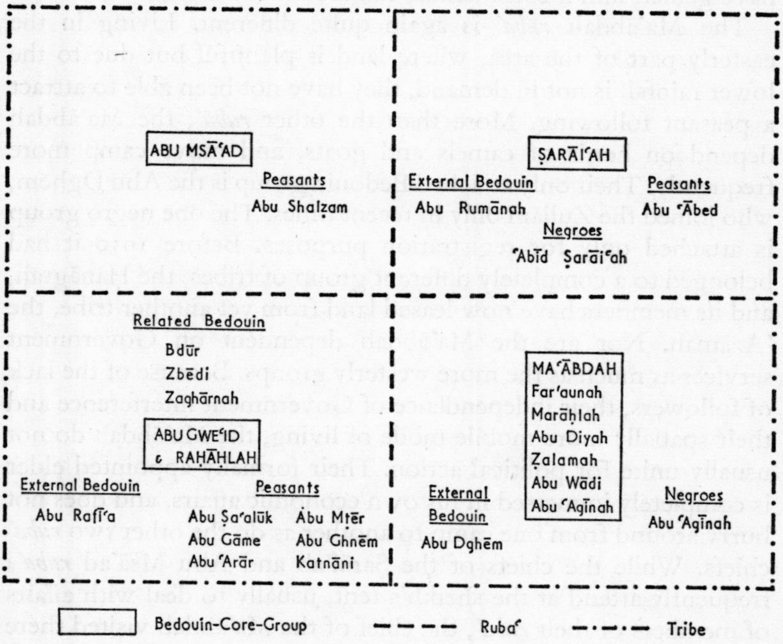

DIAGRAM 2

Co-liable groups of Abu Gweʿid tribe

can make up with their own group. It appears that the list of people who attach themselves to Ṣarāīʿah varies much more from year to year than Abu Gweʿid's. Most transfers of allegiance are not accompanied by applications to the authorities to make it official, and thus the gate of repentance is always left ajar.

The position of the Abu Msāʿad *rubaʿ* is similar to that of Ṣarāīʿah, except that it is numerically much smaller and maintains its influence mainly through the comparatively large farming areas at its disposal. Being less powerful, Abu Msāʿad tends to align itself with Ṣarāīʿah on most occasions, so much so that the sheikh once stated that Abu Msāʿad was not an independent *rubaʿ*, and that were it not for the recognition of Sulimān Abu Msāʿad as chief by the authorities, the *rubaʿ* would long ago have been absorbed by Ṣarāiʿah. Even so, Sulimān's appointment, together with his land, and his influence with the sheikhly family of the neighbouring Abu Rbēʿah tribe, whose land is adjacent to his, have gained him a considerable number of followers.

The Maʿābdah *rubaʿ* is again quite different. Living in the easterly part of the area, where land is plentiful but due to the lower rainfall is not in demand, they have not been able to attract a peasant following. More than the other *rubūʿ*, the Maʿābdah depend on herds of camels and goats, and move camp more frequently. Their only attached Bedouin group is the Abu Dghēm, who joined the Ẓullām only in recent times. The one negro group is attached only for registration purposes. Before 1950 it had belonged to a completely different group of tribes, the Ḥanāgrah, and its members have now leased land from yet another tribe, the ʿAzāmah. Nor are the Maʿābdah dependent on Government services as much as the more westerly groups. Because of the lack of followers, their independence of Government interference and their spatially more mobile mode of living, the Maʿābdah do not usually unite for political action. Their formally appointed elder is completely immersed in his own economic affairs, and does not hurry around from one camp to another as do the other two *rubaʿ* chiefs. While the chiefs of the Ṣarāiʿah and Abu Msāʿad *rubaʿs* frequently attend at the sheikh's tent, usually to deal with affairs of members of their *rubaʿ*, the chief of the Maʿābdah visited there only once during a year. But while the Ṣarāiʿah and Abu Msāʿad chiefs are their *rubaʿs* main representatives towards the sheikh, each Maʿābdah man approaches the sheikh in person whenever he has any problem which requires intervention with the authorities. The Maʿābdah do not, therefore, constitute such a politically active and organized *rubāʿ* as the three others, in the sense that they neither exercise their corporate weight nor try to maintain good relations with the authorities in order to influence their decisions. When he deals with the chiefs of the Ṣarāiʿah and Abu Msāʿad *rubaʿs* the sheikh is constantly made aware of the fact that they represent groups, while in his dealings with members of the Maʿābdah group there prevails a more personal relationship. The sheikh often felt that the Maʿābdah were closer to him than the other groups, even to the extent that at times he did not consider them a *ruba*ʿ separate from his own. When men of the sheikh's entourage were asked to draw up a list of the tribe's *ruba*ʿ*s*, they often gave only the three names of Abu Gweʿid, Ṣarāiʿah and Abu Msāʿad. When on such occasions one inquired about the Maʿābdah they would reply: 'They are of us', meaning that they were politically dependent on the sheikh. This was, of course, a one-sided view, because in practice the Maʿābdah were quite independent of the sheikh. They did not react towards him as a group; but neither was he able to influence their activities to any real extent. The sheikh knew very well that when provoked into action as a group, the Maʿābdah were very powerful, when he stated that 'they are more numerous and stronger than even the Abu Gweʿid'.

There is another fundamental difference between the Maʿābdah and the other two large core-groups of the tribe. While the Abu Gweʿid and the Ṣarāiʿah, and also the smaller Abu Msāʿad, constitute one co-liable group each, the Maʿābdah core-group is made up of at least six small co-liable groups. The different constitution of the Maʿābdah is connected to the fact that they do not usually unite for political action. Yet they constitute a political unit and are recognized as one by other Bedouin. As one tribesman put it, 'all the Maʿābdah together constitute a political party (*ḥizb*), just like the Ṣarāiʿah and the Abu Gweʿid', i.e. they are capable of uniting for common action. The full significance of the different composition of the Maʿābdah core-group will emerge later in this chapter.

The groups accreting around a Bedouin core-group and turning it into a *ruba*ʿ, differ greatly in size, and also in the interests which bind them to it. There are, firstly, the Related Bedouin Groups. The Abu Gweʿid *ruba*ʿ has three such groups, each of which maintains its independence in everyday life: each owns sufficient land of its own, which its members either cultivate themselves or lease out to landless people; each group maintains its own camp, at a distance from the chief's. The Bdūr, for instance, live an hour's riding distance from the camp of Sheikh Abu Gweʿid. The Bdūr number thirteen tents (or families) in all, a relatively large group. The Zaghārnah and Zbēdi count only two families each. Yet the latter consider themselves as independent co-liable groups, and are neither being absorbed by, nor permanently tied to, the *ruba*ʿ. They have freely attached themselves to the sheikh's *ruba*ʿ, in order to enjoy his political protection, and explain that they did so 'because in the past we were related'. But, of course, these groups enjoy the same nebulous kinship with the other *ruba*ʿ*s* of the tribe, and can at will switch over their allegiance to one of these. That this could actually happen, is shown by the Far'ūnah, of the Maʿābdah *ruba*ʿ, who have recently become closer and closer to the sheikh's *ruba*ʿ, though without any formal indication of having changed their allegiance.

One would like to speculate how such small groups had fared in the old days of tribal warfare, and whether they could then have maintained an independent existence. Today, at any rate, this does not prove too difficult, for there is only a slight chance indeed that such a group would actually be called upon to pay blood-money for one of its members, and it seems that each group is prepared to take the risk. Even should a group have to pay blood-money, e.g. for wounds inflicted in a brawl, it would not find the burden too heavy. Only in a case of killing, where the blood-money might amount to as much as IL. 2,000 to 3,000, would a small group find it impossible to raise the money required. Bedouin say that such small groups must be very wary of becoming involved in fights because of the risk of having to raise large amounts of blood-money, while larger groups do not mind as much. A man of the large Abu Ṣulb group (Abu Rqaiq tribe) put it this way: 'When we kill a man, each one of us does not pay more than a goat.' This theory may apply to premeditated attacks, such as vengeance killings, and in the four cases, attempted and successful, known to me, the deed was perpetrated by members of large co-liable groups:

Nabāri group (Qderāt al-Ṣaneʿ tribe)	numbering 30 tents
Abu al-Qiʿān (a peasant group enjoying the official status of a tribe)	numbering 30 tents
Abu Mdēghem (Hazail tribe)	numbering 30 tents
Abu Ghnēm (Abu Gweʿid and Abu Rbēʿah tribe)	numbering 50 tents

But most fights are begun on the spur of the moment by hot-headed individuals who do not pause to consider whether they might end up by embroiling their whole co-liable group in a feud. Thus during a quarrel the Zaghārnah group, numbering only five adult men, beat up one man of the Abu ʿArār group, who can muster up to 40 men. Next morning the ʿArarāt assembled all the men available and prepared to launch an attack on the Zaghārnah. This was eventually averted only by the intervention of Ẓullām notables. If the fight had actually taken place, its results might have been disastrous to the Zaghārnah.

The larger co-liable groups are mainly composed of agnatic kinsmen. Even when a man is allowed to join such a co-liable group, he does not partake of agnation. Most of the day-to-day collaboration between members of the group takes place among close agnates, often residing in a joint camp, and clusters of agnates also influence the political course of the co-liable group. A very small group will thus not materially increase its range of collaboration by joining a larger one, nor have much say in political matters concerning the whole group. It will gain assistance in a blood dispute, but will also be fully committed to policies not of its own making. As blood disputes are not very common now, men have no need to join large groups at any price. In the more turbulent past, though, isolated individuals used to seek admission to a powerful co-liable group. Thus there are now two men in Abu Gweʿid co-liable group whose grandfathers had been admitted in this manner.

On the other hand, a co-liable group's name must not cease to exist as long as a single male member remains alive. One fertile family can resuscitate a declining group. In this respect Bedouin theory and practice are in full accord. As the growth of co-liable groups will be dealt with fully at a later stage, we shall here only examine how Bedouin explain the persistence of the tiny co-liable groups.

Members of the small groups explain, and other Bedouin confirm, that formerly they had been numerous and powerful Bedouin groups, who in their present decline maintain the proud family name. And then, of course, they might again rise from the ashes and turn into powerful groups once more. Even individuals whose fathers had gained admission to a co-liable group and who persistently intermarried with its members, have not been fully absorbed into it, and Bedouin would for generations remember their foreign origin. Thus they pointed out that one man, ʿAudah ʿĀmer Abu Gweʿid, is still considered as one of the Beni ʿAṭīah, a North Arabian tribe, although his grandfather had joined the Abu Gweʿid, and he and each succeeding generation had intermarried in the group. Another example is that of the Abu Wādi group, the only Bedouin group in the tribe still considered as grafted. They originate from the North Arabian Bilī tribe, from whom the Ẓullām too claim to be descended. They appear to have joined the tribe as three men, 'brothers', at the turn of the century, and must have been considered as kinsmen. They intermarried mainly with the Abu Msāʿad and Ṣarāiʿah groups, but never thought of being incorporated into either. Instead they re-formed as an independent co-liable group. Significantly, the Abu Wādi, though allied by marriage to Abu Msāʿad and Ṣarāiʿah, hold land in an area which is cultivated predominantly by the Maʿābdah, and are politically part of their core-group.

From a long-term point of view, then, there is no such thing as an unattached family or even a single non-aligned individual in a tribe. For each of them constitutes a potential co-liable group, even if at the moment they are only very small and politically insignificant. If a man has only a son or a brother, these have to share responsibility with him, in paying and receiving blood-money. No amount of intermarriage with another group will make it share in these burdens.

In one respect the attached and related Bedouin groups differ from other accreted groups. As they own land in an area which is more or less contiguous with that of the rest of the tribe, they always remain part and parcel of the tribe. Though they can and will shift allegiance within the tribe, they cannot easily leave it for another. This is not so with the peasant groups, who are not permanently attached to any one group or tribe.

People of peasant descent make up 47 per cent of the Abu Gweʿid tribe, 534 of its 1,130 members. Table 9 shows how the peasants are divided up among the four *rubūʿs* of the tribe.

The table shows that for the whole tribe the accreted peasants are more numerous than the Bedouin core-groups. The advent of the peasants to the Beersheba Plain in such great numbers is comparatively recent, to a large extent within living memory. In 1785, the French traveller Volney reports that East of the town of Gaza

> ... on recontre d'autres bandes de terres cultivables jusque sur la route de la Mekke. Ce sont des vallées où les eaux de l'hiver et de quelques puits engagent quelques paysans à s'établir, et à cultiver des palmiers et du doura.[1]

[1] C. F. Volney, *Voyage en Égypte et en Syrie* (Paris 1825) vol. 1, p. 197.

TABLE 9

Bedouin core-groups and their accreted peasant groups in Abu Gweʿid tribe, 1961

Rubaʿ's name	*Core-group*	*Accreted peasant groups*
Abu Gweʿid	145	404
Ṣarāiʿah	123	55
Abu Msāʿad	137	75
Maʿābdah	133	—
Total for tribe	438	534

Volney does not state what arrangements these peasants had made with the Bedouin landowners, but it seems that in those turbulent times they could not have remained permanently with the Bedouin, nor do there seem to have been many of them. Perhaps Volney mistook Bedouin who cultivated their own land for peasants, for later reports do not make mention of peasants in the Beersheba Plain.[1] But Jaussen, the French missionary, who visited the area at the turn of the century, found quite a different situation:

[Les] belles pleines de Gaza... [et] Bīr es-Sebaʿ [sont] toujours cultivées par les habitants de la plaine ou par les villageois tout proches... Mais... les terrains de labour... s'étendent plus ou moins... jusqu'a ʿAïn Qedëis... Quelques bédouins de Tiāhā et des ʿAzāzmeh cultivent eux-mêmes leur lopins de terre, me disent-ils, à cause de leur pauvreté. Beaucoup cependant appellent des ḥarraṭīn ou laboureurs. Le propriétaire nourrit toujours le ḥarrāṭ; il fournit la charrue, le chameau, la semence et le terrain; le fellaḥ ne donne que son travail et il ne reçoit en salaire que le quart de la récolte.[2]

Today the situation has changed somewhat, for the peasants own at least some land. But even now, when they have to lease land from the Bedouin landowners, they can obtain it only on a year to year sharecropping basis. The agreement may be either similar to the above-mentioned type, the sharecropper getting one third of the harvest, or for each partner taking half of the net harvest, in which case the peasant provides the seeds and draught

[1] See for instance H. B. Tristram's *The Land of Israel* (London 1866) p. 377.
[2] Jaussen, op. cit., p. 246.

animals. In the past, when tribal warfare made tribal boundaries unstable, and the pursuit of agriculture rather insecure, the conditions would not have been such as to allow peasants to settle permanently with a Bedouin group. Therefore one may assume that most of the peasants referred to in Jaussen's account were natives and inhabitants of the coastal belt, mainly from the Gaza area, who were employed by the Bedouin either in the capacity of agricultural labourers or as sharecroppers. But some peasants may have formed a more permanent attachment to the Bedouin.

Only the gradual pacification of the area by the Ottoman authorities since the 1870's, has created suitable conditions for a permanent settlement of the peasants in Bedouin areas. As the tribal boundaries became settled and fixed, security of tenure and of property increased, and the peasants slowly advanced further and further eastward, always in search of land. To this day, the main preoccupation of the peasants living among the Bedouin is to obtain what they term 'sufficient' land for cultivation, which means—ever more and more. The men of the Abu Gāmeʿ group, hailing from Beni Suhailah, a village not far south of Gaza, described the process of settlement in the following terms:

> At first we only held land in Beni Suhailah, but in time our numbers increased and we lacked sufficient land. So we used to take land on the *ḥissah* system (sharecropping) from the Bedouin to the East. Gradually we advanced further East, and began to take land from the Ẓullām, who had lots of land. A man used to take land from a certain Bedouin, generally only a fraction of the Bedouin's land. In time he collected money, and when the Bedouin required some he would mortgage (*yarhan*) a bit of land.[1] Gradually a larger and larger part of the land would come into the peasant's possession, until he held a goodly-sized piece of land. Then he would sell his one or two dunam in Beni Suhailah and move over to the Bedouin. The lack of land was the main reason for our leaving the village, and not any blood-feuds or fear of being recruited to the Ottoman army.

Perhaps one should add to this that land was not scarce in the coastal belt at that time, but that the poor land-hungry peasants

[1] According to the customary law, the holder of the mortgage may use the land mortgaged till the loan is fully repaid, but receives no interest on the sums lent. Very frequently the mortgaged land remains with the lender, so that the Bedouin consider 'mortgage' as almost a synonym for outright land sale.

would be able to acquire it very cheaply from the Bedouin, who were ignorant of its market value.

It is still the land that interests the peasants who live with the Bedouin tribes. The peasants acquired land wherever and whenever they were able to obtain it, and then remained under the protection of the tribe from which the land had been bought. Thus one now finds that the members of many peasant groups are formally divided up among three or four tribes, though other groups will be concentrated in one tribe.

Table 10 provides an idea of the diverse tribal registrations of some of the larger peasant groups represented in Abu Gweʿid tribe. The numbers were culled from the official electoral roll, which lists all adults (male and female) over the age of 18.

TABLE 10

Distribution of some peasant groups among the Ẓullām tribes (by adults)

	Tribe			
Peasant Group	*Abu Gweʿid*	*Abu Qrenāt*	*Abu Rbēʿah*	*Total*
Abu ʿArār	24	40	34	98
Abu Gāmeʿ	26	10	26	62
Abu Ghnēm	11	1	11	23
Abu Ṣaʿalūk	39	4	1	44

To complete the picture one has to add that one family of Abu Ghnēm group is registered with a fourth tribe, the Qderāt al-Ṣāneʿ, while one family of the Abu Ṣaʿalūk group, though registered in the Abu Gweʿid tribe, has for years been living with the Hazail tribe. Another family of the same group used to stay permanently with the ʿAṭaunah tribe, but after its head was accidently killed in 1959 they returned to the main group. In spite of this apparent scattering, the main body of each group actually lives in one area, in which some of its members own land. Thus the Abu Ṣaʿalūk generally reside in one camp. The Abu ʿArār, who are a large group, are during the summer divided up into six camps, all of which are pitched in one limited area, enabling the whole co-liable group to maintain intimate contact with each other. The Abu

ʿArār have obtained possession over a relatively large contiguous area in the Buḥērah, a location in which members of all three Ẓullām tribes hold land. Although they are still registered with the three tribes, they constitute in fact one co-liable group.

Even though the peasant groups own some land, it would still be true if one called them 'landless', for the land is never sufficient for their requirements, and they still have to obtain the larger part in sharecropping arrangements, wherever available. There is, of course, some connection between the source of a man's land and his political allegiance, so that the peasants are in many ways politically tied to their Bedouin landowners. But this economic and political dependence on the Bedouin, does not in any way detract from the peasants' allegiance to their own co-liable groups. Cultivation never occupies them for more than several weeks in a season, and for the remainder of the time many members of the group, and mainly middle-aged family men, live in the common camps, no matter which tribe they are registered with or have obtained land from. Any shift of political allegiance, from one tribe or one *rubaʿ* to another, often in connection with changing land-leasing arrangements, does not affect the structure of the co-liable group. Officially the attachment of peasant groups to a certain *rubaʿ* has remained unchanged since 1950–4, when the Israeli authorities carried out their first registration of the Bedouin. The allegiances current at the time were laid down as a permanent administrative organization, and still are of some relevance for administrative purposes. Individuals and groups can apply for registration with other groups, but only in a minority of cases will bother to do so, especially as at a later time they might wish to switch back to the former allegiance.

Most of the peasant groups originate from the coastal strip, but some people have come from further south. From the historical traditions of the groups it appears that the Gaza area has for generations received a steady flow of landless peasants from the densely populated Nile valley, and that most of these people continued thence on their drift further north, and a few only eventually reached the Bedouin. Still this comparatively small proportion of the total population movement served to swell the Bedouin population of the Negev to approximately twice its size.

Gaza itself was claimed as place of origin by only one small group of Abu Gweʿid tribe, the Katnāni, whereas many of the peasants came from Khān Yūnis, a few miles south, among them the Abu Ṣaʿalūk group and several other smaller groups, as well as a series of groups comprising together about 1,500 members most of whom are registered with the Ẓullām, who boast common descent, a very intricate and detailed common genealogy and a full range of intermarriage. All these groups are known as Qlāʿīah, i.e. people of the fortress (*qalʿah*), a synonym for the town of Khān Yūnis.[1] As this place has been the origin of a large proportion of the peasants, including this combination of groups who are the only peasants with a political organization wider than the co-liable group, the term Qlāʿīah has often come to mean any peasant group, without reference to the place of origin. Although the Qlāʿīah are unable to make any united stand against the Bedouin, owing to their very limited resources, they still play by sheer weight of numbers an important role in Ẓullām politics.

Another important contingent of peasants comes from the village of Beni Suhailah, adjacent to Khān Yūnis, among them the Abu Gāmeʿ group. A few families living in this area come from the Ṭūr district, on the western coast of the Sinai peninsula. In other parts of the Negev these Ṭawarah are much more numerous. The Abu ʿArār apparently hail from the Qaṭīah area, already half-way to the Suez canal, and the Abu Shalẓam have come straight from the Nile delta. Thus the peasants appear to have streamed into the Negev along the coastal line, advancing from Egypt north-eastwards to Palestine. It also appears, according to traditions of some groups, that a large number of the peasants claiming to have come from villages of the Gaza area, also originally derived from the bottomless human reservoir of the Nile valley.

Except for part of the Qlāʿīah, who maintain a not very effective framework for mutual consultation in political affairs, there exist no political structures encompassing a number of peasant groups, besides that of the Bedouin *rubaʿ*. In line with this state of affairs is the fact that intermarriage between peasant groups is not very extensive, not even among groups originating from the same village.

All these groups are considered by the Bedouin to be derived of peasant stock, yet Bedouin seldom refer to them as 'peasants'

[1] See U. Heyd, *Ottoman Documents on Palestine* 1552–1615 (Oxford 1960) pp. 185–6, for the origin of this fortress. It was constructed against 'the Bedouin evil-doers [who] molest . . . travellers along the road to Egypt'.

(*fallaḥīn*). Instead they are usually classified by place of origin; although each co-liable peasant group too has its name, derived from the founding ancestor, Bedouin call them 'Qlāʿīah' (people from Khān Yūnis), 'Ghazawīah' (from Gaza), 'Suhailawīah' (from Beni Suhailah), 'Ṭawara' (from Ṭūr, in Sinai), etc. This nomenclature reflects their political approach, to consider each of the accreted peasant groups as a separate entity, and never to categorize them as peasants and thus allow for the idea that as 'Peasants' they are as a whole placed opposite themselves, the 'Nomads'. Each peasant group is thus placed on its own, and has politically to be dealt with separately, and not as part of peasant society. Yet the Bedouin are implicitly made aware of a distinct dividing line between themselves and the peasants, by the fact that there is a virtual bar against intermarriage and that the peasants are classified by place of origin, whereas Bedouin are always classified according to tribal descent. Bedouin are either Ẓullām, ʿAzāzmah or Bilī, never people of this or that area.

The political significance of the terminology becomes even evident in that all the villagers of the Hebron mountains, to the north of the Beersheba Plain, are referred to as 'Qaisīah'. Up to the First World War there occurred constant tribal wars between the Ẓullām and the peasants of the Hebron mountains, over parts of the Beersheba Plain. As a result there still exists a clear demarcation line between Bedouin and Qaisi lands, and ever since, the influx of peasants from that direction into the Beersheba Plain has been quite negligible. The term 'Qaisīah' then refers to a powerful political organization standing opposite the Bedouin, on one hand. On the other, the small number of Qaisīah in the Bedouin area have not made it necessary for the Bedouin to divide and rule them, and they have evolved no specific appellations for the several separate and localized Qaisīah groups.

CHAPTER 4

Camps and Movements

We shall now follow the different groups composing a *rubaʿ* through their annual cycle of movements, and inspect the structure of their camps at different stages of the cycle. On p. 135 is a schematized map of part of the area occupied or claimed as traditional grazing grounds by the Abu Gweʿid tribe. The area concerned extends over about 250 sq km, and is roughly rectangular in shape. A range of hills running almost diagonally from the south-western corner of the rectangle to the north-east divides the area into two parts, of roughly equal size. While the western half consists of flat cultivable loess land, similar in its characteristics to the rest of the Beersheba Plain, the eastern half is predominantly hilly country which, during the spring, provides excellent pasture, but lends itself to patch cultivation only in some narrow valleys. As one advances eastward in this area, the ground becomes gradually more and more rugged, stony and desolate, and is cut across by deep ravines. It continues to bear the same character till it reaches the perpendicular cliffs dropping a sheer 1,000 feet to the shores of the Dead Sea. While the western plain can boast three perennial deep wells, the eastern part is devoid of any permanent water sources, and the only water available is that stored in rock pools and privately owned cisterns filled by the rains. The eastern reaches of the hilly area lie outside the official limits of the reservation, but are still frequented by the Ẓullām herds, as the difficult terrain makes supervision by the Military Administration impracticable.

The peasant groups go through two annual movements. When the first good winter rains fall, groups such as the Abu ʿArār, Abu Ghnēm and Abu Ṣaʿalūk, till their land in the Plain. They own some land in the part called the Buḥērah, on which the groups pitch their summer camps, and make up the remaining part by land leased from Bedouin, mostly in the same area. As each family concludes the ploughing, now usually done by hired tractors, and sows their barley or wheat, they strike their summer tents and move to the customary winter camp site in Wadi Musīk. This valley lies on the fringes of the hilly area, and is only 5 to 7 km distant from the summer camps. Here in the hollows of the ground people find shelter from the howling winter storms and sufficient water and pasture for their small flocks of goats and sheep. The flocks are tended by the little boys and girls, who during daytime take them a small distance from camp and return each evening to the tents. As the Buḥērah is totally under cultivation, the flocks would have found no pasture there at this time of the year and trampled on the sown ground. Wadi Musīk is the uncultivated area closest to their land, and was therefore chosen by the peasants for their winter camps.

Gradually the last stragglers arrive, and each co-liable group is now united in its own camp, with only a few families staying on in other areas. At no other time is the peasant group as closely concentrated as now, but towards the end of January many of the young men will go north to seek temporary work in citrus picking. As the camps of the several peasant groups are close to one another, a few families of one group may decide to join the camp of another, because of ties of friendship or for convenience, and such a step would not necessarily affect relations with their own groups adversely. Thus in one camp in Wadi Musīk there were the 18 tents of the Abu Ṣaʿalūk group, and with them were two tents of the Abu ʿArār, whose main camp was situated but some 300 metres further down the wadi. Each group has its own guest tent where all its men assemble when in camp, and where all guests are entertained. All the members of a camp are expected to contribute equally to the expenses of the guest tent, and to take turns in providing meals for the guests. But whoever cooks the food on any occasion, the guests are those of the group. The guest tent is really the men's section (*shiq*) of the acknowledged elder's tent, and it is simply termed *shiq*. The owner of the tent has no special say in matters of hospitality, but together with the other elder men of the camp weighs the guest's worth. The standard of the entertainment accorded to a guest is often the measure of his economic or political value to the group. Thus it may happen that when a guest on whom low value is put enters a peasant guest tent, no one will stir to receive him and to prepare the obligatory coffee. Among peasants, then, hospitality is a matter for the whole group, and groups roughly coincide with camps.

Around the end of April to the beginning of May the barley

ripens, and the peasants leave Wadi Musīk one by one to move closer to their land in the Buḥērah. Here the larger peasant groups divide up into several smaller camps, in order to remain as close as possible to their land. The division is usually on the lines of kinship; male siblings and their families tend to stay together, as they sometimes also co-operate in leasing land. A few men may even move aside to pitch tents right on their own land, and later rejoin the camp after the harvest is concluded. Others will leave the camps immediately after the harvest is gathered to seek some wage labour in the north, leaving their tent and family in camp under the supervision of close kinsmen. A few very poor men will leave the camp altogether after the harvest, as they cannot afford to contribute to the expenses of the guest tent. Water does not affect the division of the camps, as each housewife fetches her daily supply of water from either the well at ʿArʿarah or Tel al-Milḥ, a distance which nowhere exceeds 5–6 km. The several camps of each group are pitched quite close to one another. The Abu ʿArār, for instance, are during summer divided into six camps, but all are situated in one neighbourhood, the distance from one to another being less than 1 km. Again there is some, but not much, mixing in a camp, as some people decide to put up their tents with personal friends or affines, but in each camp there is a dominant group which supplies it with its name. A camp is always named after its occupants, and never by locality. It will be the 'Arabs of Samārah Abu ʿArār' or 'Arabs of Sheikh Abu Gweʿid', the name referring to either the group or the elder in whose tent the *shiq* (guest tent) has been established.

The summer camps of the peasant groups remain unchanged on the same site until the return of the next rainy season. The peasants harvest the grain, thresh it in a leisurely fashion, and then store it in a number of centrally situated and guarded storage plots (*manṭarah*), which are used by peasants and Bedouin irrespective of their group alignments. Each man has his own mounds of grain and hay, which he covers with a thin protective layer of compressed earth. For each mound he pays the permanent guard of the storage plot a stipulated small proportion of the commodity stored. After the grain is safely stored away, there follows a period of almost complete leisure, which again many of the young men will use for wage labour outside the area. Women will at about this time start with preparations for the coming rains, and perhaps weave a replacement strip of tent cloth. When the rains finally begin, the peasants again cultivate their land and then move over into their winter camp at Wadi Musīk.

The camps and movements of the Bedouin take quite other forms. The small Bedouin groups do not necessarily camp close to the centre of their *rubaʿ*. The Bdūr, for instance, now have a camp numbering four to five tents, permanently located on their farm land, close to where the Plain passes over into the hilly area. In winter the camp is just transferred into a hollow in the ground, while during summer it is sited higher up, to let in the refreshing western breezes. The permanent camp is occupied mainly by older men and women, who at ploughing and harvest time are joined by the younger men and their families. Only at these times are most of the Bdūr united, while during the rest of the year their tents are spread over the land. Their main economic interest is still animal-husbandry, so that each family goes through a number of annual moves in its search for pasture. After the men have cultivated their land at the beginning of the rainy season, they move east into the spring pastures. Some of them move into Wadi Gurābah (Naḥal Dimonah), at the eastern limit of the Bedouin reservation, and some men go still further east. At a time, then, when each peasant group is concentrated in one camp, the Bedouin group goes through a stage of maximal dispersal. The spring pasture first wilts in the most easterly parts, and becomes less suited to sheep and goats, so that most shepherds retire westwards in stages, transferring their tents twice or three times in the process. They can generally hope to find sufficient grazing and water in the hilly area until the end of April or beginning of May, and then expect to feed the animals on the few stubbles remaining on the fields after the harvest. As the harvesting is done by plucking out each straw separately at its base, in order to produce as much straw as possible, there is not much left for the animals to browse on, and the large herds, of a hundred head and above, will feel the pinch very soon. These herds, especially, will have to continue the movement further west, right out of the Bedouin reservation, on which the pressure of livestock is heaviest. In past years, until the establishment of Israel, families, with their herds, used to range northwards at this time of the year. In normal years the Bedouin would reach as far as the Ramlah–Lyddah area, but in years of drought they would have to continue even further north, at times as far as the Plain of Esdraelon (Jezreel). Freedom to follow the pasture into the north has been severely curtailed by the Military Administrators.[1] Since 1959 the Military Administration has gone further, and insisted on only one member of the family accompanying the flock during its stay outside the Bedouin area.[2] Therefore, the master of the herd and his family now usually join the group's camp in the tribal area, and one of the youngsters stays with the flock. The camp thus becomes a more permanent centre of the group, while hitherto the members of the group had joined it only at ploughing and harvest time. Only the camel-herders find sufficient grazing and water in the hilly areas throughout the year, and live there in isolated camps, usually of one or two tents, and of three at the most. Other Bedouin and some peasants entrust the camel-herders with their beasts, as they do not wish, or are unable, to allocate a full-time herdsman to a small number of camels. Furthermore, this would mean that a member of the family would have to stay on his own with the camels for the greater part of the year. The Military Administration forbids camels to be pastured in summer outside the reservation.

The dispersal of a group does not necessarily mean that contact between its members is lost or weakened. The Bedouin are even more mobile than their tents, and the men are constantly away on visits or else receive visitors. While staying with one man in Wadi Gurābah, I found that about half our time was spent on visits to kinsmen. Therefore the distance between a group's tents cannot be taken as the only indication of the intensity of its interaction. The time actually spent together by the members of a group counts much more. It was also very evident that although some Bedouin took great pains to hide their affairs from other members of the group, even from their siblings, these were always well informed of their doings.

Most members of the Bedouin core-groups move about in a fashion similar to that of the small Bedouin groups; members return to their farm land for cultivation and harvesting, and when

[1] See pp. 51–2 above.

[2] In former years too the Military Administration sporadically tried to keep the Bedouin inside the reservation during the movement westward toward the end of summer, and permitted only one member of a family to stay with the flock. At other times the Administration sought, unsuccessfully, to induce a group to leave its animals in the care of one family.

the orders of the Military Administration restrict the access to summer pastures, they stay there till the next ploughing. For the remaining time, they join the cycle of movements. But in two respects they are different: members of the core-groups are unable, or unwilling, to congregate even at harvest time in one large camp, partly because their land extends over a large area, so that many will form into small camps which are situated close to their land. In part this may be due to the desire of many individuals to exercise their hospitality independently, and not in a guest tent common to so many others. The interests of a wealthy member of an important core-group are dispersed over a wide area, and do not necessarily coincide with those of others. Therefore he will sometimes pitch his tent a few paces away from another camp, be thus formally separated from it, and maintain his own guest tent. At any rate, the members of the group reside at this time relatively close to one another.

The other important difference is that the core-group's elders, the *rubaʿ* chiefs, remain throughout the year camped in the Plain and on their land, usually even staying at a single site. During summer the camps of Sheikh Mḥemmed Abu Gweʿid and of Muḥammad, head of the Ṣarāiʿah group, are pitched in the open country, so as to obtain the benefit of the refreshing westerly winds: for the rainy season, they descend into sheltered hollows not more than 200 to 300 metres away. Sulimān, chief of the Abu Msāʿad *rubaʿ*, camps in winter at the foot of Khirbet Gharrah (the ruin of one of the fortresses constructed by the Judean king Uziah to defend the sown land against the inroads of the desert),[1] where his land lies. But as this location is on the boundary between the Ẓullām and the Qderāt tribal groups, he moves in summer to a site halfway between the camps of Ṣarāiʿah and that of Sheikh Abu Rbēʿah, with both of whose groups he is linked by bonds of friendship and marriage. Here he is in the centre of activities, whereas had he remained in the vicinity of his winter camp he would have been left out of events, his *rubaʿ* being small and insignificant. As the Maʿābdah are different from the other *rubaʿs* in not having accreted groups and having a more circumscribed cycle of movement, mainly confined to the hilly area, their *rubaʿ* possesses no fixed centre.

The *rubaʿ* chiefs do not themselves work; they lease out the

[1] 2 *Chronicles*, 26: 10.

greater part of their land, and their herds are tended by sons or hired men. These chiefs, then, do not have to follow their flocks or move about, and in practice come quite close to being permanently settled. Yet they keep up their traditional way of life in tents, for the unsettled political situation does not encourage them to hurry the final step and to construct permanent homes. The considerable permanence which the camping site of a *rubaʿ* chief attains is illustrated by a remark made by the wife of Sheikh ʿAli Abu Qrenāt. Her husband had removed his tent to a new site, about 1 km distant from the old one. 'For the last ten years,' she said, 'we have camped on that one hill on an excellent site. We should have stayed on there.' The Sheikh himself explained that he was staying in one place because the Military Administration would wish him to do so, in order to facilitate their contacts with the tribe. But the Military Administration never did require the sheikhs to camp in any one place, as long as they remained within the limits of the reservation. And the heads of other *rubaʿs*, who are not sheiks and would in any case have only few contacts with the authorities, act in the same manner. If so, one should rather view the fixity of the chiefs' camps in relation to the movements of their *rubaʿs*. Where each group and, in the case of Bedouin almost each individual, belonging to the *rubaʿ* moves at different times in different directions, it is only the chief's camp that stays in place. Although the chief personally moves about a great deal, visiting his kinsmen and other chiefs, and frequently going to Beersheba on errands and for the sake of prestige, spending hours in coffee-houses, he always returns to his camp, where members of his *rubaʿ* will be able to await him. The chief's camp is the fixed centre of the *rubaʿ*, both in a spatial and a structural sense. It provides a fixed point of reference for all members of the *rubaʿ*, whereever their wanderings may take them. It is of special importance in a situation where the different types of groups represented in the *rubaʿ* observe diverging cycles of movement. Apart from serving as hub of the *rubaʿ*, the chief's camp also has structural implications for the core-group. As the Bedouin are most interested in their pastoral pursuits, the land they own does not constitute a point of local attachment. If they then wish to be free to create political and economic links with other groups, and invest women in these links, they are drawn in various directions. The permanent central camp of the group provides not only a fixed reference point for all members of the core-group, but also serves as a communication centre.

A chief's camp is, as a result of its immobility, different from the camps of others. During the ploughing and harvest seasons some of his close kinsmen and other members of his co-liable group and of his *rubaʿ* may join him, but at other times he either stays alone or there remain in his camp mainly people who do not move at all, or single families not forming part of a larger co-liable group. The camp of Sheikh Abu Gweʿid comprised at one time (April 1961) eight tents: his own; his half-brother Ḥmēd's, who kept a store in the camp and with whom lived a younger brother, afflicted with lingering tuberculosis that often tied him to his bed; Mūsa's, a father's brother's son to the sheikh and brother-in-law of Ḥmēd, a 30-year-old landless and shiftless bachelor; Salmān Raḥāḥlah's, an elderly widower caring for his invalid mother, and who had leased land from the sheikh; Gumʿah Raḥāḥlah's, who was just recovering from illness (the Raḥāḥlah form one co-liable group with the Abu Gweʿid); the sheikh's brother's son Ibrahim's, who had recently married and had not yet received a share of the family's flock, which was with his father in the hilly area; Muḥammad's, a member of the Abu Ṣaʿalūk peasant group, who acts as secretary to the almost illiterate sheikh and also leases land from him; and lastly, Ḥussēn Abu Shaʿīrah's, a refugee family from Beni Suhailah in the Gaza area, whom the sheikh had registered officially as his kinsmen, and who leased land from the sheikh. This composition contrasts considerably with that of most other camps, which are made up almost exclusively of agnates. The camp of Muḥammad, chief of the Ṣarāiʿah core-group, at all times comprises only two tents: his own and that of a landless family of peasants not affiliated to a larger co-liable group. Sulimān Abu Msāʿad's camp is made up of three tents: his own; his divorced wife's, with whom their children live; and that of his divorced sister, who had been married to a sterile man of the Ṣarāiʿah group.

There is one other situation, in which people belonging to different groups can camp together, but usually they do so only for a short while. In spring and early summer a few men may join a Bedouin camping in the hilly area, because he owns a cistern in the vicinity. For although the pasture is free to all members of the tribal group, and may even be made accessible to members of other groups of tribes, there are nowhere sources of flowing water.

So when a man digs a cistern, at a quite considerable expenditure of time and effort, no one else is entitled to make use of the water collected in it without asking his permission. Most men seal the mouths of their cisterns with cement so as to make occasional pilfering of water difficult. The owner of a cistern then practically makes the grazing in its vicinity his own, especially after the spring herbage has begun to wither. Men who do not possess cisterns in the hilly area, will often obtain permission to water from their owners, and then camp with them. In many cases, the people thus camping together will stand in the relation of affines, for groups intermarry frequently in order to gain access to pastures and water. Old Sheikh Muḥēsin Abu Gweʿid, the former chief of the tribe, owns a cistern in Wadi Gurābah, which was used by his sons ʿAbdallah and Sulimān. During the two months they spent there, they had two camel-herders of the Bdūr group staying with them, and these men remained on after the brothers had moved westwards. A third brother stayed with his wife's people, the Qabūʿah (of Abu Rbēʿah tribe), at one of their cisterns in the same area.

Another category of people who may be found living permanently in camps of other groups, are a few 'displaced persons'. They may have left their agnates because of disputes, such as Ḥamād Far'aunah, who had quarrelled with his brothers and now lives a bachelor, with no tent of his own, in the sheikh's guest tent. Or else, they may suffer from a physical handicap, and prefer the voluntary charity of friends to that which their agnates are obliged grudgingly to extend. ʿĪd Abu Gweʿid, blind and unmarried, lives permanently with an unrelated man, one Abu Bnāiah, though he frequently visits his agnates all over the area. The hunchbacked, penniless Hamlān Raḥāḥlah also is unable to obtain a wife, and moves from the hospitality of one camp to another. These men become displaced not directly by their disabilities, but by the fact that they are also too poor to marry. Most of the activities connected with life in the tent are the task of women, except the ceremonial preparation of coffee and the slaughtering of animals, so that these men do not usually maintain a tent. They become dependent on the bounty of the guest tent, they are fed, lodged and entertained there. A man of this kind will contribute in a small way to the upkeep of the guest tent by occasionally providing coffee-beans, sugar and fire-wood. He tries to make himself useful; one often finds him engaged in preparing coffee, or if someone gets up to rearrange the tent poles and cloths, he will rush to his aid. But as he does not share the expenses equally with the others he never becomes a full member of the guest tent. He cannot enter and leave at his convenience, as he has no tent to fall back on. Once he feels obliged to leave the guest tent, he leaves camp as well. Such a man can hardly fulfil the obligations of kinship and corporateness, and his moves may as often as not take him outside the range of his kin and his co-liable group. If, on the other hand, a crippled man is wealthy, he is able to obtain a wife. There are several such men, among them two tribal chiefs, and people cease to pay attention to their disability.

The description of the cycle of camps has brought out some important points. First, in spite of the different and variable sizes and movements of camps, which are related to the several and distinctive economic interests of their members, camps are composed almost entirely of agnates. Second, there is a tendency for the majority of members of a co-liable group to live, whenever conditions permit, for periods in one camp, or at least in a number of adjacent ones. Even the Bedouin core-groups, which attract people from outside the group, live in camps almost exclusively composed of members of the co-liable group. The sheikh's camp forms an exception to the rule. Third, Bedouin groups have a cycle of annual movements different from that of peasants. Bedouin make up for the greater dispersal of the group by constant exchanges of visits covering the whole range of the group and of affines. And fourth, the wide range in size of the camps indicates that ecological pressures do not set precise limits on the size of a camp. But even if there were an ecologically optimal size of camp, this would not determine the size of a co-liable group, for a large-sized group can divide up into any convenient number of camps, and it does not ever have necessarily to combine in one camp. As we shall see, the conflicting interests which the members of a group have, on one hand, in increasing its size and power, and on the other hand, in keeping it small enough to attend properly to the individual needs of each member and to delimit the extent of liability for the deeds of others, ultimately determine the size of a group and its points of fission.

The differing camping habits of the Bedouin and peasants are not due, as one might suppose, to a considerable divergence in their economic pursuits. The Bedouin do not cultivate less land than the peasants, and the peasant too keeps animals, though fewer than the Bedouin. On the contrary, from a purely economic point of view, one would expect the Bedouin with their larger share of the land to dedicate themselves more to farming than the peasants, who own little land and have to enter into unfavourable share-cropping arrangements with the Bedouin. The grazing areas, on the other hand, are open to all members of the group of tribes, including peasants. The fringes of the hilly area are actually exploited by the peasants' flocks during the rainy season, and there appears to be no ecological reason why they do not venture deeper into it.

Table 11 summarises comparative data on the farming and pastoral activities of peasant and Bedouin groups. It shows that the economic pursuits of the two sectors of the population do not differ to any great extent, and that these pursuits bear little relation to the economic advantages of each sector.

TABLE 11

Comparison of farming and pastoral activities of peasants and Bedouin* (by adult males)

Sector	*Sample (adult males)*	*Average area cultivated or leased out (in dunams)*	*Proportion of land held on lease (%)*	*Average no. of*	
				Camels	*Sheep or Goats*
Peasants	110	153	60	½	6
Bedouin	160	158†	4	1½	9

* A break-up of the data by groups is given in Appendix 3.

† The area actually cultivated by the average Bedouin works out at under 140 dunams.

These averages are based on census data for the Abu Gweʿid tribe, and are not highly reliable, because the returns were influenced by a number of considerations. In view of the considerable importance of the comparative table, I shall try to bring out the sources of bias. The figures on cultivation were collected in connection with the distribution of drought compensation, which was calculated at a higher rate for the first 100 dunams cultivated by each family. Therefore the data for the small farmers may be somewhat inflated, but large landowners were likely to camouflage the full extent of their land and that not owned by them which they had at their disposal, as they feared investigations of their titles. As the returns first went through a tribal committee, the discrepancies could be ironed out internally, and the total cultivated area for each group will be approximately correct. The number of animals may have been understated, because Bedouin did not include in their count animals smuggled in across the Jordanian border for disposal to traders from the North. In addition, the data were collected at the end of three years of severe drought, during which many animals had been sold or had died. Most people claimed that prior to that period they had owned about twice the present number of animals. It is hoped that the bias here applies equally to Bedouin and peasant returns, thus allowing us to draw conclusions.

All males from the age of 18 upward, whether stated as married or unmarried, were included in the category 'Adult Males'. The limit has been drawn somewhat arbitrarily, and can be justified only on the ground that 18 is the lowest age at which males can marry nowadays. In several cases no information on a man's marital state could be obtained. The figures on the area cultivated by a Bedouin include both land which he cultivated himself and land which he leased out to sharecroppers in the tribe, and in which he invested no labour, yet obtained his share of the harvest. On top of this, he may also hold a small area of land in leases from outside, because some Bedouin lease out some of their own land to others and then take other land on a sharecropping basis, in order to spread the risks of loss of crop in drought, which may affect local areas variably. Some of these arrangements were made by Abu Gweʿid men with men from the neighbouring Ẓullām tribes, and in such cases I obtained only figures for the areas taken on lease by the Abu Gweʿid men, but none for the land leased out of the tribe. As a man can dispose of his land, there are always some landless individuals even in a Bedouin group. In many cases, land passes from one member of the group to another. As long as a man can obtain land for cultivation from a member of his own group, one cannot consider this as land leased from outside; it is rather an internal reallocation of the land owned by the group, and is treated as such in the table.

At first sight, there seems to be only a slight difference between the farms of peasants (153 dunams) and Bedouin (158 dunams). This difference may possibly increase when one takes into account the effects of sharecropping. Against a bare 4 per cent of land leased by Bedouin from outside sources, peasants have to lease 60 per cent of their land. All of it comes from the Bedouin, for none of the peasant groups owns any surplus land which it could lease out to other peasants. The average peasant owns about 60 dunams (40 per cent of the land he cultivates). He leases over 90 dunams (60 per cent of his cultivated area), and on this land receives between two-thirds and three-quarters of the crop, i.e. the crop of about 64 dunams. Thus he gets the harvest of about 125 dunams.

The Bedouin do not lease out all of their land to peasants from their own tribe. Part of the land is given in lease to peasants from other Ẓullām tribes, and on this I have no details. It is likely, though, that a Bedouin farmer assures himself of the fruits of about 150 dunams (about 37 acres), which is a family's minimum subsistence requirement assessed by farming experts for the region occupied by the Ẓullām. Peasants have to be content with the crops of 125 dunams, because no more arable land is available. They are thus under some pressure to seek alternative sources of income outside the reservation. Until the advent of Israel outside work could only rarely be found, and the land could sustain the population of that time, so that the peasants were glad they could lease Bedouin land in addition to theirs. The conditions offered by the Bedouin landowners were not in those days considered unreasonable, for they could have worked the land themselves, with the help of seasonal labourers. Some Bedouin, I was told, hired Sinai tribesmen who would be given one-fifth of the net crop for harvesting, threshing and storing it. Under Israeli administration land became much scarcer, but gradually more sources of outside employment opened up. It became less worth the peasant's while to enter into sharecropping agreements with Bedouin landowners. Had it not been for the restrictions on movement imposed by the Military Administration, peasants would have flocked out of the reservation in search of better economic conditions. Because of the restrictions, they had no choice but to go on sharecropping for the Bedouin, and at their unfavourable conditions. When movement permits became more plentiful in 1959–60, Bedouin showed some signs of worry, but during my stay in the field they were still able to engage sharecroppers on all the land available. In 1963 there was already some land which remained uncultivated, for not only had the peasant sharecroppers left, but some young Bedouin also felt that they could make a better living by working outside the reservation.

As farming is economically unrewarding for the peasant, one might expect him to turn to herding. Access to pasture, we have noted, is free to all. A generation or so ago Bedouin were able to monopolize the pasture and forcefully prevent peasants from gaining access to it. But during British rule peasants could exploit pasture on even terms with the Bedouin, and this has remained so under Israeli rule. Yet the figures show that peasants own fewer animals than the Bedouin. As a camel has a market value of about ten sheep or goats, the relation of animals owned by the average Bedouin to the peasant would be about 2 : 1 (to be exact, 24 : 11). There is, then, some economic discrepancy between peasants and Bedouin, but it is not so significant that it could account for the basically different camping habits of the two sectors. Camels do not affect the movements of either sector, since both peasants and Bedouin use their camels mainly for ploughing, threshing and haulage, so that for long periods at a time they do not require the beasts. They then leave them for an annual payment in the care of Bedouin camel-herders, who remain all the year round in the eastern hilly area. Some Bedouin will retain one camel for riding purposes, while peasants do not usually ride camels.

Small flocks of sheep and goats are tended by the children of the owner, who does not usually combine with others to save on labour. The size of a flock will, up to a point, make little difference with regard to the herding arrangements required. Only large flocks, of around 100 animals and over, are always entrusted to an adult, often a hired shepherd. Here again the procedure adopted is the same for Bedouin and peasants, and again should not affect the movement cycle of a group.

Perhaps one should view the different movement patterns as a result not only of the respective positions of the two sectors in Ẓullām political organization, but also of diverging cultural orientations, deeply rooted in their specific historical backgrounds. The peasants still, after two generations with the Bedouin, put their main emphasis on land and farming, while the Bedouin still consider themselves primarily pastoralists. To each sector the other activity appears as complementary and peripheral to its major interest, irrespective of the proportion of income actually derived from each. The tribesmen do know the facts involved, but this does not mean that they can adjust their ideologies to conform with the facts more closely. A Bedouin feels he cannot live without animals, for he needs them at every turn, not only for economic exploitation, but also for sacrifice and guests, and for presents, and animal husbandry is a subject which he and his friends can discuss endlessly. The reverse applies to the peasant, for were he not to cultivate his plot he would be out of touch with matters which are of primary importance to the rest of his group.

It is not difficult to observe that the different emphases are part of the cultural inheritance of each sector, and of ways of life with which they grew up. They can cling tenaciously to their own emphasis only because of the high discreteness of the two sectors. The historical facts connected with the ideologies are, briefly, as follows. When the Ottoman authorities began the pacification of the Negev in the 1870's, they paved the way for a complete transformation of the Bedouin way of life. Until then the Bedouin had been busy fighting their tribal wars, often in defence of pasture, and they could not consider settling down to cultivating the land. Some large-scale clashes between tribes occurred as late as 1896. Herds were best suited to such unstable conditions, when one was never sure for how long one could retain possession of an area. At that time the peasants still preferred the comparative security and poverty of their villages to the dangers of life among the Bedouin. Only after the area had become safe and the tribal boundaries settled (the final demarcation took place only in 1917), did peasants gradually come to live in the Bedouin areas. At first there must have been a relatively clear separation of tasks, the Bedouin continuing mainly to raise animals and the peasants farming their land as sharecroppers. Land was plentiful in those days, so that the cultivated areas did not encroach on pastures (as a Bedouin would put it). As larger and larger tracts were settled, not only in the Negev, but also in the traditional summer pastures of the North, pastoralism in its pure form became gradually more difficult. In time, the Bedouin themselves put an increasing emphasis on farming. The prevailing ecological and political conditions had imposed on all inhabitants of the Negev a similar economy, namely a combination of farming and pastoralism. But the ideologies have not been modified to the same extent, and so the peasant and the Bedouin still views himself, just as in days of old, as respectively the farmer and as the pastoralist.

This is nicely brought out by comparison of the camping habits of two men. One of them, Sulimān Ṭalaqāt, is a member of the Abu ʿArār peasant group. The other is a Bedouin, Muḥammad Abu Gweʿid, elder full-brother of the sheikh. Both are roughly the same age, getting close to 50. Both own land in the Buḥērah area (Ṣdēr), Abu ʿArār about 200 dunams and Abu Gweʿid about 300 dunams. Both also own what by the standards of the Negev are considered large herds: Abu ʿArār, the peasant, about 80 sheep and goats, and the Bedouin, Abu Gweʿid, about 150 sheep and goats, and also six camels. Both employ hired shepherds, the peasant a young man of his own co-liable group, the nomad a Bedouin from another tribe. Both are quite wealthy men by Bedouin standards, in roughly comparable circumstances. The peasant camped in the 1960–1 rainy season, together with the rest of his co-liable group, in Wadi Musīk, on the fringes of the hilly area. His flock grazed at that time in the nearby area around Wadi Musīk. Around harvest time the peasant and his four brothers put up their summer tents at Ṣdēr, close to the camp of sheikh Abu Gweʿid, in whose guest-tent they participated. There they remained till they had completed the next season's cultivation, and then returned once more to their winter camp at Wadi Musīk. But the peasant's flock could not be fed for long on the stubble fields around Ṣdēr, and moved westward in stages until in late summer it reached the Tse'elim area, about 25 km west of Beersheba. This area had then been opened for the Bedouin flocks by the Administration, and the nomad's flock too entered it. During these months, the peasant regularly sent food supplies to his shepherd who could not leave the flock for a moment. But he himself went only three or four times to inspect the flock, and spent most of his time either in camp, or away on wage labour, especially during the cotton-picking season.

The nomad had first set up his lonely winter tent in the Diyah hills, in the centre of the hilly area. His herd was with him, as he both wanted to supervise the shepherd and to utilize the milk which flows richly in spring. He did not accompany the flock on its daily wanderings, as it returned to camp every evening. When the spring vegetation dried up in that area, towards the end of

March, he moved with his flock 3 km westwards to Mazraʿah, where he owned a cistern. By the end of April, the nomad had moved on to Ṣdēr. There the flock was fed on the stubbles remaining on his fields, and shorn with the help of his two sons. The herd then continued on its journey westwards, to a stubble area which the nomad and two of his brothers had leased from a Jewish farmer 8 km west of Beersheba. The nomad's tent remained at Ṣdēr, for no tents were permitted by the Administration outside the reservation, but he shuttled back and forth, spending perhaps half his time with the flocks out in the open. By the middle of August the area had been denuded of pasture, and the flocks continued on their westward trek, now relying on pastures provided by the Administration. They got as far as Tse'elim, about 60 km distance from their starting point in the East. At the end of October the nomad began completely to neglect his affairs in Ṣdēr, and came to stay with his flock for the lambing season, which was just about to start. Although his shepherd was able to cope with the increased work, Muḥammad remained with him for a full four weeks. During that time, he lived under the open sky, with not so much as a makeshift tent to shelter him from the rains which had just set in. At the same time his two adult sons were mostly away on wage labour. Back again at Ṣdēr, he cultivated his land, and by the middle of December removed his tent eastward, back to last year's lonely site in the Diyah hills, where he rejoined his flock. One of his sons was sent to bring back to camp the camels, which had spent the summer with a camel-herder to the east.

While the peasant made only two moves in the course of one year, and always camped either with, or close to, his co-liable group, the Bedouin moved several times, and during the greater part of the year stayed on his own. The divergent behaviour of the two men cannot be due to different pursuits, economic considerations, or age, for they were very nearly matched in these respects. The diverging focusing of interests of the two men alone can explain these differences in behaviour.

In this case the Bedouin moves, one might think, only according to the dictates of changing pastures, while the peasant's movements seem illogical and not conducive to the proper development of his flock. But when one follows the movements of other peasants and Bedouin, who own only small herds, say up to twenty sheep or goats, and also farm an average plot of land, the picture which emerges is usually very similar. The Bedouin stays close to his land for the sowing at the beginning of the rainy season, and then joins the common camping cycle, which takes him first eastwards deep into the hilly country, and then again by degrees westwards till he reaches his land at around harvest time; and then further west or north-westwards, until the return of the rainy season brings him back to his land for ploughing. Most of the time he will live in small isolated camps, and only towards the end of summer may he join up with a slightly larger number of tents of his agnates.

The peasant again would confine his movements to the annual transhumance, always seeking the company of his co-liable group. Winter will find him in a compact camp at the fringes of the hilly area, into which practically the whole group has gathered; in summer he goes first back on his land to reap his harvest, and then he reunites with his agnates in one camp, or in a number of contiguous summer camps on the Plain.

In this second case, it appears that the Bedouin takes unnecessary pains in his quest for pasture, for he would find sufficient grazing for his small flock in the vicinity of his land, in the Plain or at the outskirts of the hilly area, just as the peasant does. The peasant seems to move in tune with his economic activities. His economic prudence, though, is open to doubt, for in a situation where he has to lease 60 per cent of his land on an unprofitable sharecropping basis, he would do much better to minimize his farming, and instead devote himself more to sheep-raising. After all, access to pasture areas is free to all, and anybody can dig cisterns there. That the peasants do not take such a course of action has to be ascribed to the limitations which their ideology sets to their freedom of choice, and no longer to Bedouin obstruction.

The two examples of matched pairs of Bedouin and peasants have been 'crucial', in that they compared nomadic movements and camping habits of men at two extremes of the economic scale. They have elucidated a major fact: that neither among the Bedouin nor among the peasants does each man plan his cycle of annual movements and his camping arrangements solely so as to adjust himself to the changing relationship between his economic pursuits and the ecology. With regard to movements, it appears that the 'Bedouin' act as if they were still leading a predominantly pastoral way of life, and the 'peasants' act as if they were transhumant farmers. The Bedouin's ideology focuses his attention on his pastoral pursuits, and that of the peasant on his farming; and thus historical factors prescribe their respective cycles of movement.

The contrasting camping habits of Bedouin and peasants are neither due to ecological factors nor to a difference in their economies, but they have to be traced back to the unequal distribution of land ownership. In the prevailing situation the Bedouin sector of the population owns the lion's share of the farm land. It has sufficient land to satisfy its own requirements, and a considerable surplus which it can lease out to others. At the same time the peasant sector of the population which is interested mainly in farming, depends for 60 per cent of its land on annual renewable leases. With the frequently recurring droughts, poor harvests are the rule rather than the exception. The disappointment of both landlord and peasant sharecropper finds expression in mutual recriminations, and many peasants end up by changing their landlords almost year by year. Most peasants therefore lack any permanent attachment to a defined plot of land, and yet they frequently live in close, almost immobile, camps, in proximity to their agnates. There may well be some carry-over from the compactness of their former villages, though most of the peasants are the second and third generation living among the Bedouin. Yet even in their tight villages they would not have huddled as closely together, and as permanently, as they do now. This applies in particular to the winter encampments, whereas in summer the situation is somewhat more complex: among the peasants too the land is distributed unequally, and in the summer encampments the peasant groups gather around those fortunate men who own plots of land. In order to remain close to their agnates, the landless peasants prefer to lease land not too far away, and are thus indirectly bound to a fairly circumscribed neighbourhood. The attachment of a small number of peasants to the land, then, is responsible for the group's staying permanently in a relatively limited area, and for their remaining within the political orbit of the Bedouin tribal group who are its owners.

We shall later see that peasants maintain co-liable groups, on the Bedouin example, in order to give members some protection of life and limb and social security. Lacking a permanent base on the land, they keep in touch by camping closely together. They lack permanent ties to any one locality from which they could spread out and to which they could always return, so the attachment is directly made to the group in its encampment. Living together also means physical nearness, a precondition to continuity of contact between the members of the group. The peasant group keeps intact only by actually living together. Yet camping together is not by itself a sufficiently powerful agent for maintaining the group. There must also be community of interests. One way in which this is achieved is by arranging as many marriages as possible within the group, thus linking up all its members in a finely-meshed network of kinship ties. This will be shown in the following chapter.

I do not wish to convey an impression that because of their habit of camping closely together, the peasant groups are more integrated, or co-operate in more activities than do their Bedouin counterparts. Proximity may just as well engender internal frictions and disputes in a camp. There is here no higher authority which coerces members to remain in a group, so that if it continues as a going concern, this can be due only to the fact that it serves members' interests, as they see them.

The Bedouin are secure in their attachment to the land. The permanently sited camp of the chief on the core-group's land serves as a pivot on which its members hinge. This enables Bedouin to disperse widely. Yet as long as they remain within the tribal group's territory, they will not be too distant always to be able to rally at the core-group's centre in a single day.

CHAPTER 5

Marriage Patterns

MALINOWSKI shows in *Magic, Science and Religion*[1] how each transition in the life of an individual is seized upon by society and exploited for additional purposes. This phenomenon applies not only to ceremonial situations in a Melanesian society, but is part and parcel of the social life of any society. It is not surprising, therefore, to find that marriage, though essentially contracted for the founding of a family, should frequently be used to reassert and realign political and economic links of individuals. As a considerable proportion of marriages in Bedouin society is contracted within the narrow limits of agnatic groups, the choice of marriage partners becomes of crucial importance to the structuring of these groups, as well as to the manipulation of their external relations.

In Western urban society the proper choice of one's marriage partner is popularly considered a crucial step which determines in many ways the whole of one's married life. Conversely, a divorce is frequently thought to be the result not of differences that developed between husband and wife, but rather of 'unsuitability', i.e. of an initially bad choice. Compatibility becomes such an essential part of married life, that, in the popular mind, no ulterior motives should be allowed to intrude in the choice of a spouse.

A Bedouin thinks very differently about the subject. To him married life is a continuous process of living together in an intimate group within which man's most important physical and emotional needs are satisfied, and which attains its ultimate fulfilment in raising male progeny. Married life thus does not depend on the kind of marriage made, so that the choice of a spouse has, to a Bedouin's mind, relatively small significance. Bedouin claim they marry any girl, as long as she possesses the basic requirements

[1] See the essay bearing that name in B. Malinowski's *Magic, Science and Religion* (Boston 1949).

for a happy married life, good health, a balanced temperament and is not physically repulsive.[1] Thus when one man, a Bedouin of Abu Qrenāt tribe, negotiated simultaneously with two groups for a bride for his son, the young man professed complete indifference as to the outcome. He was, in fact, away on outside employment during most of the time. Another young man of Abu Gweʿid tribe, who was about ready to get married, expressed the idea thus: 'I am not concerned about my marriage. I have four sisters, so that I can marry any day.'[2] Even a happily married young man of the same tribe explained that his wife had not been intended for him, he had only been given her because his elder brother was seriously ill and unable to get married. In case the elder brother should ever be able to marry, they were holding a sister in reserve. All these customs make for depersonalization of the marriage arrangements, and thus leave the agnates free to pursue their interests.

In the Negev it is not customary for men and women to select spouses for themselves. This is the prerogative of the fathers and close agnates, who together constitute a small group of kin which will here be called a 'section'. This group jointly deliberates on the marriage of its members, and arranges them so as to serve its various interests. The candidate for marriage is hardly in a position to flout the decision of his agnates, on whom he will depend for protection and economic assistance all his life. Girls are expected to acquiesce in any arrangement made on their behalf, but a man, while not himself participating in the negotiations for his marriage, may reject the section's choice if it does not agree with his taste. But he rarely objects to the interference of his agnates, partly because his father usually also pays the greater part of the high marriage-payment, averaging between IL. 2,000–3,000 (equivalent

[1] This idea has been expressed by A. R. Radcliffe-Brown, in his 'Introduction' to *African Systems of Kinship and Marriage* (Oxford 1950) p. 46: 'The African does not think of marriage as a union based on romantic love although beauty as well as character and health are sought in the choice of a wife. The strong affection that normally exists after some years of successful marriage is the product of marriage itself conceived as a process, resulting from living together and co-operating in many activities and particularly in the rearing of children.' Although Radcliffe-Brown employs the term 'marriage' both for the arrangements leading up to marriage and for married life, the distinction between the two is made clear.

[2] Meaning that his father could any time arrange an exchange marriage for him.

to a family's income for two to three years). Until recent years it used to be well-nigh impossible for a young man to collect the high marriage-payment as his father held all the property, and there was little employment available in other areas. This enables parents and agnates to enforce their views, and thus each marriage becomes not just a union between the spouses, but also a bond between two groups of agnates, who share a common or complementary interest.

The system usually works well, because it forms a cultural configuration, in which each part sustains the others. Thus premarital chastity is enjoined, particularly on girls. It is in any case difficult for young people who are not closely related to form attachments, because the girls are allowed to see and speak only to close kinsmen, among whom some will be considered suitable marriage partners.

A young person does not conduct the usually extended marriage negotiations on his (or her) own behalf, as this would be 'shameful' (*ʿēb*). Often he does not even approach his father directly, but acquaints a father's brother or another agnate of the father's generation with his wish to marry. A girl is frequently promised in marriage at an early age: in one case such a compact concerned a seven-year-old girl, but possibly arrangements are in some cases made at an even earlier age. Marriage is often consummated when the bride is only 12 or 13, if she is then considered nubile (*mistwīyah*). At that age a girl is in no position to oppose her agnates' designs.

A bride is supposed to remain utterly ignorant of the arrangements for her marriage, and this fiction is well expressed in the marriage ritual, when the bridegroom's close agnates 'abduct' the supposedly unsuspecting bride. In practice, though, the girl will be acquainted with the choice made on her behalf and will generally submit willingly. This is not bowing to the inevitable, but to what she sees as the normal way for a girl to enter married life.

Ritual abduction of brides is practised among the Ẓullām Bedouin, but has fallen in abeyance among most of the western tribes, and is not practised by the peasants. It takes place only after the marriage arrangements have been completed and the marriage-payment paid over, and is carried out not by the bridegroom himself but by one or more of his close agnates, among them usually a brother or a first cousin. It operates not only when the bride is of another co-liable group, but also when she is of the bridegroom's own group, and even when she is a patrilateral parallel cousin. A woman's close agnates are responsible all her life for her sexual morality. This responsibility is implicit in the way a man refers to a married woman of his group in conversation: 'We have a woman [living] with such-and-such.' The close agnates have right up to the marriage been most careful not to let the girl indulge in sexual relations, and have to this purpose secluded her since puberty in her tent, as far as possible. They have an emotional investment in the girl's sexual abstinence. Therefore they must be very reluctant to let her begin her sex life, fearing that this might lead her into temptations and saddle them with the ultimate responsibility for any misdemeanour. It appears, therefore, that the ceremonial abduction of the bride signifies not only the transfer of rights over her from her close agnates to the bridegroom's close agnates, as suggested by van Gennep, to whom 'the so-called rites of . . . capture express the resistance of the losing groups'.[1] As he recognizes that such marriages take place with the full consent of the groups concerned and the loss of the bride has been compensated for by the marriage-payment—a situation arising in many societies—one does not learn why only in some this should lead to ceremonial capture of the bride. Van Gennep does not specify which 'loss' occasions rites of capture.

There is not the slightest show of resistance by the 'losing group', which collaborates actively at the ceremony with the 'captors'. The insistence of the bride's group on performing the capture rather indicates that it has given something beyond what it was morally entitled to: it has given a woman to another family or section, whereas a woman ideally remains all her life also a member of her group of origin. The capture relieves the giving group of the onus of its transgression, and at the same time constitutes an acknowledgment by the receiving party that it has indeed overstepped its rights. The woman has been captured by force, as it were, and therefore she ought to be allowed to return to her father's tent. The fact that the receiving group has voluntarily carried out something resembling an illegal act, shows that it is willing to concede the woman the right to return to her parents. But then, her father has renounced his claim to her by the

[1] A. van Gennep, *The Rites of Passage* (London 1960) p. 124.

acceptance of the marriage-payment and would be obliged to send back the woman to her husband's family.

There has, then, been an agreement to transfer a woman from one family to another, but at the same time both the families admit that a complete transfer cannot be effected. The resulting arrangement is, from the viewpoint of the families concerned, quite unambiguous: the woman must live, work and bear children for her new family, but she must also retain her ties with her family of origin. Both parties have shown themselves willing to make concessions to each other, so that the marriage ought to link them in an amiable relationship.

This argument can be illustrated by a description of a marriage which I attended, and of its antecedents. In 1952, Sulimān (A1) transferred the motherless daughter b1 of A3 to Sālem (A6). She was at the time about six or seven years old. Sālem, whose wife (a5) was a kinswoman of the girl's father, had entered an agreement with Sulimān (A1) who acted as the girl's representative, that he would bring her up for his son (B2), and had paid IL. 1,000 as compensation for her loss. In 1960 both men agreed that in four years' time the girl would be physically ready for marriage. But then the young man (B2) decided that he wanted to marry urgently, and after some wrangling Sulimān agreed to permit the marriage. A week before the marriage was to take place, the girl (b1) was taken back to her guardian's tent, even though she had been living with the groom's father for nine years.

On a Thursday evening[1] I arrived at Sulimān's guest tent,

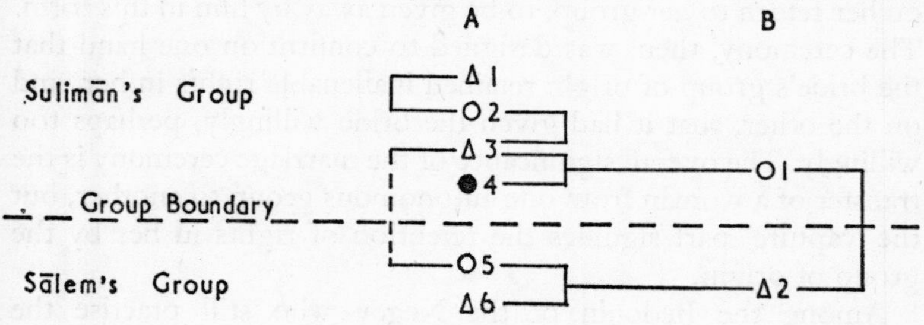

DIAGRAM 3

Background to a Bedouin marriage

[1] I.e. Muslim Friday eve, as a day is deemed to begin on the preceding evening. In Arabic, Friday is named *yaum al-gumʿah*, which can be translated

where the groom's father was already waiting, armed with his rifle. Upon a gesture by Sulimān, Sālem rose and walked off in the direction of his camp. Soon after, the bride's guardian instructed me to drive up a nearby hillock, and there we saw three women walking along, all covered by one black cloak. They turned out to be the bride, her sister, and her father's wife (a2), who was Sulimān's sister. When we had come close to the women, Sulimān shouted out for the bride to come in a hurry, as her camel was ready. The woman in the middle then stepped out from under the cloak, muffled her face thoroughly, and clambered into the car. Then Sulimān got out and told me to drive off, anywhere. I had not gone far, when the groom's father appeared and signalled me to stop, brandishing his rifle menacingly. He got into the car, did not even turn towards the girl, and told me to drive straight to his tent. On the way, he fired a shot or two in the air. No member of Sulimān's group was present when the marriage sacrifice was slaughtered soon after.

The account shows clearly the close collaboration of the bride's and bridegroom's representatives in the 'capture'. The bride had been living for many years with the bridegroom's family, who were furthermore her relatives. Yet it was arranged for her to go back to her group, so that the abduction could take place. Though both sides were apparently in agreement to carry out the ceremony, I was under the impression that the abducting party was perfectly willing to forego the procedure, as it already considered the bride as belonging to its family. The bride's guardian insisted on her return to her group, to be given away by him in this form. The ceremony, then, was designed to confirm on one hand that the bride's group of origin retained inalienable rights in her, and on the other, that it had given the bride willingly, perhaps too willingly. The overall significance of the marriage ceremony is the transfer of a woman from one autonomous group to another, but the 'capture' part signifies the retention of rights in her by the group of origin.

Among the Bedouin of the Negev who still practise the ceremonial abduction of brides, it also signifies a girl's sudden transition from closely-guarded maidenhood to womanhood and

---

as 'the day of uniting', and is therefore considered to be auspicious for marriage.

sexual activity, and relieves her close agnates of the obnoxious obligation of having openly to permit her to engage in sexual activity. A passage quoted by Robertson Smith in support of his contention that the ceremony is a survival of an ancient practice of capturing wives from other groups, confirms precisely my argument: '. . . the bride declares that she would be disgraced if she allowed her husband to enjoy her favours in the encampment of her father and brothers'.[1] In fact, though, the captured bride may marry a close kinsman, whose tent may be pitched in her father's camp, and therefore she is often then brought back into her father's camp, and the marriage consummated there.

That the practice has almost disappeared among the western tribes of the Negev is not due to a different economic structure which makes the rigorous exploitation of marriages less imperative than among the Ẓullām. Although territorial marriage links are no more important to the western tribes, they can still exploit marriages for other interests. Rather has the ceremonial abduction of brides been discontinued because of the ridicule showered upon it by the settled Arab population, with whom the western tribes had more contacts than the Ẓullām. When people are certain that no outsiders would attend a wedding, the ritual may still be gone through. At one wedding of the Tarabīn al-Ṣāneʿ tribe, the chief had to persuade his people to go on with the ceremony in spite of my presence.

Personal attachments between young men and women may develop and, if a match is considered suitable by the close agnates, their wishes may be taken into account. If the marriage is not approved, the couple can only have recourse to elopement. In practice, such cases are not very frequent, and in many instances involve men who belong either to small poor groups or whose social distance from the woman's group is great, as for instance when they belong to another tribal group. In general, though, marriage partners are selected by a young man's or woman's close agnates, and he or she abides by their decisions.

Yet after the marriage has been concluded, the young couple are considered to belong, first and foremost, to each other. This becomes evident in the separate marriage tent (*birzeh*) set up for them, in which the new wife remains for at least three days, and

[1] W. Robertson Smith, *Kinship and Marriage in Early Arabia* (London 1903) p. 99, quoting from Kitāb al-Aghāni, 9, 150.

often up to seven days, a period during which she may see only her husband, but neither his nor her kin. Often the new couple start off with a tent of their own, and only if they are unable to afford one immediately is a part of the groom's father's tent partitioned off for them. A few months later, but usually after the birth of the first child, the young couple ask to become fully independent, and the man's father sets him up with some animals and land, in lieu of his part in the inheritance. This is usually much less than an equitable share. The young people will not necessarily camp with the father (except in peasant groups), although the men will quite frequently visit each other. The young husband from now on devotes much thought and care to his family, his children, his herds and his land. Even when he meets other men of the camp in the guest-tent or visits another camp, a great part of the conversation revolves around these subjects; with close kin he will discuss his family affairs, and in a wider circle his problems of herding and farming. True, he never neglects to visit his kinsmen, since this is a major obligation, but his family and property are uppermost in his mind. He is attached to his wife, who maintains his property and is the mother of his children, while she too grows more and more into his family. Yet the wife's attachment to her family of origin remains as long as members of it are alive.

A crucial example of the clear-cut separation between the arrangements for marriage with the attendant forging of political and economic ties, and the recognition of the separate nuclear family, is the manner in which Bedouin society deals with elopement. Firstly we shall examine the formal approach, as reflected in customary law and opinion. When a man abducts a girl—and every elopement is considered by the girl's family to be an abduction—her agnates immediately give chase and try to kill the culprit even when the girl's connivance is evident. If the girl is found to have lost her virginity, she too should be killed. Many stories are told about the relentlessness of the pursuit, such as that of a father who sought out and attempted to kill his daughter's abductor, even after her death.[1] Bedouin are convinced that a girl's marriage arrangements are the concern of her group, and that whoever infringes its rights must suffer the penalty.[2]

But on the other hand, custom provides the elopers with an institutionalized way out, for they can put themselves under the

[1] See ʿĀref, *Qaḍā*, p. 135. [2] Ibid., p. 128.

protection of an important person, such as a sheikh. This notable should not be embarrassed by the request for help; on the contrary, he should feel proud that he has been chosen as protector. Custom expects him to do his utmost to get the agnates to consent that the elopers be allowed to marry, and generous sheikhs have been known to provide the marriage-payment out of their own pockets. The newly-weds then have to live with strangers, and usually return to their agnates only after many years.

An actual abduction or elopement occurred in 1960 in the Abu Rbēʿah tribe. Involved were a divorced woman and her father's shepherd, a penniless young stranger. After the man could not obtain the father's consent to a marriage, the woman induced her lover to elope with her. They took refuge with sheikh Abu Qrenāt, but as this man did not wish to waste his money on the woman's marriage-payment, he kept the couple for three days and then conducted them to another sheikh. From this man they were passed on to a third notable, who knew that the girl's father had informed the police of her abduction, and therefore feared to harbour them. He surrendered them to the police. As the girl was found to be three months' pregnant the police preferred no charge against the man and returned the woman to her father. But the man kept away from the Bedouin reservation, fearing the girl's agnates might still try to shoot him.

Even though the young couple failed in their attempt to marry against the wishes of the woman's agnates, the case shows how two institutional procedures work each in its own direction: while normally arranged marriages serve the interests of agnatic descent groups, the procedure for the resolution of elopements endorses the establishment of families even where a section's interests have suffered. An eloping woman stands to lose the connection with her group of origin, and the man must also flee from the wrath of the woman's agnates. But the couple are assisted to establish a family elsewhere, and some years later may succeed in bringing about a reconciliation. Even the firmly established patterns of marriage contain in themselves rules which allow transgressions to set in train part of normal processes. Similarly, killers fleeing from the avengers were in the not too distant past offered refuge in other tribal areas. The strangers then often settled permanently with their protectors, and remained even after becoming formally reconciled with their enemies. These 'external'

Bedouin often provided invaluable connections between the highly discrete tribal groups.

The exploitation of marriages for purposes besides the direct one of founding a family, is common to many societies. Bedouin sections can exploit marriages in their interests more systematically and consistently than corresponding groups in societies which permit pre-marital sexual experimentation and in which potential spouses have a say in their own marriage. This cultural configuration is peculiar to the Bedouin of the Negev and of Sinai. Bedouin marriage patterns in other regions may be quite different. The Rwala tribes of the Syrian desert, who have been described by several perceptive travellers, have a pattern of marriage in which men usually select their own bride. Except in the families of great chiefs, agnates do not seek to arrange marriages to suit ulterior interests, the marriage-payment is relatively smaller and divorce is much more frequent than in the Negev.[1]

The rules of marriage observed in the Negev are in most respects identical with those accepted all over the Arab Middle East, and enshrined in the legal code of Sunni Islam. They define which unions are to be considered as incestuous, and set limits to the range of marriage. Basically any union which could fall within the boundaries of an extended family is proscribed. These include, according to the Qur'ān (4, 23), a man's sister, descendants of sisters, father's, mother's and grandparents' siblings; a wife's mother, son's wife, stepdaughter, all direct affines, such as marriage of two sisters at one time (though subsequent marriage, or marriage of two brothers to two sisters is permitted), or to a wife and her father's or mother's sister at one time. Marriage to a foster sister is also prohibited.

The outer limits of marriage are also broadly those imposed by Islam. A Bedouin may not marry a woman professing another religion, though some legal schools of Islam permit a male to marry Jewish or Christian women and convert them to Islam. A Muslim woman cannot marry a non-Muslim. There is also in

[1] See the following descriptions: J. L. Burckhardt, op. cit., pp. 48, 61–4; A. Musil, *The Manners and Customs of the Rwala Bedouins* (New York 1928) pp. 135–40; C. R. Raswan, *The Black Tents of Arabia* (London 1936) pp. 36 f. The last book contains a rather romanticized account of Bedouin life, but is based on intimate acquaintance with the Rwala.

Islam a very ambiguous rule against marriage between unequals (*kuf'*), which would sanction the strict injunctions among the Bedouin against intermarriage of Bedouin, peasants and negroes.[1]

Within these limits, Muslims are formally given a wide field from which to choose marriage partners. But there is said to exist a 'preferred' type of marriage which, though not anchored in religion, is nevertheless common throughout Arab lands. This is marriage of a man to his father's brother's daughter (the *bint ʿamm*). Patai found this type of marriage

. . . in central, southern and northern Arabia, in Jordan, Palestine, Syria, Iraq, Kurdistan, Iran, Sinai, Egypt, Anglo-Egyptian Sudan, and North Africa. It exists among the nomadic tribes, in the settled rural population and in a somewhat less pronounced manner, among the townspeople.[2]

This custom, then, has often been considered to be a right, even though infringements cannot be contested in courts of law.

In this background we shall examine the marriage patterns of Bedouin and peasants. The rules of marriage of both sectors are identical, so that differences in their actual marriage practices may well be correlated with differences in other aspects of their social structure.

The absence of clear-cut rules of endogamy and exogamy invests Islamic marriage with a considerable resilience. Marriages may range over a wide field and are readily adapted to varying conditions. Thus Bedouin may, firstly, exploit the advantages of marrying out of their agnatic descent groups. Fortes sees the main advantages of marriage out of a group, from the point of view of an individual, to be that:

. . . extra-clan kinship makes a number of breaches for the individual in the rigid genealogical boundary of the maximal lineage and clan. . . . He has not only channels of communication with other clans, but sources of material aid and moral support outside his clan.[3]

Where the individual's advantages are mainly 'material' and 'moral', the groups connected by intermarriage derive in addition political advantages, by being able to join forces. The drawbacks of having marriages within the group, on the other hand, have

[1] For Islamic legal rules see A. A. A. Fyzee, *Outlines of Muhammadan Law* (Oxford 1955) pp. 87–93.

[2] R. Patai, 'Cousin-Right in Middle Eastern Marriage' (1955) p. 385.

[3] M. Fortes, *The Web of Kinship among the Tallensi* (Oxford 1949) p. 286.

been reduced considerably in Bedouin society. For here personal choice of marriage partners has been almost eliminated and almost no property moves with women. When several members of a group compete over their own women, the senior men who negotiate marriages can usually correctly assess the risk of dividing the group against itself. As not only the parties directly concerned take part in the discussions, the competing claims can usually be settled in a satisfactory fashion.

A numerical comparison between the proportion of marriages contracted by males with women from within their co-liable groups and outside it, shows that the practices of Bedouin and of peasants differ a great deal (Table 12). The table compares three of

TABLE 12

Marriages inside and outside co-liable groups, by male peasants and Bedouin (N = 166)

Category	*Inside Group*	*Out of group*	*Total*	*As %*	
				Inside group	*Out of group*
Peasants	45	30	75	60	40
Bedouin	27	64	91	30	70
Total	72	94	166		

the larger groups of each category with at least 15 marriages to a group. Smaller groups of both categories have not been included in the calculation, because in them the actual possibilities for marriage inside the group were often reduced or non-existent. The difference in the marriage patterns of peasants and Bedouin is striking, and it is statistically highly significant.[1] Also, the marriage patterns of peasants in the Negev are quite different from those of Arab peasants from other parts of the country, as the following comparison of in-group marriage shows.

From Table 13 it appears that the in-group marriages of the Bedouin show at a similar level to those of Arab peasants in other parts of the country, while the peasants of the Negev show a quite different pattern. No figures for villages of the Gaza area, from

[1] $\chi^2 = 12{\cdot}93$, dfl, $p > 0{\cdot}01$.

TABLE 13

Comparative data for marriage inside co-liable groups in the Negev and in Palestinian Arab villages (by males)

	Negev				*Ṭurʿān*	
	Peasants	*Bedouin*	*Arṭas*	*Ramleh 5 villages*	*Moslems*	*Christian*
Sample	90	124	264	631	578	211
Marriages in Groups	51	30	89	207	182	45
As %	57	24	33·7	32·8	31·5	21·3

The figures for the Negev here include both large and small co-liable groups, in order to facilitate comparison with the other areas. Figures for the Palestinian villages are taken from Rosenfeld's analysis.* For the Ramleh villages, the figure for 'Sub-clan marriages' was inserted, instead of that for 'clan marriages', the smaller groups being of similar size to the groups of the Negev chosen by me as units.

* H. Rosenfeld 'An Analysis of Marriage and Marriage Statistics for a Moslem and Christian Arab Village', (1957) p. 46.

which most of the peasants originate, are available, but one may assume that they would not be too dissimilar from those of other villages. If this is true, then the marriage patterns of the Negev peasants cannot be treated as a carry-over from former conditions, and one can legitimately look for correlations with other aspects of their social structure.

The figures by themselves give only a slight indication of the deep-seated economic and political differences between peasants and Bedouin. One must beware of being misled by statistics into the belief that the same factors, at differential rates, affect the marriage patterns of both categories. There may be different constellations of factors at work in each category, so that the figures obtained for Bedouin and peasants may not be directly comparable. We shall now attempt to sort out these factors, firstly in terms of the interests governing the different types of marriage among peasants and Bedouin, and then, in terms of the structural relevance of these patterns.[1]

We have already seen how the lack of land affects the peasants.[2]

[1] Marriage data for all groups analysed are set out in Appendix 4.

[2] See pp. 90–9 above.

We shall now examine how peasants use marriage within their groups as a means of reinforcing their community, to overcome the handicap of having no base on the land. This they achieve by forging more and more affinal links between members, so that their co-liable groups turn into groups of cognatic kin. Conversely, there is little inducement for peasants to contract marriages outside their groups. As women do not inherit land, there are no grounds for marrying women from other groups in order to acquire property. Other peasant groups have generally been, and in particular during periods of increased immigration into the Bedouin area, rather additional competitors for land than political allies against the Bedouin landowners. There was, and still is, no intermarriage between peasants and Bedouin, mainly perhaps because the latter were committed to constant intermarriage among their own groups, in order to maintain their political superiority and safeguard their economic interests. The overall result has been that most peasants have become isolated minority groups, each of which is bent on strengthening its internal structure, on linking up all its members in various ways.

The Abu Ṣaʿalūk peasant group can provide an example of the numerous intricate links tying together the members of a group. The Abu Ṣaʿalūk[1] appear, according to their own traditions, to have drifted from North Africa via Egypt to Khān Yūnis in the Gaza area. They moved into the Ẓullām area at around 1910 and the first to arrive were, as one man put it, 'six men, brothers and cousins (*awlād ʿamm*)', who gradually acquired some land in the Buḥērah tract. They now comprise about 110 souls, and are divided into six sections (*qōm*,[2] pl. *qwām*), all descendants of the six founders. A section is a group of agnates among whom there is an appreciable number of adult males, most of whom are connected through an ancestor one or two generations removed. A section in some cases also contains more distantly related agnates. The most important feature of the section is that it is the only agnatic group in the Negev, in the sense that its members are both kinsmen and political collaborators. Kinship connections are not

[1] Ṣaʿalūk (the Beggar) is said to be the nickname of the group's ancestor, whose 'real name was lost'.

[2] In classical Arabic, the term *qaum* connotates a group, often in the sense of nation. In general Bedouin usage a *qōm* is a band, and also a raiding party, while in the Negev it refers to the sections of agnates.

usually traced beyond second cousins. Sections also form the nuclei for the wider associations of men. A section may sometimes constitute a co-liable group for its members, but in other cases several sections share in co-liability.

All the tents of the Abu Ṣaʿalūk are pitched in winter in a single camp in the hilly area, and in summer five of the six sections maintain one camp in the Buḥērah area, except for individual families which may remain for a while close to their leased land. All Ṣaʿālkah consider themselves agnatically related. This may or may not be so historically: at any rate they have, through persistent intermarriage, all become cognatic kinsmen of one another. Even the Ṣāleḥ section (the descendants of A6) made up of four brothers who have actually gone to live in another area with the Abu Qrenāt tribe, contracted two exchange marriages with the other sections of the Abu Ṣaʿalūk. Eighty per cent of such marriages of males as I have been able to record have been contracted within the co-liable group, thus connecting all sections in a network of multiple kinship ties. To chart the many interconnections between all the members of the group would be a well-nigh impossible task, but by following through the kinship links of just one member one can obtain an idea of the various ways in which the group is interlaced with kinship. Diagram 4 shows the kinship ramifications of one man, Muḥammad Abu Ṣaʿalūk, and I emphasize at the outset that he was not exceptional in this respect. The diagram is abbreviated, showing only persons representing sections or through whom links have been made. Muḥammad (C9) is linked up with the other four sections of the camp by a series of four marriages contracted by women of his section: C1 = c8; C4 = c13; C6 = c16; C7 = c15. An additional link to section A2 is provided by his late brother's wife (c3), who is now living with him. He himself is married to a father's brother's daughter (c14), which does not have any effect on his section's structure as she has no brothers. All these links are in Muḥammad's own generation, but in addition he has also forged one link into the succeeding generation, by marrying d2. Then also his centenarian mother (b7) is living with him, one of the only two surviving members of the ascending generation, through whom especially intimate ties with A2's section came to be established. During my stay with the Abu Gweʿid tribe in 1960–1, Muḥammad was already considering how to arrange the marriage of his eldest son, and also toying with the idea of himself taking a third wife from among his kinsmen.

One clearly sees that Muḥammad was actively and almost continually engaged in spinning out his already numerous kinship links and in this manner he was contributing to the strengthening of a network of moral obligations embracing the members of his co-liable group. One has only to imagine all the other members of the group pursuing the same aims, each man on the face of it seeking to augment his own position in the group by extending his kinship links, in order to realize the density of the network of obligations towards fellow-members of the group in which they enmesh themselves. These manifold obligations of kinship constitute a means for holding the group together.

In the last chapter we saw that, in the absence of a solid and permanent communal base, peasants can keep their groups intact only by actually living in common camps. But this is not in itself sufficient to keep the group going. There must also be common interests, whose day-to-day pursuit activates members in association, in one context or another, in order to ensure the group's continuity. For only groups whose members interact frequently can normally persist through time. Now the co-liable group is not frequently called upon to perform its primary task, which is to deploy its power corporately, mostly in violent disputes. In between such states of emergency, in which the group rallies for common action, there may occur long stretches of inactivity, during which each member or section will attend to his own affairs. But in practice the group is sustained through these inactive periods because its members, in the interim, interact in other fields of common interest. In the economic field the interests of the individual peasants do not coincide, for each family leases land from any available source, if not too distant, and there is a certain amount of competition and of 'secret negotiations' involved in each sharecropping agreement. Acting as a group in matters of land would not further the peasants' interests *vis-à-vis* the Bedouin landowners; on the contrary, it would arouse the landlords' antagonism. Neither are the peasant groups in a position to initiate political activities against the Bedouin, dependent as they are on them for land. Nor is there any other sphere in which the group could interact regularly in the interest of its members. With so few common interests to motivate day-to-day

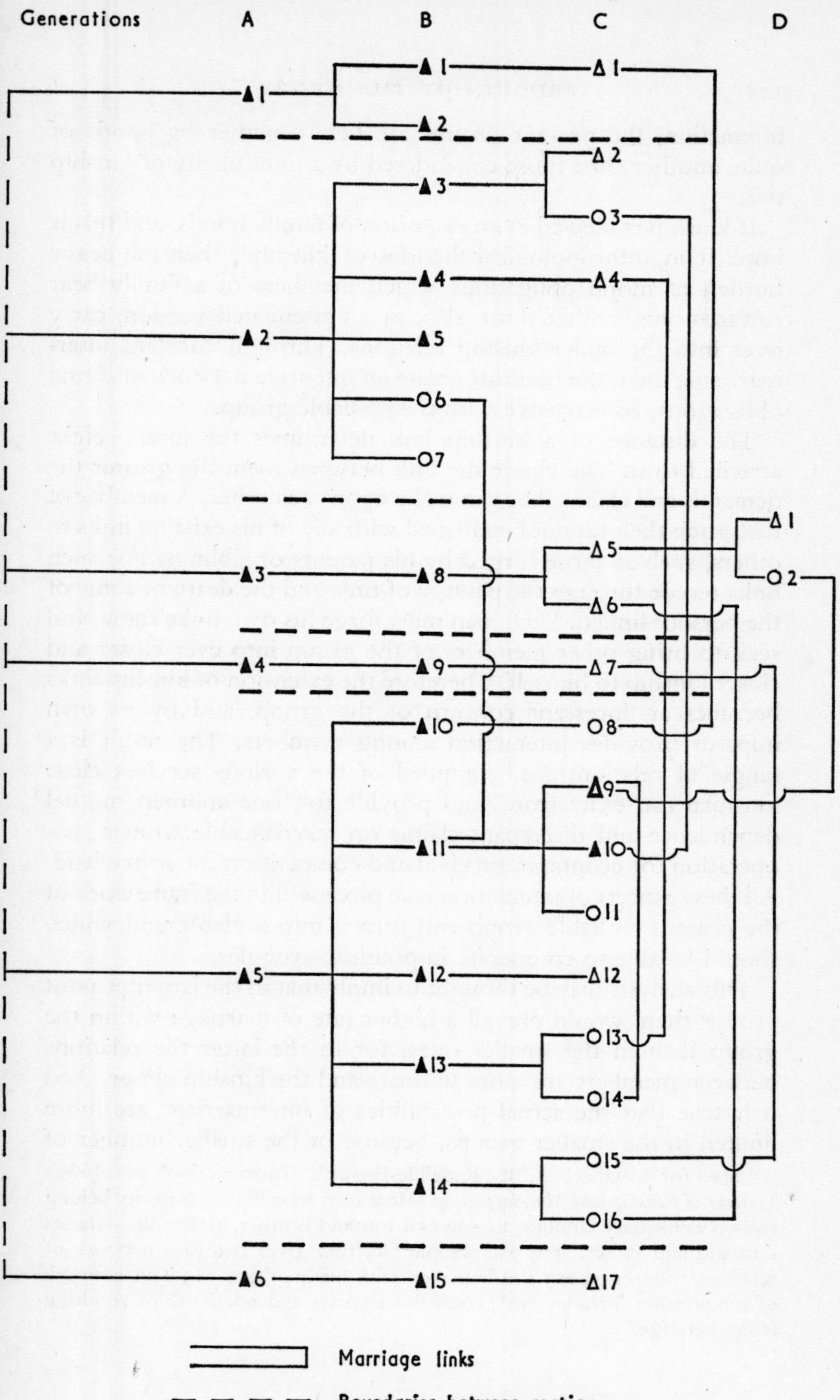

DIAGRAM 4

Kinship links of one member of Abu Ṣaʿalūk peasant co-liable group

interaction, the peasant groups are held together by bonds of quite another sort: those engendered by a multiplicity of kinship ties.

If kinship is viewed as an extension of family bonds, and this is implicit in anthropological theories of kinship[1], then the heavy burden of moral obligations which members of a family bear towards one another must also, in an attenuated version, carry over into the wider kinship relations. Through constant intermarriage, then, the peasants create an intensive network of moral obligations, co-extensive with the co-liable group.

The distance of a kinship link determines the jural weight attached to it. The closer the link between men, the greater the demands and claims they can make upon each other. A member of the group then cannot be satisfied with any of his existing links to others, such as those forged by his parents or siblings. For such links recede through the passage of time and the death of some of the persons linked. Each man must forge his own links anew, and seek to bring other members of the group into ever closer and closer kinship to himself. Therefore the extension of kinship links becomes an incessant concern of the group, and by its own impetus provides interaction among members. The result is a tangle of relationships, compiled of the various services close kinsmen can exact from, and provide for, one another: mutual dependence and discrepant claims on marriageable women, co-operation for economic survival and competition for scarce land. All these aspects of interaction take place within the framework of the peasant co-liable group and turn it into a viable unit which should be able to co-operate in political struggles.

This analysis may be thought to imply that in the larger peasant groups there would prevail a higher rate of marriage within the group than in the smaller ones, for in the latter the relations between members are more intimate and the kinship closer. And it is true that the actual possibilities of intermarriage are more limited in the smaller groups, because of the smaller number of

[1] See, for instance, A. R. Radcliffe-Brown's 'Introduction' to *African Systems of Kinship and Marriage*, p. 6: 'Most men who live to maturity belong to two elementary families, to one as a son and brother, and to the other as husband and father. It is this simple fact that gives rise to a network of relations connecting any single person with many others. . . . This network of relationship includes both cognatic relations and relationships resulting from marriage.'

suitable marriage partners available at any one time. Yet they too have a degree of intermarriage and exploit its limited possibilities to the utmost. The Abu ʿĀbed peasant group provides a good illustration of this. They came originally from Beni Suhailah, a village of the Gaza area, and do not own any land. Diagram 5 shows the internal marriages contracted by the living members of the group. In a set of four marriages, the members of the group completely exhausted their possibilities of intermarriage, and all four marriages are to the most closely related women permitted. These marriages took place in the following manner: two were arranged between patrilateral parallel cousins (C3 = c2 and

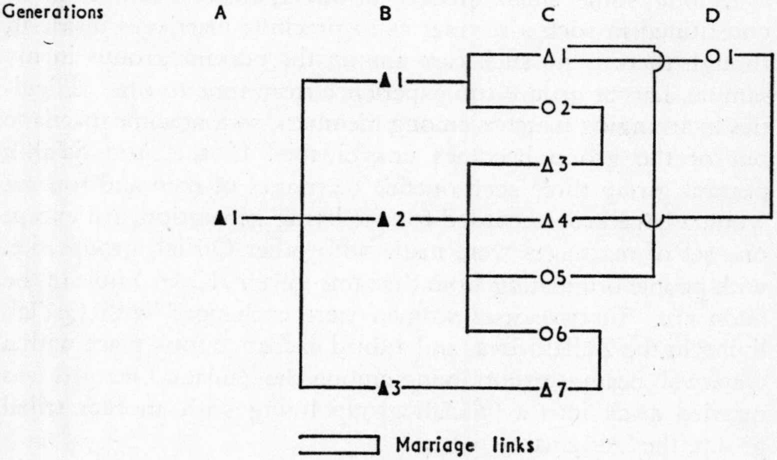

DIAGRAM 5

Internal marriages of Abu ʿĀbed peasant co-liable group

C7 = c6), and two others constitute an exchange marriage, in which a father obtained his patrilateral parallel cousin for himself in exchange for his own daughter as bride to his bride's brother (C1 = c5 and C4 = d1).

The fact that small peasant groups also seek in-marriage to strengthen affinal, and therefore ultimately cognatic ties, sheds additional light on some of the points in the above analysis. With each generation that passes, the ties of agnation grow more distant and the corresponding kinship obligations become weaker and less specific. Each generation then makes its best efforts to reinforce agnatic links by interlacing them with the closest possible affinal links. This process has to start at the earliest possible moment, that is when father's brother's daughters become available for marriage, for a pattern once set creates reciprocal obligations. When a family gives a woman in marriage to another, it will often try to obtain another woman in return, even if it be in the following generation. Conversely, this means that if the pattern of marriages is once directed outside the group, it may create further obligations of intermarriage with the group concerned, with alternating claims and counterclaims. Peasants are afraid of having their hands tied in this way, as this might tend to weaken the links with their own groups.

Among some small groups, however, membership may be constituted in such a manner as to preclude marriages inside it, though there is no such case among the peasant groups in my sample. Larger groups too experience from time to time difficulties in arranging matches among members, so that some marriage out of the group becomes unavoidable. In the Abu Ṣaʿalūk peasant group three such outside marriages of men and four of women have been recorded for the living generation. All except one set of marriages were made with other Qlāʿīah groups, i.e. with people originating from the same village, Khān Yūnis in the Gaza area. In two cases women were exchanged with Qlāʿīah living in the Ẓūllam area, and a third exchange took place with a Qaṭāṭwah peasant group living among the Ẓūllam. One girl was married away into a Qlāʿīah group living with another tribal group, the ʿAẓāzmah.

The Abu ʿArār group shows six outside marriages of men in the present generation and three of women. All three women were married out in exchange for women of other peasant groups, two within the Ẓūllam territory and one to another part of the Bedouin reservation. The other women brought in were also of peasant descent. Only in one case was a woman clearly brought in against payment of marriage-payment and not in exchange marriage.

The Katnāni group, originally from Gaza, numbering only seven men, have through an exchange marriage become linked to another small group of the same origin, the ʿĒr. The Katnāni camp a little distance from their affines who are attached to the Abu Rbēʿah tribe.

Where peasants married out of their co-liable group, they were in many cases forced into this by a temporary absence of marriageable women in their groups. In many cases such marriages were expedients for groups of close kin who were unable to find a suitable pair of siblings within the group with whose close kin an exchange of women could be arranged. As exchange marriages do not require the actual cash expenditure of the fully paid up marriage-payment, peasants often prefer an exchange marriage to another group to the alternative of making payment for a woman of their own co-liable group, while their own marriageable girl might have to wait a long time before getting married. Although three-cornered exchanges can overcome this difficulty, and do actually occur, they involve such lengthy and complex negotiations, that simple exchange marriage is preferred even if it means being linked to another group. Particulars of exchange marriages are difficult to obtain, as people are particularly reluctant to talk about an arrangement which they know is not approved by Islamic law.[1]

Although marriages of peasants out of their co-liable groups are often the result of the absence of suitable marriageable spouses inside the group, these marriages are also employed in the interests of the close kin who make the arrangements. These interests are twofold: Firstly there is the desire to maintain relations with other peasant groups of the same local origin, and among such groups this may often mean the continuation of already existing kinship links with erstwhile neighbours. These links may remain dormant for years, but may then become very valuable points of anchorage to people who never know for how long they will be able to stay in one place. When the groups concerned live close to each other, their affinal links may help them towards political co-operation, as was shown in 1961, when seven separate co-liable groups of Qlāʿīah began to co-ordinate their political efforts versus the Ẓullām Bedouin chiefs. Smaller peasant groups, such as the Katnāni, may also by intermarriage enter into close relations with other peasant groups in order to secure their political assistance. Some of the links made on a basis of common origin can also extend to groups now residing in distant areas, as is shown by the

[1] The Arabic legal term for exchange marriage is *shaghār*. It is expressly forbidden by some legal schools. Yet it is practised in the Negev, and elsewhere in Islam, and some Bedouin consider it to be the most widespread form of marriage arrangement. See also W. Robertson Smith, *Kinship and Marriage in Early Arabia* (London 1903), p. 112.

Abu Ṣaʿalūk marriage into ʿAzāzmah territory. These links may shade over into a second type, those connected with the smuggling activities of the peasants. As the success of smuggling operations depends on whether lines of communication can be kept open, such links are strung out along the smuggling trails, and are made with groups of varying origin.

Some outside marriages of peasants, then, are exploited for economic and political ends, with the result that a certain number of affinal links are distributed over a very wide area, partly inside and partly outside the territory of the tribal group from whom the peasants concerned obtain farm land. These links are scattered in this fashion because the peasants, unlike the Bedouin, do not invest marriages in the tribal group's pastures, and also because their frail attachment to the land gives them a considerable measure of spatial mobility.

The pattern of peasant marriage inside the co-liable group has been connected with their economically insecure position in their enforced dependence on Bedouin land. At the time of my field work in 1960–1, this situation was undergoing rapid change. Increasing opportunities for wage labour were open to the peasants outside the reservation and the more liberal issue of movement permits mitigated their economic dependence on Bedouin land. Some peasants moved out of the reservation closer to their places of employment. Among them were the Ṣāleḥ section of the Abu Ṣaʿalūk who, even some years earlier, had camped apart from the rest of the group, in the Abu Qrenāt tribal area. Muḥammad Abu Ṣaʿalūk himself (C9 in diagram 4) found work as a watchman in an orange grove near Reḥovoth and moved his family there. All these men insisted that they visit their kinsmen in the Negev at frequent intervals, but inevitably their connections with other members of the group became weaker.

The altered situation is reflected in recent marriages. During my stay in the Negev in 1963 I was told that two Abu Ṣaʿalūk men who had moved to Lydda had taken the unprecedented step of marrying local women there. Their new links had begun to draw these men away from their group of origin.

The marriage patterns of Bedouin groups are qualitatively very different from those of peasants, and we shall now examine the former in more detail. A very far-reaching difference is, firstly, that all Ẓullām Bedouin consider themselves as inhabiting a common territory. This is expressed in a somewhat vague genealogy, which makes all Ẓullām the descendants of three men, the founders of the three large tribes, or of four men if the small Kishkhar tribe is included. The latter's few tents were until recent years scattered over the barren mountains of the Central Negev, where they are territorially distant though not separated by intervening tribes from the other Ẓullām tribes. Only in 1960 was this tribe partly transferred to the Beersheba Plain. Each of these Zullām tribes has a version of the tribal genealogy which differs slightly from the versions of the others. Here are those I obtained in the Abu Rbēʿah and Abu Gweʿid tribes:[1]

1 2

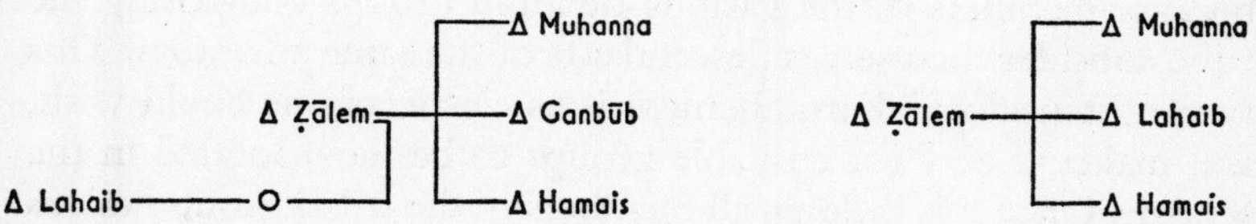

Source: Abu Rbēʿah Tribe Source: Abu Gweʿid Tribe

DIAGRAM 6

Ancestry of the Ẓullām group of tribes according to versions of Abu Rbēʿah and Abu Gweʿid tribes

The four names recurring in these genealogies are the traditional ones of the four tribes, which are still employed by the Ẓullām among themselves when they wish to refer to the whole of a tribe:

Lahaib, pl. Lahāibah—Abu Gweʿid.
Muhanna, pl. Mahāniah—Abu Qrenāt.
Ganbūb, pl. Ganabīb—al-Kashkhar.
Hamais, pl. Hmēsāt—Abu Rbēʿah.

The name by which a tribe is known to the outside world is that of the leading core-group, which usually provides the tribe's chief.

[1] It is worth noting that A. Musil, *Arabia Petraea* (Vienna 1908) vol. 3, p. 44, gives the Abu Qrenāt version of the Ẓullām ancestry, while ʿĀref, *Taʾarīkh*, p. 27, seems to quote an Abu Rbēʿah source.

Ẓālem (the oppressor) is the ancestor after whom the whole tribal group is named. All the versions agree that he arrived in the Negev after having to flee from his tribe, the Bilī, of the Red Sea littoral of Saudi Arabia. The common ancestor indicates that the Ẓullām tribes occupy contiguous territory, while the variations in the names of his descendants may reflect the fact that none of them enjoys political supremacy over the others.

The Bedouin co-liable groups are all attached directly to their tribal ancestor, whether they are core-groups or small powerless groups, and in this sense at least they are structurally equal. The groups do not necessarily claim to be descendants of sons of the tribal ancestor, for, as one man put it, they 'have not learned to write and could not retain in their memory all the descent lines (*silsilah*)'. In sociological terms, one forgets the descent lines because members of the various Bedouin groups composing the tribe consider themselves descendants of the same ancestors. This type of genealogical arrangement is as elastic as one could wish, and makes it easy for co-liable groups to be incorporated in the scheme. Once this is done, all members of the tribal group rank as agnates to one another, and they have a charter for intermarriage.

The group of tribes is essentially a territorial and ecological unit, so that marriage in the tribal group means marriage within a geographically distinct area.

When one surveys marriages from the viewpoint of the tribal group, the most salient facts are firstly that all marriages are contracted in Ẓullām territory. In Abu Gweʿid tribe there occur only three Bedouin marriages out of a total of over 130, with members of the Qderāt group of tribes who occupy territory to the west of the Ẓullām. All these cases concerned families who had come to live permanently with the Ẓullām. Secondly, within the area the marriages are spread out widely, and practically all marriages are made between people of Bedouin descent. The overall result of this seemingly fortuitous distribution of marriages over the area has been to create kinship ties between all Ẓullām Bedouin groups, thus providing them with a framework for communication and concerted political action, should this be required. The Ẓullām are able to realize their unity by contrasting themselves with the peasants, and this contrast confronts them in daily life in the landowner–tenant relationship, in the bar against marriage with peasants, and in their sentimental emphasis on pastoralism. Yet relationships with peasants are not usually tainted with animosity. It is the category of peasants, and all that is associated in their minds with it, that provides the Bedouin with a background against which they view themselves as being different, and against which they assert their unity.

In order to obtain a better focus on Bedouin marriage, we must approach it from a section's viewpoint. We observed that repeated intermarriage among the sections of peasant co-liable groups tends to reduce the distinctions between them and vests power in the total co-liable group. But among Bedouin, sections not only remain distinct within the framework of the co-liable group, but they also act very vigorously in many contexts. Here too it is the section that makes decisions with regard to marriages of its young members. In these contexts, members who are not close agnates of the candidates for marriage are not necessarily consulted. We saw that the peasants arrange their marriages with emphatic single-mindedness: the varied interests of the Bedouin sections range so widely, that the allocation of marriages to each interest becomes a complex matter and the section must exercise strict economy with their short supply of marriageable men and women. In practice, this is achieved by dealing with requirements as they arise. When a gap appears in the marriage links of the section, it will try to fill it up with the first possible marriage. A section may not even be aware of the interest to be safeguarded, but view the decision as a result of kinship obligations or of friendly relations with the group concerned.

Let us identify the several interests at work in the marriages of two sections. I have selected rather large sections, because they are in a better position than the smaller ones to allocate marriages to all ends desired, and thus provide fuller illustrations of the diversity of ends. One of the sections is of the Ṣarāiʿah co-liable group (diagram 7), the other is the sheikh's section of Abu Gweʿid co-liable group (diagram 8). The latter section was included to demonstrate also the way in which marriage may be exploited by sheikhs, to meet problems which do not exist for other sections.

For the purpose of linking groups, it is of little importance whether a link has been created by a woman marrying out or by a woman marrying into the group, although admittedly it is of considerable importance to an individual whether he disburses marriage-payment or receives it. It is of little concern whether communications from one group to the other run through a daughter's or sister's husband or through a wife's brother or father, as in both cases they pass through the same number and type of kin. For this reason, one may consider both marriages of males and of females as linkages, when looking at them from a group's viewpoint. Through the practice of exchange marriage, the two types of links will actually coincide in many cases, thereby often increasing their effectiveness. We shall begin by analysing marriages contracted inside the co-liable group, and then survey other kinds of marriages.

There are, first, marriages among first patrilateral parallel cousins, the closest union permitted in Bedouin society, and in Arab society in general. It appears that all the marriages that have been contracted within both sections (marked in dotted lines) are of this type, and of course few marriages of other types will usually become available within a section. Since a man has an actual say in the marriage of his brother's daughter, it is not surprising to find that the practical possibilities of such matches are often exploited. A small difference in age between the spouses, even when the woman is the senior, will not be considered an obstacle to marriage, but in the one exception found in our examples, that of Sulimān Ṣarāiʿah, (D18), not only was he seven years younger than his bride (d17), but she was also given in exchange marriage, so as to provide a wife for her brother (D11). Exchange marriage is often allowed to override other considerations, as it absolves people from an actual marriage-payment. But this does not mean that such marriages are not exploited for structural purposes. It is clear, however, that a man will usually be able, with the assistance of other members of the section, to compel a recalcitrant brother to acknowledge the 'rights' of the parallel cousin.[1]

Secondly, there are marriages with other sections of the co-liable group. Here Bedouin begin to employ their marriageable men and women sparingly and each large section of the co-liable group is connected with the others by a single marriage link, which may be renewed after lapses through death or divorce, if there are marriageable members available. The two sections in our example forged links with the other large sections of their co-liable group, but never more than one at a time, although further marriages could easily have been arranged in a society in which marriage of

[1] Marriage in the section will be discussed in Chapter 8.

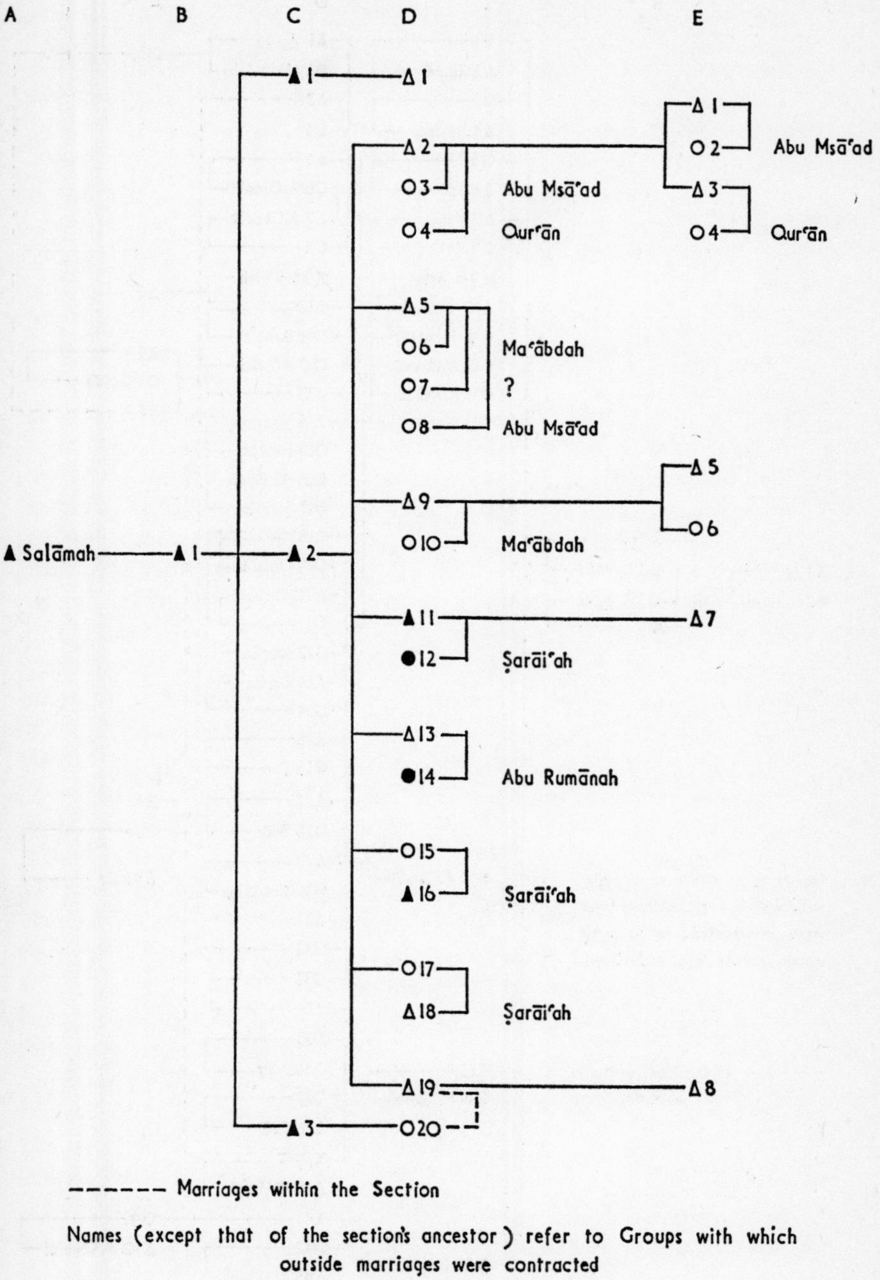

DIAGRAM 7

Marriages of the Salāmah section of Ṣarāi'ah co-liable group

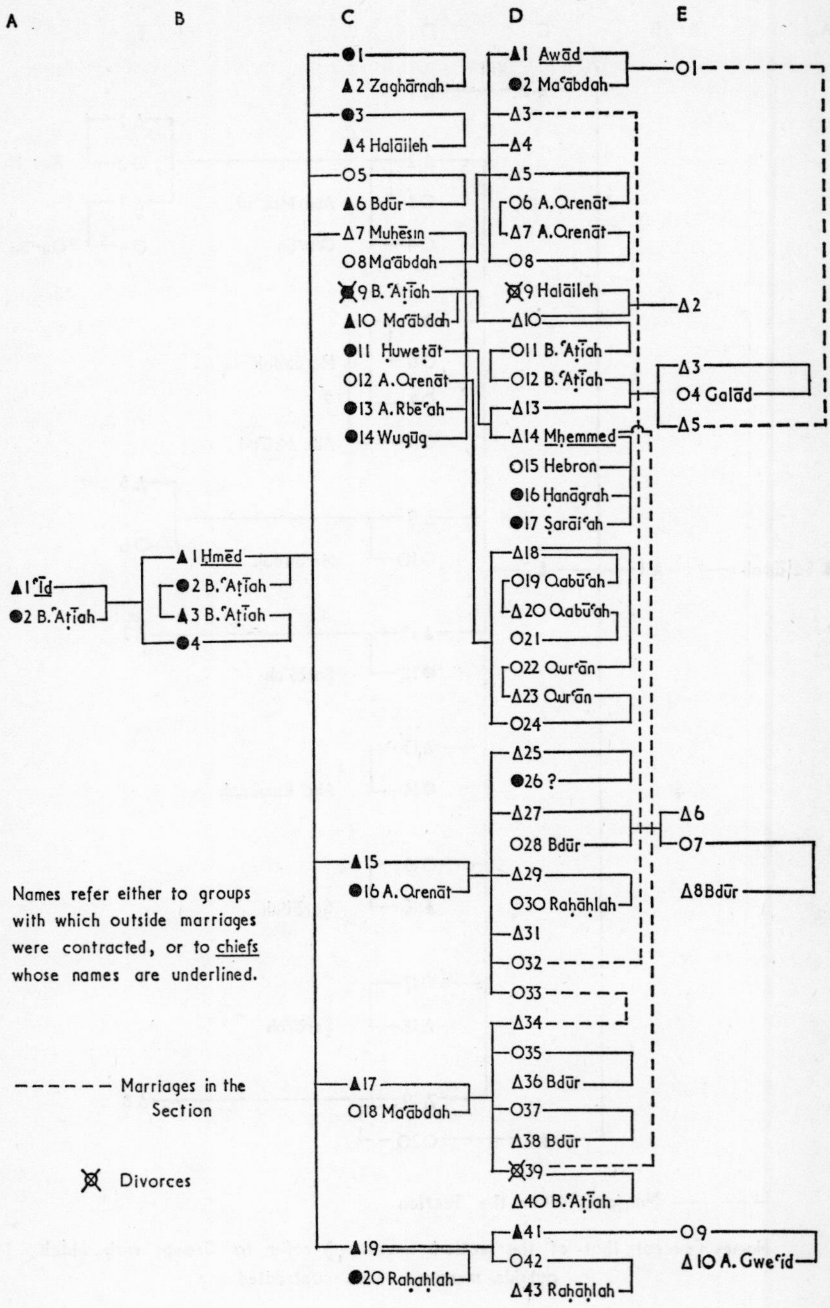

DIAGRAM 8

Marriages of the Sheikh's section of Abu Gweʿid co-liable group

a man to his brother's wife's sister is permitted and occurs (see diagram 8, D10 = d11 and D13 = d12). Ṣarāiʿah linked on to the two other large sections of his group, to one by the exchange marriage D11 = d12 and D18 = d17. The link d15 = D16 makes the connection to the third large section of the group.

The Abu Gweʿid section is similarly linked to the other large section of the co-liable group, which bears the patronymic Raḥāḥlah. In the ascending generation the two sections were apparently linked by the marriage C19 = c20. That link was then continued down into the following generation by the marriage D43 = d42, to a father's sister's daughter. That marriage seems to have been made around 1925. Some twenty years later the family with which it had been made had produced only one male descendant and had also grown apart from the main concentration of male agnates in the Raḥāḥlah section. A new marriage, that of D29 = d30, was now contracted in order to provide a link between the two clusters of men now dominant in the group.

This series of three marriages illustrates the manner in which the links between large sections are maintained through time. Such marriages are arranged deliberately, so that an affinal link compensates to some extent for the increasingly distant kinship ties between agnates of successive generations. The renewed link, with its obligations of co-operation and mutual aid between the kinsmen concerned, provides a constant flow of communications between members of the sections, and ensures that both sections will try to maintain existing political relationships and resist temptations to fission.

The Abu Gweʿid section also maintains marriage links with the smaller sections participating in the co-liable group. One such connection, that with the Beni ʿAṭīah, can be traced through three generations; first the chief Ḥmēd (B1) married b2, the sister of Sālem (B3), a refugee of the Arabian Beni ʿAṭīah, who obtained the chief's sister (b4) in return.[1] Sālem (B3) formally joined the Abu Gweʿid co-liable group, and his descendants have remained members and continued to intermarry with the chief's descendants, C7 = c9, and in the present generation the two half-brothers (D10 and D13) married the Beni ʿAṭīah sisters (d11 and d12), and their brother (D40), now the only remaining adult male

[1] B3 and b2 were no kin of a2, though originating in the same tribe. The latter's marriage is discussed on p. 142.

ʿAṭīwi (singular of Beni ʿAṭīah), was given an Abu Gweʿid woman in marriage (d39).

The marriage D10 = d9 is of a similar nature. The Halāileh were also refugees of Beni ʿAṭīah origin who joined the Abu Gweʿid khams a generation ago. Their father (C4) received in marriage one of the then tribal chief's daughters (c3). They now constitute a thriving section of the co-liable group. There exists a third small section of foreign stock within Abu Gweʿid co-liable group. It is now represented by two brothers, who state that their grandfather was a member of the North Arabian Ḥuweṭāt Bedouin who found refuge with the Abu Gweʿid and joined their co-liable group. As far as I could make out, there has been no intermarriage between this family and the Abu Gweʿid; instead they contracted marriages with the Maʿābdeh, another core-group of the Abu Gweʿid tribe, and have settled in the latter's area. A fourth section, now comprising two adult men, is that of Ḥmēr (E10). It was generally conceded that these men were of Abu Gweʿid descent, but that the precise kinship connection was no longer known. A member of the section tried one evening to work out whether it was closer to Abu Gweʿid or to Raḥāḥlah, but soon gave up in despair: how could he unravel this problem when he did not even remember his own grandfather's father's name? Ḥmēr himself has established a link to the chief's section by his marriage to e9.

Finally, there are four members of the co-liable groups who are each the only remnants of a section. While one of them married a woman from the Halāileh section, three others are still single, though they are now well in their thirties.

These facts tell us something about the nature of this type of marriage link. Up to the end of the Turkish era, the Abu Gweʿid and other large groups must have been eager to accept refugees from distant tribes who could swell their numbers and increase their fighting strength. Such men were formally accepted as members of the khams and often were attached to the group through marriage. The individuals and small groups thus accepted were, on their part, glad to join a powerful group which could effectively protect their lives and property. The large groups are to this day ready to take in new members. Thus one man said to me: 'We do accept new members to the khams. This is done by a formal announcement in the tents of three big men. Even you could ask to be admitted.' It did not occur to him that the last time an outsider had joined the co-liable group had been about fifty years ago. If no new members have joined since those days, this is due mainly to an altered political environment. Under today's secure conditions, members of small groups have no need to obtain physical protection by joining larger groups. Nowadays they are reluctant to give up their political independence and to become committed by policies in the shaping of which they had only a small share. The small sections within a large group, on the other hand, make no efforts to secede, because to do so they would have to act against the wishes of the leading sections and incur their displeasure. It is very difficult to work for separation under the alert eyes of a large section. Nor would they be able to play any important political role as autonomous units. Only large sections attempt secession. It is thus not surprising to find that the large sections of a co-liable group, who make a point of establishing marriage links with each other, do not regularly intermarry with the small sections, whose members in turn will often be constrained to marry outside the group.

A third type of marriage link is that between a core-group and a smaller Bedouin group, in which the latter is not drawn into co-liability but only into a less rigid political connection; the two groups become 'related'. For large groups the interest which governs these linkages is that of gaining political allies. Small independent groups of Bedouin from the tribe seek these alliances at times when their numerical strength is at ebb; the alliances remain intact even when a group's power is again rising, but tend to dissolve when the group has become large enough to rival its former ally as a core-group. Links with related groups may be continued over a long period, such as the link between Abu Gweʿid and the Bdūr. The Bdūr group is somewhat smaller than the Abu Gweʿid, but is still a quite formidable group, and is considered to be descended of the tribal ancestor. The marriages with Abu Gweʿid can be traced back over four generations (in diagram 8: E8 = e7; D27 = d28; D36 = d35; D38 = d37; C6 = c5. See also diagram 14). The marriages between Ṣarāiʿah and Abu Msāʿad are of a similar nature (diagram 7: E1 = e2; D2 = d3 and D5 = d8). The Abu Msāʿad, who were formerly a large group and at one time provided the tribal chief, managed to salvage during their decline a comparatively large part of their lands, and are therefore especially welcome as allies.

Another marriage of this kind, which took place over a generation ago, is that between the Abu Gweʿid chief's sister and a member of the Zaghārnah (C2 = c1), a Bedouin group of the tribe that was then quite strong and is still noted for its quarrelsomeness.

Groups of Bedouin originating outside the tribal group, usually coming in as fugitives, who were allowed to settle in the tribal area, often reinforced the political connection by marriage links. The Abu Dghēm, refugees of the Bilī Bedouin of Saudi Arabia, were during the twenties taken in by the Maʿābdah and contracted several marriages with them. Their relationship with the Maʿābdah is now akin to that between 'related' groups. As previously noted, even individual refugees from foreign tribes do not nowadays find it necessary to obtain formal membership in large co-liable groups, and often cement their looser connection to such groups by intermarrying with them. A case in point is that of the daughter of one Abu Rumānah to a man of the Ṣarāiʿah section (diagram 7, D13 = d14). Abu Rumānah is the only surviving adult male of a group, originally of the Ḥuweṭāt Bedouin of Sinai, which had joined the Ẓullām in his grandfather's time. The marriage links with such groups facilitate their absorption, until their full incorporation into the tribe.

The core-groups seem to pay careful attention to their alliances with these different related Bedouin groups, for they are linked in marriage not only to the relatively large ones, but also to those which seem to be on the verge of extinction. An alliance with a group the size of the Bdūr adds considerably to a group's political weight, and it is quite understandable that the Abu Gweʿid cultivate their links with the Bdūr. That the very small groups too are allotted some of those strictly rationed marriage links, may be attributed to two considerations: firstly, that such groups only undergo a temporary eclipse and may within one generation regain much of their weight, and that therefore the attachment of such floating groups is a worthwhile investment; and secondly, that being 'strangers' to the tribe (and as long as they remain in that category), they possess a great deal of structural and spatial mobility, and can be usefully employed as political and commercial go-betweens. Men like Abu Rumāneh can undertake delicate undercover missions from one political group to another, much more readily than others, as they are not personally involved in power politics. They can provide rival chiefs with information that permits them to co-ordinate action and thus enables them to go on sulking. They can maintain commercial relations extending beyond the confines of political groupings and settle competing claims on smuggling routes. Their range of experience and their judgment are wider than that of the average Bedouin and chiefs value their advice. Yet their influence is founded on their subordinate and undefined position in the power structure. They depend on being indispensable to the larger Bedouin groups, and thus can be relied on always to take their part and not to sell out to either peasants or the authorities. This dependence finds expression in their strict adherence to Bedouin custom and legal precept.

Although the related Bedouin groups also require the political assistance of the core-groups, this is not nowadays a matter of life and death for them. For in these times of public security, even the fiercest quarrels cannot degenerate into outright warfare or feuding, and in the end all disputes have to be settled peacefully. Therefore a related group will welcome the political backing a core-group can provide, yet can also manage reasonably well without this. The small Bedouin groups, then, are not forced to seek the protection of the larger ones, and they can withdraw from the alliance at convenience, so that the partnership is not too unequal and is based on the mutual interests of the groups concerned. Thus both the core-groups and the small Bedouin groups wish to give greater stability and continuity to these alliances.

The related Bedouin groups are not bound to their core-groups by the well-defined obligations and the interdependence that prevail between members of co-liable groups. Even though agnatic connections are assumed to exist, except in the case of groups which have not yet been incorporated in the genealogical scheme, these connections are not traced, and political alliance cannot be couched in terms of the detailed concrete obligations due among agnates. Therefore the partners in political alliance hope to give it the necessary stability and continuity by the creation of actual marriage alliances. These are gradually transformed into matrilateral kinship, the obligations of which may not be as binding as those of agnation, but do still morally bind the groups concerned to stand by one another. As the agnatic links are so very vague, marriage links have to be fostered and kept going with greater care than among people who recognize that they are bound together by agnation. In the case of a large related group it may even be necessary to have more than one link at a time, in order to maintain pervasive moral bonds, as is shown by the marriages between Abu Gweʿid and the Bdūr.

All these types of marriage link discussed hitherto are of great political importance to the sections concerned, and have been deliberately arranged to serve the interests of whole sections. Yet we saw that sections use these marriage links with strict economy and allocate them only singly and to the most pressing requirements. They have to do this so as to be able to set aside marriage links for economic purposes. Both the Ṣarāiʿah and Abu Gweʿid own land in the Plain, close to the western limits of Ẓullām territory. But for their herds they also need the use of cisterns and pastures in the Hilly Area. Only links to the more easterly groups, which specialize in the exploitation of the Hilly Area, can assure them of access to cisterns in different parts, as may be made necessary by the vagaries of rainfall. A Bedouin tries therefore to create as many links as possible to the Ẓullām groups ranging into the Hilly Area, regardless of their tribe. But as the Maʿābdah occupy the traditional pastures of Abu Gweʿid tribe in the Hilly Area, there is a good chance that more marriage links will be made with them than with any single other group. Sections have only been able to set aside a small number of marriages for economic links. With all their efforts the Ṣarāiʿah have managed only four such marriages (E3 = e4; D2 = d4; D5 = d6; and D9 = d10), two of which link them to different sections of the Maʿābdah, while two more were made with the Qurʿān group of Abu Rbēʿah tribe. Even the more numerous Abu Gweʿid section has made only five links of this type during the present two generations (E3 = e4; D1 = d2; the exchange marriages D5 = d6 and D7 = d8, the exchange marriages of D18 = d19 and d22 against D20 = d21 and D23 = d24). Here also one of the marriages went to the Maʿābdah, while one each was made with the Qabūʿah and Qurʿān groups of Abu Rbēʿah tribe, and one to the Galād, attached to Abu Qrenāt tribe. Map 2 gives an idea of the spatial distribution of the economic marriage links of the two sections.

It also shows the approximate area occupied by each of the three tribes in Ẓullām territory. One observes that each tribe has a strip of land running from east to west, so that each tribe holds some land in the Plain and some in the Hilly Area. In the easterly parts of the Hilly Area even the rough tribal boundaries disappear, for they provide only a few weeks of spring pasture. If the Ṣarāiʿah and Abu Gweʿid core-groups and their retainers wish to make use of cisterns in all the better parts of the Hilly Area, they must create

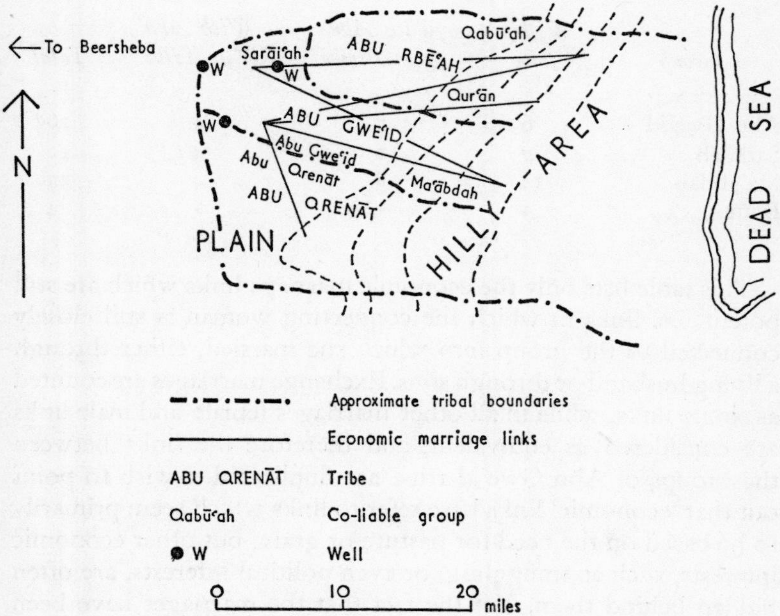

MAP 2

Territorial division of Ẓullām tribes and economic marriage links of two sections of Ṣarāiʿah and Abu Gweʿid

marriage links not only with the Maʿābdah, but also with the other two tribes. The Maʿābdah again must have links with the two neighbouring tribes, but also rely, though to a smaller extent, on the summer pastures in the Plain, and on the grain raised there, and thus have an interest in maintaining their links to the other *rubaʿs* of their tribe. In Table 14 the economic marriage links of all sections of the four largest Bedouin groups of Abu Gweʿid tribe have been assembled. In this context, the Abu Msāʿad are not being considered, because their economic interests are different from the others. This small group has almost no animals and is not interested in pasture, for its members obtain a comfortable living by leasing out their farm land.

TABLE 14

Economic marriage links of four Bedouin groups of Abu Gweʿid tribe

Group	*Within tribe*	*With Abu Qrenāt tribe*	*With Abu Rbēʿah Tribe*	*Total*
Abu Gweʿid	6	7	3	16
Ṣarāiʿah	7	1	4	12
Maʿābdah	15	8	4	27
Bdūr	3	—	1	4

This table lists only the economic marriage links which are still potent, i.e. links in which the connecting woman is still closely connected to the group into which she married, either through a living husband or through sons. Exchange marriages are counted as single links, while in all other marriages female and male links are considered as equivalent, and therefore the links between the groups of Abu Gweʿid tribe are duplicated. I wish to point out that 'economic' links here refer to links which seem primarily to be based on the need for pasture or grain, but other economic interests, such as smuggling, or even political interests, are often hidden behind them. Yet the fact that the marriages have been made into other parts of the common territory, provides the widest common denominator to all these marriages. As the details of a few links could not be ascertained, the figures are to be taken as approximations.

The first point to emerge from the table is that more marriage links fall within Abu Gweʿid tribe than to the other two tribes. This is connected with the tribe's annual movement cycle, which normally takes the Bedouin herds through territory mainly occupied by their own tribesmen, from the Hilly Area to the Plain and from there further westward and right out of Bedouin territory. The tribe is, among the Ẓullām, not just an administrative and a political unit, but is still a territorial entity. Within the territory of the tribal group, the tribe owns a more or less clearly-defined continuous area, which can in good years satisfy its members' requirements of winter and early summer pasture. The relatively numerous economic marriages linking the tribe's Bedouin groups reflect this situation. In less favourable years, pastures are more difficult to obtain, and economic marriage links in the other Ẓullām tribes are activated. Significantly, such links are contracted not only with neighbours; the tendency is to spread them as widely as possible, so as to secure access to an extended range of pastures. Thus the Ṣarāiʿah have forged links not only with the adjacent Abu Rbēʿah tribe, but also with the more distant Abu Qrenāt tribe, and similarly, the Abu Gweʿid have in addition to their various links with the neighbouring Abu Qrenāt created ties with groups of Abu Rbēʿah tribe ranging in the Hilly Area. The Maʿābdah, themselves occupants of the Hilly Area, have taken care to intermarry with groups of the two other tribes living in that area, as well as being linked with groups living on the Plain for access to early summer pasture. Conversely, no marriage links for pasture have been made between groups in the Plain which can provide early summer pasture for their herds on their own stubble fields, although they may occupy adjacent territories. No such links exist, for instance, between the Abu Gweʿid and the Ṣarāiʿah, the two large groups of Abu Gweʿid tribe living in the Plain, whose lands interpenetrate and whose members maintain cordial relations with one another.

That the Abu Gweʿid group has contracted more marriages outside the tribe than inside it, may be due to a temporary situation, in which some economic marriages within the tribe have fallen vacant. It is definitely not connected with this group's political predominance. Most of the marriages into Abu Qrenāt tribe were, in fact, made by the Raḥāḥlah section of the Abu Gweʿid, and not by the leading sheikh's section, so that no case can be made out for a particular political relevance of these links.

The economic marriage links constitute a network of relations criss-crossing the tribe and the tribal group. If viewed in conjunction with the political links between the members of the *rubaʿ*, then all the Bedouin groups of a tribe are connected with one another, either directly or through the core-groups to which they are attached. But the tribe is not the limit of their links; they are also spread widely over the other Ẓullām tribes. Through its links each group is more or less firmly fastened to a certain point in the political framework of a tribe, yet with the help of its alternative links in the tribal group it can temporarily shift its position within this elastic structure. A group can, and will sometimes, align itself politically with the groups of a neighbouring tribe. Such alignments are usually short-lived, for ecological and administrative pressures will sooner or later bring back a group to its tribal fold. On one hand, the herds will make their seasonal moves largely through tribal territory, and this presupposes reasonably good relations between the groups constituting the tribe. On the other, the administration will only on rare occasions, and for weighty reasons, change a group's administrative affiliation to a tribe, and such cases as occurred were always bound up with a resettlement of such groups in other areas.[1] The Ṣarāiʿah have repeatedly in the past made common political cause with the Abu Rbēʿah group, their neighbours to the East, against their own tribe. Yet they never severed the connection with Abu Gweʿid tribe; the administrative affiliation and the pastoral requirements always drew them back towards it.

The marriages of tribal chiefs are different from those we have examined hitherto, in that they neither serve the direct political nor the economic interests of their co-liable groups. The chief derives his power nowadays from numerous sources, the most important of which are his influence with the Administration and the size of his personal following in the tribe. In a system of indirect rule, such as that of the Military Administration in the Negev, these two sources of power are to a large extent interdependent. For while the tribesmen judge the chief by his accomplishments with the authorities, his influence with the authorities rests on the manner in which he is able to carry out their instructions in the tribe. One means by which a sheikh is able to increase his effectiveness in the tribe is to build up his own family, so as to have as many sons as possible. In the internal affairs of Bedouin, it is physical power that counts most, the potential of self-help, so that a group's effectiveness depends on the number of able-bodied males it can put into the field. In this way, a chief's influence over the members of his co-liable group depends on the number of his personal supporters. A man's most stalwart followers are his sons, whom he can morally and materially coerce into supporting him.

[1] Thus when the Abu al-Qiʿān group was transferred from the Shuval area to the foothills of the Hebron mountains in 1958–9, it was at the same time detached from Hazail tribe.

If his family comprises a considerable number of grown-up males, they become a separate section of the co-liable group. The chief is then situated at the centre of concentric circles of influence: with the help of his family section he can more readily influence his core-group. His core-group, usually the largest in the tribe, will have preponderant influence on the decisions of the tribe, while his tribe stands behind him when affairs of the tribal group are concerned. This machinery of power will usually remain latent, its mere existence guaranteeing in most situations the chief's effectiveness.

As chiefs have such a big stake in sons, most of them contract polygynous marriages, and usually retain only fertile women, i.e. women who bear sons. While all Bedouin desire polygynous marriages, relatively few of them have more than one wife at a time. Thus among the 255 families of Abu Gweʿid tribe, only 19 men (7·5 per cent) have been, or still are, married polygynously. (Taking Bedouin only—of 130 families, 12 are polygynous.[1]) The marriages of 22 men who have from 1948 to the present day been tribal chiefs, on the other hand, are made up as follows (the list states the simultaneous marriages, and excludes consecutively contracted ones):

7 men married one wife
3 men married two wives
7 men married three wives
5 men married four or more wives.

In conjunction with polygyny, some of these chiefs contracted frequent short-lived marriages (one chief, Sheikh Salmān Hazail, attained a total of 39 marriages), and in this fashion begat numerous progeny. On an average, chiefs have eight living children, as against a general Bedouin average of three to four children.

Every Bedouin wants to become head of a family of men, but the sheikhs have better chances of attaining this end because of their higher than average income. Chiefs are also under greater

[1] Polygyny became illegal in Israel in 1951, but this had little effect on Bedouin marriage patterns. No Bedouin have yet been charged in court with bigamy.

pressure to do so, in order to maintain their influence in the tribe. The venerable former sheikh of Abu Gweʿid tribe (C7) stated categorically that he 'married in order to increase his descendants and thus to become more powerful. Even so,' he added, 'one knew that even when one begot many sons only a few were likely to reach maturity and beget children.' Thus of his own 12 brothers, only he and three others had grown up to marry wives. In this context, women who have been proved to bear males make desirable wives, and no stigma attaches to their being divorcees.

Let us now analyse the marriages of the Ẓullām chiefs. Here is an almost verbatim report about the marriages of the present chief of Abu Gweʿid tribe, and one can see that the Bedouin narrator was mainly interested in the males born of the marriages. When the sheikh (D14, diagram 8) was chosen in 1948, he was married to a father's brother's daughter (d39). She bore him a son who died in early infancy and a daughter, and she was divorced a short time after his accession. He married three other wives, and was the only member of the tribe who had been married to three wives at once during the last years. His second wife (d15), who is the only survivor of the three, is a townswoman from Hebron. Hers is the only marriage between a Bedouin and a non-Bedouin in the tribe. She is the mother of three sons. The third wife (d16) was of the Ḥanāgrah, a tribal confederation located in the Gaza area. She had been repudiated by another chief, to whom she had borne male children. She bore the sheikh one son before she died. The fourth wife (d17) was a widow from the Ṣarāiʿah group (shown as d12 in diagram 7), who had a son in her first marriage. But she died within a year of her marriage to the sheikh, without having had a child by him.

The chief of Abu Qrenāt tribe has also married four wives. Two of them are women from other core-groups of his tribe, and the third wife comes from the sheikh's group of Abu Rbēʿah tribe. His fourth wife is of the Abu Gweʿid core-group (d9), who had been married to a member of that group (D10) and been divorced after bearing him a son. She has since borne four male children to Sheikh Abu Qrenāt, who considers her as his head wife and receives guests in her tent.

The sheikh of Abu Rbēʿah tribe professes to modern standards, and has married only one wife of his own group. The chief of the fourth Ẓullām tribe, al-Kashkhar, has married three of his tribeswomen and a fourth wife had been of the ʿAzāzmah confederation, the closest neighbours of his tribe in the Negev mountains.

Sheikh Muḥēsin, the former chief of Abu Gweʿid tribe (diagram 8, C7),[1] claims that he took his seven wives 'from wherever he could obtain them'. I was able to elicit particulars only about six women, four of whom had borne him living sons. His first wife (c9) was the daughter of a father's sister (b4), who had married a Beni ʿAṭīah man, a member of the co-liable group. She bore him one son, was later divorced and remarried to a Maʿābdah man. Another wife (c8) came from the Maʿābdah core-group, the only one still living. He did not marry a wife of the tribe's other large core-group, the Ṣarāiʿah. The three other Ẓullām tribes contributed one wife each. One of them had been of the Abu Rbēʿah group (c13), the other from a core-group of the Abu Qrenāt tribe (c12), and the third from the leading group of the Kashkhar tribe in those days (c14). Another marriage was contracted still farther afield, with a woman of the Ibn Gāzi branch of the Ḥuweṭāt, a tribal confederation ranging over Northern Sinai, the Red Sea littoral of Saudi Arabia, and Jordan.

Notwithstanding old Sheikh Muḥēsin's claim, the plural marriages of chiefs fall into distinct patterns. It is true that in several cases they married male-bearing women, but these were not chosen for this reason only, the marriages all set up significant links. Marriages of chiefs, at least those made after their accession, are different from those made by other members of their sections, in that they are all made to further tribal politics. The chief does not have to marry women of his own group, nor does he have to worry about linking the related Bedouin groups, for this has already been done by his section. He creates political links to the other core-groups of his tribe, as both old Sheikh Abu Gweʿid and Sheikh Abu Qrenāt did. Such marriages are no longer economic links, for they attempt to create personal links between the chief and the core-groups concerned. This comes out most clearly in the unique marriage of the present Abu Gweʿid chief with the Ṣarāiʿah woman, as the two core-groups have no complementary interest in each other's pastures in the Plain. Then there are personal links between all the chiefs of the tribal group, clearly

[1] Sheikh Muḥēsin led the tribe from 1917 to 1947, when he handed over to his son ʿAwād (D1), who died the following year. Sheikh Muhēsin died in 1963.

shown in the two marriages of Sheikh Abu Qrenāt to Abu Gweʿid and Abu Rbēʿah women, and old Sheikh Abu Gweʿid's marriage to women of the three other Ẓullām tribes. The latter's marriage to the Abu Rbēʿah woman was again unique. Abu Gweʿid men used to state categorically that there was 'no marriage between them and the Ṣarāiʿah, the Abu Msāʿad and the Abu Rbēʿah'. All three groups live on the Plain, and have consequently no need for each other's pasture there. Abu Gweʿid men did not, therefore, consider marriage with these groups a useful thing, and the marriages of their chiefs with the Ṣarāiʿah and Abu Rbēʿah women were exceptional in the sense that they were contracted for other than the usual reasons. One finds this forging of links between the chiefs of a tribal group in other parts of the Negev, for instance among the chiefs of the Ḥkūk group of tribes, who are connected through the chief of Hazail tribe.

Finally, chiefs were almost the only men to contract marriages outside their tribal group. In past days the most far-flung marriages were usually connected to political relations between tribal groups or confederations. The Abu Gweʿid chief once stated that 'the Ẓullām used in the past to raid the Beni ʿAṭīah who live near Ḥaql in Saudi Arabia and the Ḥuweṭāt of Sinai and Jordan'. The two most distant marriages made by former Abu Gweʿid chiefs were precisely with these tribal confederations (A1 = a2 and C7 = c11), and seem to have been connected with attempts to restore peaceful relations. But raiding relations with distant tribes ceased after the first World War, when the newly-established states in the Near East barred Bedouin from crossing international boundaries.

Nowadays such far-flung marriage links are rare and may be connected to commercial relations of the chiefs, many of whom engage in smuggling activities on a considerable scale. These extend into Jordan, Sinai and the Gaza strip, but the chiefs do not necessarily rely on marriage links to local tribes, for most tribes are represented by their own members in the neighbouring territories. Three of the four core-groups of Abu Gweʿid tribe, Ṣarāiʿah, Maʿābdah and Abu Msāʿad, have one or more members living in Jordan; and part of the Bdūr group, who are closely allied to the Abu Gweʿid core group, also now reside in Jordan. Most of the large peasant groups, such as the Abu ʿArār, Abu Ṣaʿalūk and the other Qlāʿīah groups, have members living both in Jordan and the Gaza strip. These arrangements began to emerge in the early forties, when Transjordan had become increasingly separated from Palestine, and wartime scarcities made smuggling across the border a profitable business. But they became fully developed only since the establishment of Israel. During the hostilities of 1948–9 a large proportion of the Ẓullām retreated temporarily into Jordanian territory, and on their return to the Negev found themselves living on the frontiers of two states between which no normal commercial transactions took place, and whose economies were differently organized. It is thus not surprising that the Ẓullām groups, Bedouin and peasants, left some of their members behind in Jordan, with the intention of establishing a brisk trade. In this situation there was no longer need for the chiefs to forge marriage links to local groups in these areas.

Bedouin co-liable groups have their own land, and are, through their core-group's permanent camp, connected with a fixed communal base, and can thus freely disperse in pursuit of their pastoral activities. As it is very important for them to gain access to pastures all over the Hilly Area, they seek to make as many marriage links as possible with groups of all three tribes specializing in the exploitation of that area. They were able only to invest a limited number of marriages in these economic interests, because political requirements had to be satisfied first, and these swallowed up a considerable proportion of the available marriages.

Marriage links do not play such a vital part in holding the Bedouin co-liable groups together as among the peasants. The co-liable groups hold most of their land in one relatively compact area, and they acknowledge bonds of agnation even if they do not trace them in detail. The marriage links between sections of a group reactivate the lapsed kinship connection where the sections have become separated several generations ago, and even reinforce agnatic ties where they are still traced. The obligations of close cognatic kinship here too, just as with the peasants, bring the sections of the group closer to one another, and keep divisive tendencies in abeyance.

The Bedouin co-liable group unlike the peasant group does not lack interests to keep it together for concerted action in violent disputes. For the Bedouin, the need to unite is always there and in order to maintain their political and economic supremacy over the peasants they have to maintain a large concentration of power. Bedouin have a big stake in retaining the peasants as sharecroppers, in keeping them disunited politically, and in representing them in relations with the authorities. Formally, in a *rubaʿ*, peasant groups and small Bedouin groups unite around a powerful Bedouin core-group. While the small Bedouin groups ally themselves with the larger core-group on a basis of mutual interest, to increase their power, the peasants hope to obtain political protection from the core-group in the first place. From the security of this protection, they can then venture out and lease land, often directly from members of the Bedouin core-group. The Bedouin groups allied in a *rubaʿ* not only extend protection to the peasant so as to enable him to till their land in peace, but also unite in order to present a large concentration of power to the peasants. By keeping the peasant groups separated from each other, they can maintain political ascendancy even where the total manpower of the protected peasant groups exceeds theirs.

The *rubaʿs* in the tribe not only unite *vis-à-vis* the peasants, when occasion demands, but also compete among themselves for greater influence in the tribe. This applies especially to the relations between Abu Gweʿid and Ṣarāiʿah core-groups, each of which seeks to tilt the balance of power in the tribe in its favour by attracting the third large core-group, the Maʿābdah. This fight on two fronts, against the peasant subjects on one hand, and to gain advantage over the other *rubaʿs* on the other, keeps the Bedouin groups of a *rubaʿ* on the alert. The need to preserve their interests through co-operation as a *rubaʿ* activates the Bedouin co-liable groups continuously.

The chief of Abu Qrenāt tribe competes with the Abu Rbēʿah chiefs for hegemony over the Ẓullām, each trying to draw the smaller Abu Gweʿid tribe to its side. Although the Abu Qrenāt chief went as far as to support the political aspirations of the Qlāʿīah peasant groups of Abu Rbēʿah tribe to establish a separate tribe, he drew the line at economic concessions. Neither of the competitors offered his peasant tribesmen improved sharecropping conditions.

Among Bedouin, then, common interests sustain interaction in several ranges of political organization. Therefore marriage links do not have to take the whole load of ensuring the continued existence of the co-liable groups, and many of them can be set aside to serve non-political interests.

The foregoing analysis of marriage patterns may have given the impression that links are made to serve, for once and for all time, a single, stable and fixed interest, and that perhaps they do not easily adapt themselves to changing conditions. If so, the impression is due to the relatively unchanged conditions in which the Ẓullām tribes have been living until recent years. Their distribution on the land has hitherto remained undisturbed, their demographic structure appears to have remained almost stationary until the last decade, and their traditional economic pursuits are even now being deliberately maintained by the authorities. The political and economic impact of Israeli society on the Bedouin is increasing but, for the time being, traditional interests are still present, and the original intentions behind the older marriage links are still observable.

Although marriages are arranged to link sections for specific interests, they are not for ever confined to the same interest. A marriage always links the sections concerned in a general kin relationship, which can become the vehicle for varied common interests. While in one social constellation a link may be exploited in one interest, changing conditions can alter the nature of the interests. If the linked groups can adapt themselves to the altered conditions, the already existing marriages will support the resultant new interests, provided they are common to, or complementary for, both groups. In this fashion, links which had hitherto been economic, can in an emergency be invoked for political co-operation. This is true not only for Bedouin, for whom the flexibility of links is an essential part of all such relationships, but it is also true for peasant marriages. The marriages linking some of the Qlāʿīah peasant groups facilitated their political struggle against the Abu Rbēʿah chiefs and their allies, from 1960 onwards.

CHAPTER 6

Personal and Joint Interests in Marriage

THE various interests served by marriage links could be observed with great regularity in the sections examined in the preceding chapter. But this poses the question whether it is possible for a group to pursue its interests as consistently and apparently successfully as is indicated there. One would expect chance factors, or various factors governing social behaviour in other fields, to affect marriage patterns to a considerable extent, and to deflect at least part of the marriages from a purely interest-oriented course.

Chance might be thought to enter the picture in the form of a personal preference of the bridegroom-to-be, who may even fall in love with a girl unacceptable to his section. In rare cases, girls can also resist a hateful marriage against the wishes of the whole section. Sometimes two men may wish to cement their ties of friendship by intermarrying.

Personal preferences must occasionally prevail, and where they are incompatible with sections' interests may lead to elopement. But in certain cases, personal preferences can be accommodated within the framework of interests, and in others they may bias people in favour of one interest as against another. Let us examine in which conditions personal preferences of spouses-to-be can be reconciled with the interests of their sections in peasant groups.

While a peasant is expected to marry a girl from another section of his co-liable group, this may still leave him a choice between several marriageable girls, especially in large groups. His close kin would not wish him to marry a girl he dislikes, but neither would they permit him to marry out of the group as long as a suitable spouse was to be found in it. Within these limits there may often be considerable scope for free choice. A man's agnates have the means to keep him within the limits, for they can induce his father to withhold the marriage-payment if he insists on choosing an undesirable wife.

When peasants marry out of their group, they can exercise considerable freedom of choice. The groups from which the bride is selected will have to be in a similar position, in having either no marriageable male available at the moment, or in being able to arrange an exchange marriage. This in itself is not sufficient inducement to part with a girl. There must be previous acquaintance between the sections concerned, such as grows out of smuggling associations and political collaboration, in order to make a marriage link desirable. This narrows down the field considerably, yet leaves the final choice to a personal preference, such as the attributes of the bride-to-be or friendly relations between the parents on both sides.

Among Bedouin the situation is more complex. When a member of a large co-liable group has a marriageable patrilateral parallel cousin, he will be given little choice but to marry her. Where links to other sections of the co-liable group or to allied Bedouin groups have to be maintained, the choice of marriage partners is not much wider, and may in many cases also be confined to one specific girl. But there is a wider field of choice when it comes to economic links, for these can be made with any one of a large number of groups. While the interests of a section require access to wells in a specific part of the Hilly Area, the actual choice of marriage partners can be freely exercised within that field. There it will follow such chance factors as personal friendships or kinship ties. Some types of marriage link then have characteristically narrow fields of choice, while others allow a greater element of personal selection, but personal preferences are rarely permitted to take precedence over sectional interests in the choice of marriage partners. Interests determine the more or less delimited field within which a marriage has to fall and in this field only can personal preferences be indulged.

When a section arranges a marriage link, it obviously acts under the assumption that the link will remain useful for a long time to come, and that it will not within a short time be terminated by a divorce or death of one of the partners to the union. This is especially important where a marriage link opens access to such permanently valuable assets as cisterns and pasture, or establishes a political alliance between groups. Where such long-range advantages are at stake, one would expect the members of the section to do their utmost to continue the link into succeeding generations; for the descendants of its present members will also wish to enjoy the benefits obtained through these links. Later in this chapter we shall examine the connection between interests and kinship. The perpetuation of long-term interests, however, also has direct bearing on the problem confronting us now: how much tension the various types of marriage link can stand, and how divorces affect the interests of the parties concerned. Such an analysis may shed some more light on the nature of the various interests, on the specific qualities of these interests, and on the impact of these interests on various levels of the social structure. The analysis of marriage links has hitherto been mainly concerned with the varieties of interests pursued by people in the Negev. The discussion will henceforth be more concerned with the qualitative aspects of each interest.

Divorce is formally made very easy in Islam, and enforced by a simple pronouncement on the husband's part. He is not even required to produce valid reasons for the divorce.[1] In practice, however, Islamic jurists have hedged in divorce by numerous procedural qualifications; and the reasons for the divorce are highly relevant, because they determine whether the marriage-payment has to be partially or fully restituted.[2] Bedouin very frequently remark on the facility of divorce, yet this does not indicate a high rate of divorce. Such statements are rather meant to bring out the superiority of husband over wife in a marital union, and the ascendancy of the agnates over the cognates in political relationships. The fact that only the husband has the right to pronounce divorce is viewed as the crucial test of his superiority, while in other respects the union is founded on a division of tasks between the sexes and on a balance of rights and obligations. Agnation is affirmed in the rule that the children of a terminated union must become members of the husband's section, and thus also of his other political associations. All this was nicely brought out by a man of the Kishkhar tribe:

When a woman is dissatisfied with her husband, she cannot do a thing about it; but when he finds fault with her, he just divorces her. But although the wife can be so easily divorced, the husband has to supply everything to her. She does not work outside [the camp], she only

---

[1] See Fyzee, op. cit., pp. 123 ff.

[2] In Israel Muslim divorces are subject to the Ottoman Family Law, 1917. For text and commentary see S. D. Goitein and A. Ben Shemesh, *Ha-mishpat ha-muslimi bi-Medinat Israel* (Jerusalem 1957) pp. 225 ff. and 303 ff.

cooks, launders and keeps house, while the husband has to exert himself and supply everything to her: her clothing, her sustenance, the tent and its equipment.

When a man divorces his wife, the children, big and small, always belong to him. It is shameful (*ʿēb*) to leave the children with a divorced wife, even when she is of the same co-liable group. If she has a baby, the man pays her a sum to suckle it until she weans it at about the age of two, when she returns it to the father. She is not to marry during that period.

There is no need to point out that this statement does not reflect actual behaviour, but is an ideological formulation. In particular, where marriages link together the interests of groups, it must be difficult for a spouse, even a husband, to escape from the bonds of a marital union. Yet some unions inevitably end in divorce, and this must adversely affect the interests of the parties. A man who is constrained to continue an unsatisfactory union, can find some consolation in the hope that he may perhaps later on marry another wife. And if the wife becomes quite unbearable, he can still have resort to a divorce. Even though a divorce does obvious damage to the interest which brought about the marriage, it does not affect all types of links to the same extent. Some links are more brittle than others.

Marriages of peasants in their co-liable groups carry a heavy load in holding the group together. Therefore their claims that divorce is rare among them and that it occurs less frequently than among the Bedouin may be true: my numerical records do not enable me to substantiate these claims.

With regard to Bedouin, my information on divorce is more detailed for the Abu Gweʿid co-liable group than for any other and the analysis will here be confined to the Sheikh's section of that group. For references to persons see diagram 8.

Economic links are very vulnerable as they do not generally coincide with other interests of the sections concerned. When a union of this kind breaks up, one can no longer expect to utilize the watering facilities or the stubble pasture of one's affines. ʿAlayān Abu Gweʿid (D18) showed that he was aware of this danger. He is married to a woman of the Qabūʿah group (d19), of Abu Rbēʿah tribe, whose kinsmen have given him permission to water at their cisterns in the Hilly Area. He used to camp for extended periods near his affines. His wife was sick and had to spend increasingly long spells in hospital. There was only ʿAlayān's younger sister (d24) to take care of his three small children and the herd, so in 1961 he decided to remarry. He anticipated that this act, though not a divorce of his wife, would eventually lead to a breach with her kinsmen. Therefore, he exchanged his sister (d24) for a girl (d22) from the Qurʿān group, also of Abu Rbēʿah tribe, which possesses cisterns in the same area. He thus made sure he would be able to replace one economic link, which was about to deteriorate, by a similar one. Yet he did not intend to dissolve his first marriage. It appears, then, that ʿAlayān must have considered the first link to be very brittle: once disturbed it would no longer assure the water supply for his herd. In any case access to cistern water cannot be claimed as a right. The owner would in normal circumstances hardly be able to refuse either members of his section or a direct affine. Nevertheless, such access is granted as a favour.

Political alliances among large Bedouin groups are also potentially fragile. We saw in the preceding chapter that, on one hand, the smaller groups could easily transfer their political allegiance from one core-group to another, and, on the other hand, that the core-group does not completely rely on the political assistance which the smaller group might be able to extend. Both groups make efforts to strengthen the alliance, by forging a number of links in the same generation. This is the case with the alliance between Abu Gweʿid core-group and the Bdūr group, where in one generation three marriage links were made (diagram 8: D27 = d28; D36 = d35 and D38 = d37), one of which was an exchange marriage. A similar relationship prevails between the Maʿābdah core-group and the allied Abu Dghēm group. The latter originate from the Saudi Arabian Bilī tribal confederation and appear to have joined the Ẓullām, who also claim to be of Bilī descent, around the turn of the century. The elders of the Abu Dghēm are linked to the Maʿābdah by two marriages (diagram 9, B5 = b6 and C1 = c2). Three more marriages with Maʿābdah have been contracted by younger people (D6 = d7, D8 = d9 and D13 = d14). Diagram 9 shows all adults of the two living generations, and so demonstrates vividly that two to three marriages per generation constitute a considerable proportion of all marriages of the relatively small Abu Dghēm group. The duplication of links in both these cases is necessary in face of the fragility of the

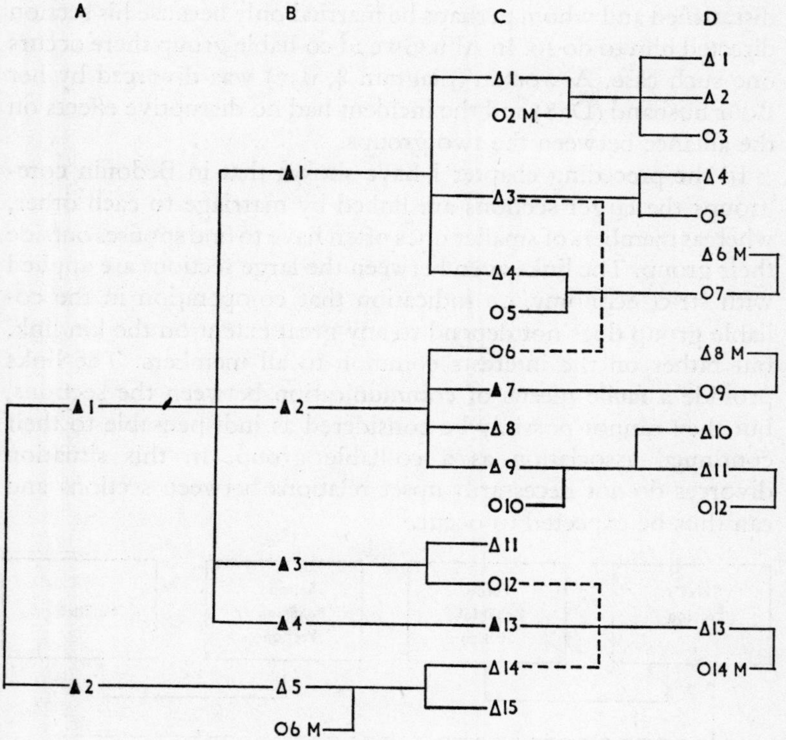

-------- Marriages in the group M Maʿābdah marriages

DIAGRAM 9

Abu Dghēm co-liable group, showing political marriage links to Maʿābdah core-group

alliances and it ensures that even if one link snaps, either through death or divorce, the alliance can still hold by the other links. A divorce does not, then, undermine the alliance, and this tends to make it easier for a man to repudiate a wife with whom he is dissatisfied and whom perhaps he married only because his section directed him to do so. In Abu Gweʿid co-liable group there occurs one such case. A woman (diagram 8, d37) was divorced by her Bdūr husband (D38) and the incident had no disruptive effects on the alliance between the two groups.

In the preceding chapter I have shown that in Bedouin core-groups the larger sections are linked by marriage to each other, whereas members of smaller ones often have to find spouses outside their group. The links even between the large sections are applied with strict economy, an indication that co-operation in the co-liable group does not depend to any great extent on the kin link, but rather on the interests common to all members. The links provide a facile means of communication between the sections, but they cannot possibly be considered as indispensable to their continued association as a co-liable group. In this situation divorces do not necessarily upset relations between sections and can thus be expected to occur.

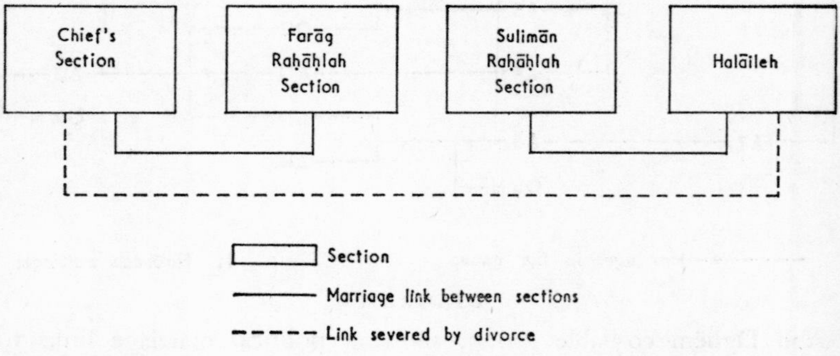

DIAGRAM 10

Marriage links between the larger sections of Abu Gweʿid

Diagram 10 shows the marriage links between the larger sections of the Abu Gweʿid core-group. The chief's section is connected by one marriage to the descendants of Farāg Raḥāḥlah, the second large section of the group. One marriage links the Halāileh with the Sulimān Raḥāḥlah section. There is no link between the chief's section and the smaller sections, nor is there one between the two Raḥāḥlah sections. A link between the chief's section and the Halāileh was severed by divorce about twenty years ago, and has not been re-established since (diagram 8, D10 divorced d9). Similarly, in the ascending generation, Sheikh Muḥēsin divorced his Beni ʿAṭīah wife (C7 divorced c9). In both cases the women were soon remarried outside the group, with Abu Qrenāt and Maʿābdah men, and the case was closed. The day-to-day relations between the sections of the co-liable group continued as before. Neither the absence of marriage links between the smaller sections, nor the occurrence of divorces, bring about splits in the group. But one ought to point out that marriages regularly link the dominant sections of the group and that links of this kind have not been terminated by divorce, for here there is a chance that a dispute between the sections might occasion secession from the co-liable group. A large section can pursue its political aims independently and can, after time has healed the wound caused by the secession, again collaborate with its group of origin in their common interests.

In the Maʿābdah core-group matters lie somewhat differently, as can be seen in diagram 11.[1] Here marriages link the sections,

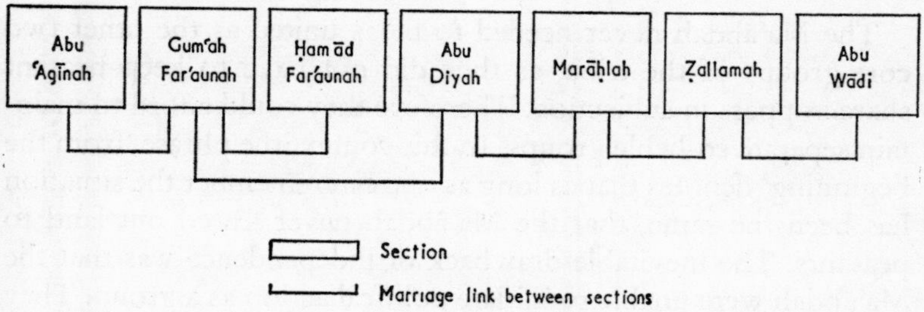

DIAGRAM II

Marriage links between the constituent sections of the Maʿābdah Bedouin core-group

large and small, of the core-group, one is tempted to say, almost methodically. Although most of the sections are rather small (the Marāḥlah number only three men) each section maintains a

[1] The diagram takes account neither of the variations in size between the sections, nor of the fact that marriages which have been continued in descending generations have temporarily duplicated links between sections.

marriage link to at least one other section, so that all sections are linked serially. An additional link joins the two Far'aunah sections. It is significant that the Far'aunah and the Abu ʿAgīnah, the two largest sections, are linked directly to each other; most of the sections, it can be seen, are linked only indirectly to one another.

The specific pattern of marriage links between the sections of this core-group is connected to its political constitution. It will be recalled that these sections constitute independent co-liable groups, except for the two Far'aunah sections which together make up the largest of the six co-liable groups. A Bedouin explained the situation to me like this:

The Maʿābdah were from the beginning independent of each other. Most of them are descended of the same ancestors, except the Abu Wādi who, like the Abu Dghēm, are of Bilī origin, but joined the tribe much earlier. The Maʿābdah are divided into small co-liable groups. There is among them no single large group that can wield preponderant influence because of its size, but they have a leader, ʿIyādeh Abu ʿAgīnah. All the Maʿābdah together constitute a party (*ḥizb*), like the Ṣarāiʿah and Abu Gweʿid. They do not line up behind one of the other two parties; they are independent. They intermarry with both the Abu Gweʿid and Ṣarāiʿah.

The Maʿābdah never needed to be as united as the other two core-groups of the tribe, as they did not have to keep peasant sharecroppers in subjection. Therefore they could afford to maintain separate co-liable groups. In this context the phrase 'from the beginning' denotes that as long as one can remember the situation has been the same, that the Maʿābdah never leased out land to peasants. The inevitable drawback of independence was that the Maʿābdah were unable to initiate political action as a group. They could lend their political weight either to the Ṣarāiʿah or the Abu Gweʿid in any activity these core-groups initiated. They were wooed by both these core-groups and were linked in marriage to the leading sections of both. The Maʿābdahs' strength lay in being able to remain independent of the other core-groups. They had to be careful that some of their groups were not drawn into an exclusive alliance with one or the other core-group. A consensus of opinion on a common policy was essential to their existence as a core-group, and the marriages between the constituent sections of the Maʿābdah provided the communicative links for this purpose. The Abu ʿAgīnah are only the second largest section of the Maʿābdah, but ʿIyādeh Abu ʿAgīnah was 'leader of the Maʿābdah' because being linked in marriage to both the Ṣarāiʿah and the Abu Gweʿid, he was well placed to deal with both core-groups and to maintain their influence in an equilibrium.

The marriages between the Maʿābdah sections have, in this situation, to carry a relatively heavier load than the intersectional marriages of the other two core-groups: without them sections of the Maʿābdah could easily become aligned with one of the core-groups. It is not surprising to learn that, as far as my information goes, none of the marriages between sections of the Maʿābdah has yet ended in divorce.

The break-up of a marriage within the section, usually a patrilateral parallel cousin marriage, does not disturb it profoundly at the time, though it may affect its development in future.[1] During the earlier stages of a section's life-cycle, the members are still close kin: they acknowledge political and economic obligations towards each other, they determine one another's marriages and share in the advantages of the section's marriage links. A cousin marriage does not at this time bring the members of the section into a still closer relationship towards each other, and the brothers who decided to arrange a marriage between their children should not fall out over a divorce caused by discord between the young people, especially if there are other close kinsmen who can hold them in the framework of the common section. One divorce of this kind occurred in the Sheikh's section of Abu Gweʿid group, when the Sheikh himself (diagram 8, D14) divorced his father's brother's daughter (d39) after his accession. The woman was almost immediately remarried to D40, the only living male of the related Beni ʿAṭīah with whom, it will be recalled, the Abu Gweʿid have been intermarrying for the last three generations. In this fashion the woman was removed from the section, and at the same time she renewed a previously vacant minor link. The divorce itself occasioned no dispute among the members of the section, and the woman was even allowed by her former husband to retain her little daughter.

We have seen that the repercussions of divorces on interests are not the same in every case. This is due to the qualitative differences between the various types of links. Economic marriage links are

[1] See Chapter 8.

fundamental to economic collaboration, but not because they are made with spatially distant people. Indeed, Bedouin often move along their economic links, and will frequently stay close to their affines, though they do not actually join the affines' camps. The fragility of economic links is rather due to their being in most cases unsupported by other interests, and related to economic, i.e. scarce, resources. They tend more than any other type of link to become confined to the men directly linked by marriage, so that for instance watering privileges are not made equally available to all members of the affinally linked section. Thus while ʿAlayān Abu Gweʿid (D18) stayed for extended periods at the cisterns of his father-in-law, of the Qabūʿah group, his brother Sulimān (D10) took advantage of the kinship connection only during a few weeks late in spring, when the rainwater collected in puddles had evaporated.

Links between allied Bedouin groups are diffuse in every sense of the word. They result in few concrete obligations and are instead vested with the strong emotional appeal of kinship. They are political links, i.e. they seek to combine men for increased strength so that when made between multi-sectional co-liable groups, the alliance is assumed to cover not only the sections directly linked by marriage, but in addition to encompass the whole group. In times of peace and quiet such an alliance can function smoothly, even where not all sections of the two groups are linked. As the allied groups also maintain marriage links with several other groups, it may well happen that in an emergency the alliance proves to be unreliable, and that one of the groups follows another link. We have already noted how readily one type of link can be transferred into another when altered conditions demand it. Thus the Bdūr, though closely allied to the Abu Gweʿid, also have two economic links to the Maʿābdah core-group, which they might one day be tempted to convert into a political alliance with the latter. To ensure the stability of an alliance, then, the core-groups will frequently invest in it more than one link, and try to spread them over the various sections of the related group. The Abu Gweʿid have done this in their alliance with the Bdūr.

The links between sections of a co-liable group serve more than the section immediately linked. People realize that such links contribute to the effective co-operation of the co-liable group as a whole, and that each link is only one in a number of marriages connecting all the sections in the framework of the co-liable group. The marriage links are, of course, superimposed on the numerous joint interests of the members of sections, requiring co-operation on a wider than sectional scale. When one looks at political activities from a section's viewpoint, there are several ranges in which it can co-operate with other groups. For some purposes a section may only require the support of one other section of its co-liable group, as for instance, in a short brawl. At other times it will need the assistance of the whole co-liable group, as for payment of blood-money. Sometimes it may be in need of additional succour and turn for this to the allied group, as in the political manœuvres of one *rubaʿ* against the other. In extreme circumstances it may even obtain help from groups with which it usually entertains only economic relations. At each level of political action there must be either community of interests, or else reciprocal interests, if co-operation is to become effective. These determine the extent and range of political co-operation in each case and not the fact that one has direct marriage links to the groups whose help one wishes to enlist. Where political collaboration of groups is concerned, a marriage link in itself cannot sway the decisions of whole groups.

A marriage link acts as a very effective communicative device between groups, because the woman who conveys the communications is so intimately bound up both with her husband and sons, and with her father and brothers. She has the interests of both groups at heart and would suffer most from an estrangement between the two groups. At the same time she is on the inside of both groups, and thus able to assert her influence over the sections through the men to whom she is closely connected, as well as through the women. Thus when a man visits his sister, or perhaps a woman her father, information of importance to both sections is exchanged, assistance solicited and new errands entrusted to each side. Time and again I accompanied Bedouin on ostensible visits to their sisters. (Women could come with me only when accompanied by their husbands or guardians, so that I witnessed fewer of their visits, but they are also very frequent.) After spending some time in the man's part of the tent, my companions then retreated to the closed woman's part of the tent, to meet their kinswomen. Days after, I would often hear bits of information about the political machinations of another tribal chief, about moves of the other group's camps, about the current prices of smuggled commodities, about imminent marriages, and so forth. The marriage link had in these instances been used to convey information or to discuss or co-ordinate affairs concerning both sections.

A father's brother's daughter marriage has no impact beyond the confines of a section. In its implementation the woman's father usually has to subordinate his personal interests in a higher marriage-payment from a suitor outside the section to his other interests in retaining in future the co-operation of the other members of the section. It is thus a test of the section's will to co-operate, and is also a conscious attempt to hold it together for another generation. The two families concerned show by the marriage that they have made common cause of their future, for both are equally interested in the welfare of the new couple. Therefore they are also willing to combine their efforts at present. Here then the marriage does not constitute a link, but instead is part of a section's structural development.[1]

In the previous section we have been discussing all marriage links as if they were newly-made ones, and contracted by sections to suit their interests. Yet many marriages are arranged between sections which are connected by previous marital links, and which have therefore become cognatic kin to each other. Many marriages are, for instance, made between crosscousins. Bedouin explain cross-cousin marriage in Lévi-Straussian terms:[2] when a group obtains a woman in marriage it incurs an obligation to return another woman in her place, either in the contemporary or in the succeeding generation. In the latter case it would have to return one of that same woman's daughters. It is obvious that by following this procedure a man should always have first claim to the hand of his father's sister's daughter, for thus a woman's daughter would be restored to her group of origin. If the principle were applied consistently and without interference from any rival principle, the marriage of a man with his father's sister's daughter would prevail over any other type of marriage, as can be shown in diagrammatic form.

[1] A fuller discussion of this matter is to be found in Chapter 8.

[2] See C. Lévi-Strauss, *Les structures élémentaires de la parenté* (Paris 1949) pp. 167 ff.

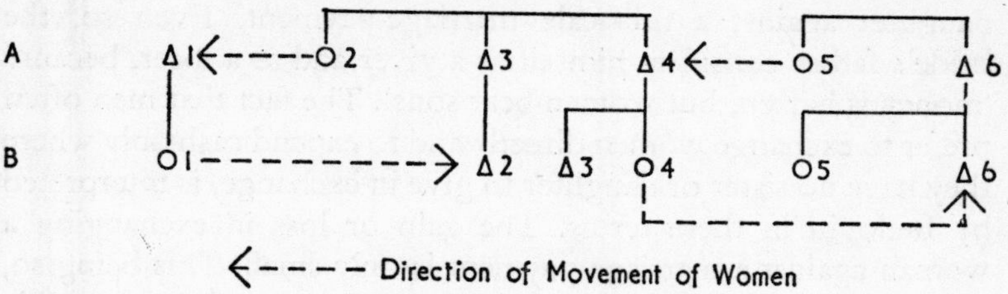

DIAGRAM 12

The theoretical operation of the principle of replacement of women

Here, the only proper way to arrange a second generation marriage would be that between a father's sister's daughter and a mother's brother's son (B2 = b1 and B6 = b4). A man could then marry neither his father's brother's daughter (B2 to b4), nor his mother's brother's daughter (B3 to b5). We have already met with numerous examples of men marrying their father's brother's daughters in preference to their father's sister's daughters, both among peasants and Bedouin (see, for instance, diagram 4). There also occur cases of mother's brother's daughter marriage (as in diagram 4, C10 = c3). This does not mean that the principle of the replacement of women is invalid, but rather that its efficacy is restricted by the presence of other, perhaps more important, social factors.

In the Negev the principle of replacement of women, or long-term exchange of women, as it may also be termed, cannot be of very great moment: when a woman is given in marriage no debt relationship is thereby established between the families, but instead she is exchanged for a high marriage-payment. It appears that in the Negev the marriage-payment, though varying a great deal, fluctuates between an average of IL. 2,000 to 3,000 (about £240 to £360) and occasionally rises as high as IL. 5,000 (about £600). This sum, which usually must be fully paid before a man may consummate his marriage, is roughly equivalent to an average family's income for two to three years. It is considered as full compensation for the woman, as is evidenced by the fact that it is of the same order as the amounts paid in compensation for a killing. The bride's father is considered to have been fully reimbursed for the loss of the woman and entertains no claim to her labour or children thereafter, except to be given the woman's daughter against a full-scale marriage-payment. Even so, the bride's father considers himself as a giver and as a loser, because 'money is barren, but women bear sons'. The fact that men often prefer to exchange women directly and to expend cash only where they have no sister or daughter to give in exchange, is interpreted by Bedouin in these terms. The gain or loss in exchanging a woman against a marriage-payment is only small. This being so, the principle of replacement of women is not able to override other more powerful factors in the social structure. Only where a section is faced with a choice between several equally important interests is the principle of replacement likely to tilt the balance in favour of one interest rather than another.

One should not assume that the claim on a father's sister's daughter is abandoned only in favour of another type of cousin marriage, as might be suggested by the frequent occurrence of father's brother's daughter marriage. There are many cases in which a marriage passes by all those close kinswomen and strikes out into a completely new direction. Thus the sheikh's section of Abu Gweʿid co-liable group has made one economic link with the Maʿābdah, which was not continued by a return marriage in the following generation. Both the sections concerned had men and women between whom marriages could have been arranged, yet they disposed their marriages otherwise. In the Sallām section of Ṣarāiʿah co-liable group, one man married a woman of the powerful Qurʿān group, from Abu Rbēʿah tribe, yet none of the numerous children of this marriage contracted a marriage with their mother's people. Such cases are found in most groups, and they all seem to have one thing in common: the marriages of the ascending generation were made as economic links. And while their descendants also stood in need of economic links, these were in many cases forged by marriages into other groups and into other parts of the Hilly Area. Economic links seem to take little account of already existing kinship ties and they shift from one group to another with great facility.

Economic links are more susceptible to switching from one group to another than any other type of marriage link. In order to understand this we must take another look at the nature of these links. Economic links affect the distribution of the relatively scarce water supply in the cisterns of the Hilly Area, or access to the little summer pasture remaining after the barley in the Plain has been

Photo: Dan Rattner

PLATE V

Above: A winter tent is being erected; the roof (*raffa*) comes first, then the walls

Below: A winter encampment of al-Asad tribe; the tents are pitched in hollows

PLATE VI

Above: Sale of tent-cloths at the Bedouin market at Beersheba, end of October 1961, just before the rain set in

Below: Building Sheikh Muḥēsin's tomb, August 1963, at ʿArʿarah

harvested. If there remains any surplus the owner's close agnates have first claim on it. Therefore the water supply or summer pasture available to an affine may dwindle with an increase in the herd of its owner or of his section. On the other hand, there are numerous groups of all three Ẓullām tribes spread out over the Hilly Area with any of which a Bedouin from the Plain can intermarry, and conversely, people living in the Hilly Area may seek their summer pasture in any part of the Plain. While some sections increase others decline in numbers, so that they can share more of their water and pasture with others. There are then good grounds for transferring economic links from one group to another, irrespective of the already existing links, and there is also a wide selection of persons with whom an economic link can be negotiated.

One should not view this process of switching links as a means of obtaining access to a wider range of groups and their economic facilities. Sometimes a man's descendants make an economic marriage link into a new group while the link established by his marriage is often still vital and active and becomes available to the following generation as a cognatic kinship tie. But there is a basic difference between such a cognatic tie and an affinal link. A marriage link gives direct representation to a man of one group in the other, as he has a member of his immediate family living with it and being part of it. A man can wield considerable influence over the other group through his sister or through his wife, who not only has the ear of her husband or brother respectively, but also has direct access to the women of the other group. Where a man has to employ the good services of cognates with the other group, which in the best case would be through a father's sister or a mother's brother, he does not obtain direct access to a member of the other group. For even when a man speaks directly to his kin in the other group, his communication is filtered, as it were, through an intermediate member of his family and thus weakened.

In political matters, where a section is involved corporately, the two ties would be similarly valuable, and a father's link would serve the son just as well. An economic link, however, concerns primarily the men directly connected, and therefore only the closest possible ties become useful. For should a cognatic tie have to compete with an affinal link for the allocation of scarce economic resources, then the latter must always prevail. It is not surprising, then, to hear Bedouin state that 'an affine is better than an agnate' (*Al-nasīb aḥsan min al-qarīb*). The pursuit of economic interests, then, entails the forging of personal marriage links by each generation. As these have to follow the available supply of cistern water and pasture, these requirements may in some cases lead to the shifting of marriages away from one's cognates to non-related people. Where claims for replacement of women, or other claims on girls based on existing kinship, come up against economic interest, the latter is bound to prevail.

Marriages of peasants out of their co-liable groups show superficial similarities to Bedouin economic links, in that they are often confined to one generation and not continued in the succeeding generation. They are also often tied to economic interests, and in such cases the families directly connected enjoy the main advantages of the link. But there seems to prevail amongst peasants greater awareness than among Bedouin of the transience of both economic and political interests, which indeed is true with regard to the more short-lived smuggling associations and the peasants' general political dependence on the Bedouin. This connects with the fact that most of their marriages outside the co-liable group are arranged as exchanges. Exchange marriage can, in this context, be viewed as an arrangement by which obligations to replace women are cancelled out immediately, and thus no incentive is provided to foster kinship relations in the succeeding generations. An exchange marriage creates a strong relationship of interdependence between the families concerned while it lasts, but after it lapses, either through divorce or death of one of the linking women, it provides no built-in incentive to a renewal of the kinship by further intermarriage.

If economic interests cannot be served by a renewed marriage among kin, the relationship will be allowed to lapse. As time passes the kinship becomes more distant and gradually fades into oblivion. Distant kin who are of the same age and sex, will retain loose ties of friendship. Among both Bedouin and peasants such 'friends' (*rafīq*) will enjoy chats whenever they meet, will arrange to attend feasts in company, may plan other activities together, and may confide secrets to each other. In some cases friendship may lead to renewal of marriage links, but in others it may only be a stage in the erosion of kinship ties.

The discussion of economic interests has shown that not all

kinship ties are equivalent, and that the more distant they are the less they can convey economic interests. At this stage of the analysis it becomes imperative for us to have a closer look at kinship, in order to define more clearly what is meant by the frequent references to 'close' or 'distant' kinship.

Kinship must be viewed as the interpenetration of the permanent relationships growing out of an individual's participation in a series of families. Living in a family is perhaps the most intense, multiplex and continuous relationship possible to human beings. These relationships create almost unseverable bonds, which can hold little diminished even in the absence of face-to-face relations. We shall not now concern ourselves with the different types of relationships maintained in a family, but only with the extensions of these relationships. For this purpose we shall consider the family as a unit, comprising husband, wife and unmarried children. The two adult members of the family, even after their marriage, still retain an unbreakable membership in their families of origin. Marriage has given the husband and wife full access to each other's families of origin, but has only to a much lesser extent established direct rapport between the two families of origin. When their children marry, the parents will strike up intimate relationship with the spouses of their children. This relationship is later consolidated by the birth of children. The parents will again establish only casual relations with the spouses' families of origin. While the husband and wife were still living in their families of origin they participated in the intimate relationships which their parents had with persons who had been members of their families of origin, that is their parents and siblings and the latter's children. All these relationships become mutually accessible to husband and wife, so that their kinship network becomes co-extensive, and becomes that of a family and not that of any individual within it. The relationships could be, and in some societies are, extended further, always in the same symmetrical fashion. Among Bedouin, though, there are objective factors which keep kinship within these well-defined limits. The range of effective kinship of a family can, in other words, be stated thus:

1. The immediate family of which one is a member at the time.
2. The families of origin of husband and wife, and the families of their children.
3. The families in which the members of the husband's and wife's

families of origin had participated, or the families of which their children's spouses had been part.

For convenience we shall refer to these categories as primary, secondary, and tertiary degrees of kinship.[1]

This may at first sight seem a very limited range of relationships to include under the term 'kinship', but it can actually comprise a considerable number of people. All these people would be kin to the family which we made our starting point, and could be called upon to bear greater or lesser obligations on its behalf, and of course be entitled to make similar demands of it. One can perhaps better visualize the extent of a kinship network, by assuming an imaginary family, made up of a husband, wife and two children. If all the kinship ties of this family were made with equally small families, and assuming also that three generations of adults are alive at one time, then our family will, at its zenith, have access to approximately sixteen families of kin.[2]

Let us now see how it is possible to observe the extent of kinship among the Bedouin in practice. During spring and early summer the Bedouin were most widely dispersed, and their camps at that time comprised usually only two or three tents. People felt the need to visit one another at frequent intervals during that time.[3] In the large peasant camps and in the late summer camps of Bedouin, families congregate in agnatic clusters, and while they also meet cognates during that time, one would be hard put to decide which meetings with people are due to their spatial proximity, which to kinship or membership of groups, and which to chance encounters. But in spring all the visits a man made had to be

[1] This nomenclature is identical with that adopted in G. P. Murdock's *Social Structure* (New York 1949) pp. 94–5.

[2] Murdock's count (op. cit., pp. 94–5) of 33 kinds of secondary, and 151 kinds of tertiary, relatives is sociologically irrelevant. It is based, on one hand, on the introduction of biological criteria (he separates consanguineal from affinal relatives, although on p. 92 he recognizes that 'the point of departure for the analysis of kinship is the nuclear family' [as a whole]). On the other hand, he ignores biological factors, such as the limits to an individual's life span, which make it unlikely for a man to have at one and the same time both a great-grandparent and a great-grandchild.

[3] This trait was first noted by C. Niebuhr, *Travels Through Arabia* . . . (Perth 1799) vol. 1, p. 164, among the Bedouin of Sinai, whom he visited in 1762: 'These Arabs, although scattered in separate families over the country, seem to be fond of society and visit one another frequently.'

deliberate, as they entailed special journeys, and were, incidentally, easy to follow. During March and April, I spent most of my time in the company of one Bedouin, ʿAbdallah Abu Gweʿid (diagram 13, C12), and often joined him on his journeys which took him to people all over the Hilly Area and the Plain. I also met the visitors to ʿAbdallah's tent. Most of them were chance visitors, passing that way on their business, who would each be treated to the three thimblesfull of black unsweetened coffee. Others would stay longer, often overnight, and would partake of meals, and I gradually learned to identify these.

On the first camping site in the Hilly Area, one of ʿAbdallah's seven brothers (C16) had pitched his tent next to his. ʿAbdallah's mother (b10) had come to stay with him, to help his wife (c11) during this very busy time. There were many tasks which women should preferably attend to, such as milking the ewes, gradually weaning the little lambs and making into butter the surplus milk produced at this annual peak period. ʿAbdallah had engaged a young shepherd as he had no son big enough to do the work for him, while he had to keep up a visiting routine that left him little time to devote to his herd. A frequent visitor to the camp was another brother's son (D1), who then would also see his mother's sister (c17), who was brother C16's wife. Then another brother (C14) joined the camp, and there was also a visit by a brother (C18) whose camp was pitched only about 3 km away. In honour of the latter ʿAbdallah prepared a festive meal at which he slaughtered a kid.[1]

In spite of all the urgent work in hand, ʿAbdallah was half the time away on visits to those close kinsmen who had not yet come to see him. He went twice to see his father (B9) who was for the time being staying with his son, the Sheikh (C21), on the Plain, his brother (C15) living in the same camp, and his remaining brother (C19) now camping in the Hilly Area. During that time ʿAbdallah's mother (b10) and wife (c11) were too busy to be able to leave for visits of their own.

One day ʿAbdallah's father- and mother-in-law arrived. The father-in-law (B6), being a busy tribal chief, did not stay long, and after

[1] Meat is only eaten on festive occasions, and is always consumed communally. To slaughter or 'sacrifice' (*dhabaḥ*) an animal, usually a sheep, in honour of a guest is to Bedouin the embodiment of true hospitality.

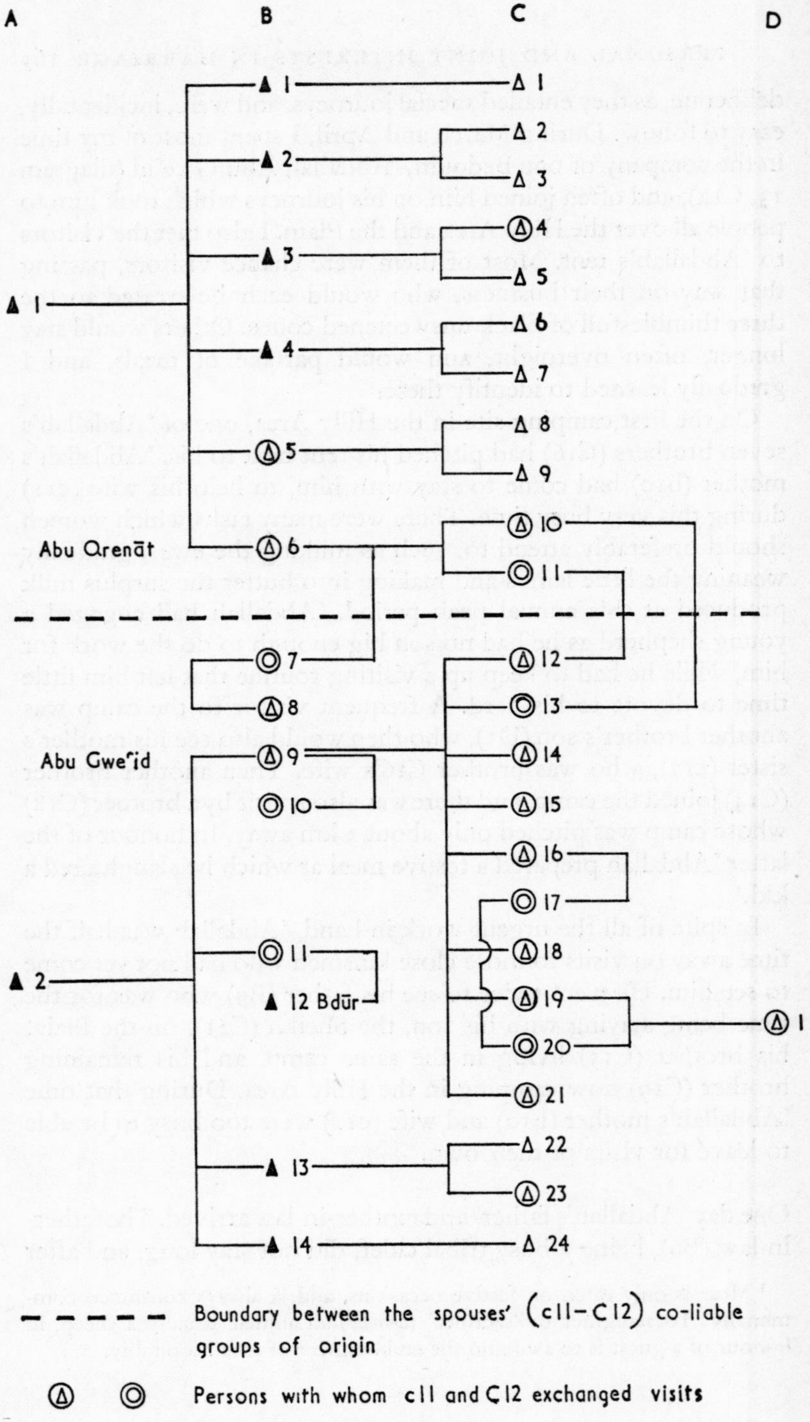

DIAGRAM 13

Range of obligatory visits of a family and its kin

sipping the three cups of coffee drove back to his camp. The mother-in-law (b7) greeted ʿAbdallah and his brother (C16, who had, incidentally, been her first husband) affectionately, kissing them on both cheeks. She stayed overnight and the following morning took back her daughter (c11) and ʿAbdallah's precious baby boy. The official reason supplied was that the young woman had an irksome tumour, and should spend some days of rest with her parents. ʿAbdallah and his wife were living very happily together, and the visit to her parents was certainly not the result of a dispute, though in many other cases women readily leave their husbands for visits to their kin whenever a quarrel occurs. The visit of ʿAbdallah's wife must be seen rather as a means to refresh her relations with her family of origin and her close kin. She spent a fortnight with her parents and I had no information on her rota of visits while there. But she was certain to see her father's only living brother (B5), and some of her many father's brothers' sons. During that time she also must have met her mother's brother (B8) when he came to see his sister.

By the middle of April ʿAbdallah had moved a short distance westwards to al-Dabbeh on the outskirts of the Hilly Area, where his father owns two cisterns. His brothers C16 and C14 moved with him. Soon after they were joined by brother C18, and then their father (B9) came to stay with them for a while. One day the Sheikh (C21) and his brother (C15) made a return visit to ʿAbdallah, who prepared another feast in their honour. All the brothers visited each other conscientiously, without consideration of relative rank, wealth or age. When later on the Sheikh (C21) omitted to visit his brother (C16), he was thoroughly piqued and retaliated by ostentatiously avoiding the Sheikh's guest tent. But all the brothers visited their old father and never expected him to reciprocate.

ʿĪd al-Aḍḥā (the Feast of Sacrifices), one of the two major events of the Muslim's year, fell in 1961 towards the end of May.[1] ʿAbdallah was at that time staying in the Sheikh's permanent camp in

[1] *ʿĪd al-Aḍḥā* lasts three days, from 10th to 12th of the month *Zū a-Ḥiggah* of the Muslim lunar calendar.

Diagram 13 has been abridged, so as to feature chiefly living adults, most of whom represent families. Women have been shown only where they provide additional kinship ties.

the Plain, and from there one could observe the tents of the other brothers. For it was harvest time, and they had all moved to their fields, and had thus reached their annual point of maximal proximity. On the second day of the feast ʿAbdallah asked me to accompany him on a number of visits. We set out at about 9 a.m., partook of the Sheikh's sacrifice, and then started on what turned out to be a *tour de force*, in which ʿAbdallah tried to visit kinsmen who were camping further away. First we went to see his brother (C19) although his camp was not very distant, for in the last series of visits his camp had been left out. After eating his meat, we continued on our way to ʿAbdallah's in-laws. First we visited the mother-in-law (b7) and then went on to her son (C10), who is married to ʿAbdallah's sister (c13). A short time before they had fallen out with the husband and father (B6) and set up their tents with another *rubaʿ* of their tribe. Thence we went to visit the father-in-law (B6). At each stage of our journey we were compelled to gorge ourselves with more meat, for in every guest tent the feast is celebrated by the slaughter of sheep and goats.

All these visits were exchanged with kin who had formerly been members of ʿAbdallah's and his wife's families, and would come under category two of our list.[1] There are no obligatory mutual visits between more distant kin, but they often form close friendships. During the spring ʿAbdallah was kept fully occupied by visits to his closest kin, but at other times he would also meet some of his first cousins. Not all cousins would be equally appreciated, for he had his preferences, and it appears that there was no bias in favour of agnates in this, not even where they were members of his own section. The 'friends' (*rafīq*), as they were called, were distributed over the whole range of kinship. ʿAbdallah was on very intimate terms with only one of his numerous father's brother's sons (C23), and had an even closer relationship with a father's sister's (b11) son, a member of the allied Bdūr group. As there were no first cousins on the mother's side there is a gap in our evidence, but there is sufficient material to show that men often have close ties with their matrilateral cousins, as for instance the above-mentioned Bdūr man's relationship with ʿAbdallah. It appears that this kind of selective visiting is apportioned fairly evenly among the two paternal and the two maternal lines of kinship. In addition, ʿAbdallah is also very friendly with one, and one only,

[1] See p. 163 above.

of his wife's father's brother's sons (C4). His mother-in-law's siblings have no adult descendants, but as ʿAbdallah has only been married for under three years, one would not expect him to have formed all-round affinal friendships yet. Although the friendships are based on kinship, they also depend on additional factors, such as similar age and the absence of too compelling mutual obligations.

Friendship is not the rule among kinsmen of this range. The relations between these 'tertiary' kin are not maintained by mutual visits but by the fact that each pair of cousins is connected directly to an intermediate family. If no direct visits are exchanged between most of the persons in the cousin category, they are bound to meet frequently in the tent of the intermediate family with which they exchange obligatory visits. If ʿAbdallah's parents-in-law retained his wife for so long a period as a fortnight, then surely they must have had in mind also that she would, during that time, meet their other visiting kin coming to their tent, and refresh her relations with them. ʿAbdallah could raise no objections to her going, for he too would in some future contingency derive benefits from the good relations thus maintained. The four lines of kinship of ʿAbdallah's wife will gradually merge with his own, mainly because of their children, and provide the family with a common set of kinship ties.

It appears that tertiary kinship is, in Bedouin society, the effective limit of kinship, for the obligatory exchange of visits regularly brings together kinsmen up to this range. 'Kinship' relations going beyond that range are either eclectic extensions for the sake of friendship, or are interest-determined associations expressed in terms of kinship. Such associations may coincide with sections of persons who consider themselves as kin to each other, but may also go beyond this range altogether, and can analytically be clearly distinguished from kinship.[1] The most important, though perhaps not immediately obvious, conclusion to emerge up to now from our analysis is that the range of kinship is, from the viewpoint of a family, multilaterally symmetrical. It extends to the same range on the husband's and on the wife's sides, and sooner or later merges into one common network of kinship for their family. To suggest a differential range of kinship for husband and wife would be unthinkable in Bedouin society. It would be like saying that a

[1] In this chapter we shall analyse only kinship; the following chapter will deal with the distinction between kinship and the associations based on it.

sister who marries out of her section has a different range of patrilateral kinship from her brother, or alternatively that she sheds part of her kinship ties upon marriage. This would be tantamount to denying the efficacy of political marriage links.

The analysis of visiting among Bedouin has only supplied us with a useful index to the range of kinship, but all these relations have hitherto been treated as if they were qualitatively similar to one another. Kinship ties are not all equivalent. It is indeed one of the distinctive characteristics of kinship that each relationship is qualitatively different from the other. The relationships of ascendants and descendants remain those of superiors and inferiors, even after they have become members of different families, but the relationship is much attenuated after separation and may even become a benevolent one. The parents have shot their last bolt by marrying off their children according to their interests, by obtaining the daughter's marriage-payment or providing the son's marriage-payment and rendering him his share in the inheritance. Henceforward the relationship should become more easy-going. Relations between grandparents and grandchildren are even less clouded by mutual expectations and are mostly very affectionate, and may be impaired only in the rare cases where a grandfather still wields power in his section. Relations among cousins are patterned on those of brothers, in that they are egalitarian, but they do not have the fierce competitive element of the latter. It is thus an essential attribute of a kinship network that the more distant the connection, the less intense it is. Although the tertiary ties are more relaxed than the closer kinship ties, they always retain something of the nature of the familial relationships from which they derive. It appears that time plays an exceedingly important part in the qualitative differences between varying degrees of kinship. Through the passage of time, especially, affinity becomes transmuted into kinship, and the initially still severe relationship prevailing between fathers and their children even after their marriage, becomes more affectionate.

Part of the specific qualities of each kin relationship are the particular rights and obligations associated with it. These are not usually stated as explicit rules, but instead are understood in a generalized fashion as moral values whose contravention is shameful. As the obligations incumbent on kin are not formally defined, there is no limit to the variety of matters in which one may expect their assistance, and this cannot easily be refused as long as the relationship is kept up. Yet assistance cannot be demanded as a right, but only granted as a favour which should be reciprocated by another on some future occasion. This seems to be another characteristic of kinship, as compared with associations for interests.

Exchanges of visits are obligatory on kinsmen, yet are not necessarily related to any definite practical interest. Kin should behave toward each other with great consideration and warmth and be prepared to give unlimited aid to each other. Kinship initially imposes only one concrete obligation: to maintain relationships. This obligation is complied with in regular exchanges of visits, which help to keep the relationship vigorous and effective. But kinship does not depend on visits, for kinship cannot be repudiated or severed and Bedouin consider it as an innate bond of blood. This can be clearly seen in the very rare cases in which co-liable groups formally expelled members. In Bedouin ideology, expulsion (*tashmīs*) is the greatest calamity that can befall a man. It leaves him without protection, with no one to avenge him or to pay the blood price with him. In reality, though, one recognizes that bonds of kinship are unseverable. Thus one group of Abu Rqaiq tribe expelled a man who had committed several killings, but the members knew that the culprit's father's brother, his only living close kinsman, still maintained relations with him. Indeed, some members approved of the relationship, which they thought was quite inevitable. When the father's brother told me about his nephew's history, he refrained from using the legal term for expulsion and instead said non-committally: 'we threw him out (*ṭlāʿnā ṭlūʿ*)'.

Kin relationships do not necessarily serve interests. Yet when the need arises a great variety of concrete contents can be superimposed on them. Kin relations can be exploited for any type of interest, and this versatility is one of their greatest assets.

Economic links can be viewed as an instance of the kind of help one may obtain from one's kin. As the ownership of the land and wells is vested in families, rights over their exploitation are extended to people according to the principles of kinship: they spread out symmetrically in all lines of kinship, but are graded according to distance of the relationship, and they are always granted as favours to persons with whom one maintains friendly relations.

The use of economic resources is accorded to all kin, whether agnates or not. But where there is a clash of interests between equally close kin of different lines over their exploitation, the owner's affines have to yield place to his agnates with whom he is tied up in political interests, in addition to the economic ones. An estrangement with agnates would jeopardize these other interests as well, and therefore there is bound to be a permanent bias in their favour and against the other lines of kinship.

The relationships growing out of marriage links between large allied Bedouin groups differ in many respects from those stemming out of economically inspired marriage links. This may best be brought out by an actual example, such as the alliance between the Abu Gweʿid and Bdūr co-liable groups. We shall not consider marriages between small groups in this connection, because it is much more difficult to isolate in their analysis the various overlapping interests.

Diagram 14 shows within the two groups only those persons, both living and deceased, who were involved in intermarriages. The earliest traceable marriage was that of Ḥmēd (A2), who was chief of the Abu Gweʿid tribe apparently until his death in 1917, with a Bdūr woman (a3) whose name is unknown to me. That woman's brother (A4) took a Raḥāḥlah woman (a1) in marriage. In the following generation again two marriages seem to have been arranged across the two groups: the Abu Gweʿid chief's sister (b3) and another Abu Gweʿid woman (b4) whose particulars I could not elicit, married men of two Bdūr sections (B6 and B7). In the succeeding generation, once more two Abu Gweʿid women, the sisters c2 and c3, married Bdūr men (C5 and C4). It can readily be seen that in these last four marriages the principle of reciprocity was completely set aside, for all the women married in one direction, from Abu Gweʿid to Bdūr. In addition marriages seem to have begun to shift from one section (the descendants of B7) to another (B5's descendants). The one-way marriages were not offset in the following generation, for the marriages C1 = d3 and D2 = d1 constitute an exchange, in which one man gave his daughter in return for the other's sister. It will be seen that in this generation the shift-over of marriages to B5's descendants was completed, and B7's only male descendant was unable to obtain a wife from the Abu Gweʿid. The change in direction can probably be ascribed to the altered relative importance of the Bdūr sections concerned. While in the past B6's and B7's sections were the larger ones, Selīm's (B5) section has now outgrown the two others. The Abu Gweʿid in each successive generation sought to marry into the main cluster or clusters of men of the day.

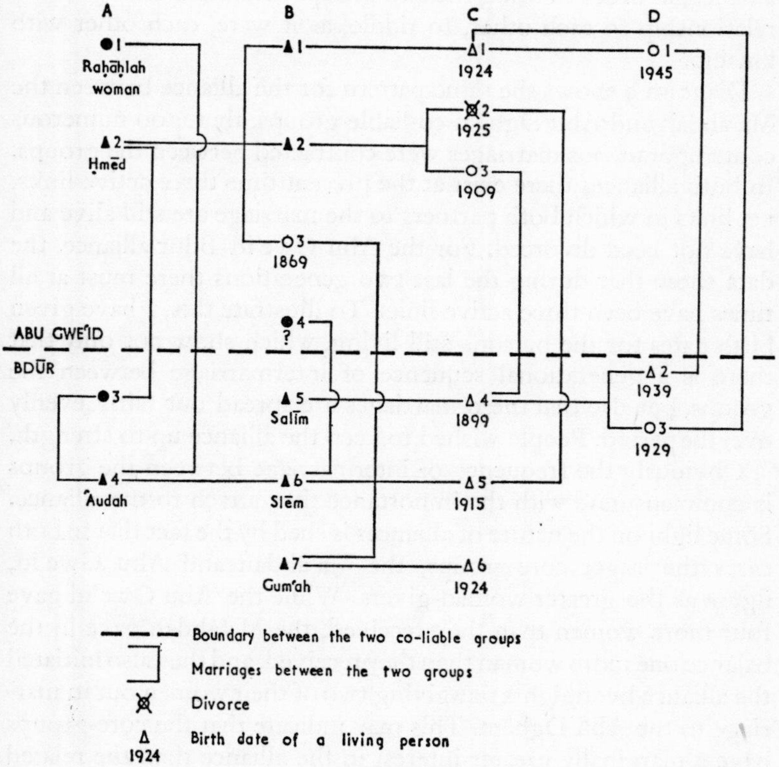

DIAGRAM 14

Marriages between Bdūr and Abu Gweʿid co-liable groups

According to the principle of replacement, women should move in alternative generations in opposite directions, or be exchanged simultaneously. When analysing economic marriage links, we found that in many cases a descending generation made no return for a woman given to the older generation in marriage because the economic interests necessitated a shift of the link elsewhere.

In alliance links, too, the interests supplant the principle of replacement of women, but in a very different manner. Here not only were links between groups continued for several generations, but there also were four marriages additional to the alternating movements of women from one group to the other. It appears that the groups tried to cram a considerable number of marriages into the alliance, in order to bring the two groups into the closest possible relationship to each other, to riddle, as it were, each other with kinship.

Diagram 9 shows the same pattern for the alliance between the Maʿābdah and Abu Dghēm co-liable groups: there too numerous contemporaneous marriages were contracted between the groups. In both alliances there exist at the present time three active links, i.e. links in which both partners to the marriage are still alive and have not been divorced. For the Abu Gweʿid–Bdūr alliance, the data show that during the last two generations there must at all times have been three active links. To illustrate this, I have given birth dates for the persons still living, which show not only that there is a generational sequence of intermarriage between the groups, but also that these marriages are spread out fairly evenly over the period. People wished to keep the alliance up to strength.

Obviously the frequency of intermarriage between the groups is commensurate with the importance they attach to the alliance. Some light on the nature of alliances is shed by the fact that in both cases the larger core-groups, the Maʿābdah and Abu Gweʿid, figure as the greater woman-givers. While the Abu Gweʿid gave four more women than they received, the Maʿābdah gave in the balance one more woman than they received, and they also initiated the alliance by straightaway giving two of their women out in marriage to the Abu Dghēm. This may indicate that the core-groups have a marginally greater interest in the alliance than the related Bedouin groups.

The numerous intermarriages between the allied groups result in a special relationship which is recognized by other Bedouin, who consider some groups as being 'closer to each other' than to any other group. Each of the three core-groups of Abu Gweʿid tribe has one such 'close' (*qarīb*) group, and one only:

Abu Gweʿid	Bdūr
Maʿābdah	Abu Dghēm
Ṣaraiʿah	Abu Msāʿad

and similar alliances are known in the other Ẓullām tribes. Theoretically a core-group might make alliances with numerous smaller groups, and indeed women are often given to even the very smallest groups. But an alliance can only be made with one large group, because of the high investment of marriages required; an alliance always has to be renewed. Alliances are only one of the interests for which marriage links are made, so that not all marriages can be expended on alliances.

If an alliance is so eagerly sought by the larger Bedouin groups, it must serve important interests. Its main advantages are probably that it provides for close political collaboration between two groups, without their having to extend the tedious obligations of co-liability to each other. A co-liable group is expected to bear such heavy commitments for each of its members, that membership must remain circumscribed. Otherwise there may be chronic apprehension that it may split after a major crisis, and that the circumstances of the splitting may make collaboration between the parts impossible for a long time. An alliance is neither as far-reaching, nor as morally binding on the partners, as co-liability. Yet it can play an important part in the internal politics of the tribe. Each core-group competes with the others for ascendancy in the tribe, so that an alliance augments its manpower, and in these usually peaceful political manœuvres a related Bedouin group can be relied upon to stand by its ally. It will never be expected to render assistance in fighting, or payment of blood-money, though individuals may help out their close kinsmen in the other group.

'Closeness' (*qarābah*) is by Bedouin associated with agnation. It is a very non-committal way of expressing the political relationship between allied groups. Bedouin do not define it more clearly, and do not employ the term 'alliance' or any other explicit term. But the members of the allied group give some cognizance to the special relationship, which they express, like other political relationships, in agnatic terms. The collaboration between the allied groups is not so strong and stable that it could be expressed in terms of common descent from a single named ancestor, but they view it vaguely as a relationship between agnates. One does not consider every member of the opposite group as an agnate, except those who are one's kin. But among these even matrilateral kinship is transformed into agnation. Thus the sons of Sheikh Muḥēsin Abu Gweʿid and C6 considered each other as father's brother's sons (*ibn*

ʿ*amm*), although the latter is the son of the former's father's sister. Similarly, Sheikh Muḥēsin's sons referred to D2 as brother's son (*ibnākh* [*sic*]), although he is the son of a father's brother's daughter. When I asked D2 about this point he confirmed laughingly that Sheikh Muḥēsin's sons were indeed father's brothers (ʿ*amm*) to him. In fact they would not address each other by the kinship terms, for being of roughly the same age, they addressed each other by their first names. This brings out the equality among age-mates.

Alliances, then, are to some extent supported by kinship ties, as is shown by the piling up of marriages. But the agnatic idiom in which the relationships between allied groups can be stated, suggests that they also involve the two co-liable groups concerned in a corporate fashion. This collaboration, however, is solely based on mutual goodwill due among kinsmen, and lacks the explicit and defined mutual obligations of corporate associations.

Here again it has been shown that it is not kinship which determines the marriage between kin, but the permanent interest in maintaining a political alliance. The principle of replacement of women is also disregarded where these interests are concerned.

Photo: Dan Rattner

PLATE VII

Left: Man of al-Asad tribe pounding coffee in a wooden mortar (*gurn*)

Below: Group of women chanting on a feast-day

Photo: Dan Rattner

Photo: Uri Gavish

PLATE VIII

Above: Bdūr men racing their camels

Below: Sword-play by Ṭalālqah tribesmen

CHAPTER 7

Sections and Co-liable Groups

UNTIL now the term 'section' has only been loosely defined,[1] as a small number of close agnates who arrange their marriages by mutual consultation. We noted that among Bedouin a section operates as a political unit, while among peasants it tends politically to fuse into the more inclusive co-liable group. In some cases a co-liable group is composed of a single section, but often it comprises several sections. It may have become apparent that a section in the political field is not always completely identical with the domestic group of that name. This chapter will be devoted to a fuller analysis of sections and co-liable groups.

Sections and co-liable groups owe their continued existence to the administrative constellation reigning in the Negev today. The Ẓullām Bedouin make every effort to keep the authorities in the dark about matters of land ownership and about their internal tribal politics, and their activities in these spheres require a political organization. The authorities can as a rule intervene directly only when a dispute among Bedouin has resulted in a flagrant infringement of the law. Yet the authorities' power is effective to the extent that no single individual or group can accumulate permanent concentrations of power[2]. Thus, while there is still a considerable scope for the exercise of force in the Negev, power is distributed fairly widely and evenly among men. A man still has to ensure the safety of his family and his property, and can attain this end only with the help of his fellows. The measure of his security is the number of fighting men he can call to his aid. Such help can best be obtained on a basis of mutuality so that each man assumes similar responsibilities on behalf of others and his interests are safeguarded to the same extent as those of others. Necessity and interest induce Bedouin to organize for political purposes.

This organization takes the form of corporate sections and co-liable groups. One must be clear why other forms of organization, namely kinship and camp membership, do not serve these

[1] In Chapter 5. [2] See Chapter 2.

purposes. In the last chapter we saw that a family's kinship relations extend to the extended paternal families of husband and wife, and to their mothers' families. With these kin one exchanges visits and one expects them to help out in various matters. The sharing of pasture and cisterns proceeds according to the closeness of kinship and even a non-committal alliance of groups can be fostered by, though not entirely based on, kinship ties. Indeed, one may turn to any kinsman for help in matters which can be settled without involving too many persons at a time. Thus among both peasants and Bedouin, one can obtain from a close kinsman food and shelter, or money loans without interest. Political activities, however, are based on the collaboration of a number of people in a framework wider than that of a single family. Put in the most general terms, political activities are concerned with order and security, and by their very nature involve the fighting out of violent disputes. In such matters great advantage is gained by combining in large numbers. Now a man's primary kin, the closest kinsmen available in an emergency, are relatively few in numbers. More distant kinsmen would not be heavily committed to him, or their commitment might clash with one towards other kinsmen, perhaps closer ones. The differentiation of kinsmen by generation into ascending-superior and descending-inferior, also militates against co-operation of men on a basis of full mutuality.

The most important of matters which are dealt with on a basis of camp membership is the maintenance of the guest tent (*shiq*) and dispensation of hospitality. The expenses of the guest tent should be shared equally by all tent-owners, though in practice the wealthier members of a camp often contribute larger shares. In many camps each tent-owner takes his turn in furnishing food for guests, no matter who first invited them. This includes the slaughter of animals for honoured guests. Peasants adhere to this formal rota more closely than Bedouin, who frequently compete for the right to entertain their special guests. There is a strong element of competition for status in the lavish expenditure on entertainment of guests, which is incompatible with the mutuality of political obligations. Impoverished men may feel unable to participate in a big guest-tent, and will camp off the beaten track so as not to be burdened with too many guests. An elderly Qlāʿi peasant left the common camp of his group at the wells of Tel al-Milḥ after harvest-time and put up his tent in an isolated spot north of Tel ʿArad. He claimed that he moved away because he was unable even to contribute his share of fire-wood to the group's guest tent.

At harvest-time the members of a Bedouin camp, or of a chief's camp, which may be composed of both Bedouin and peasants, often assist each other in the wearisome business of reaping the barley, which entails plucking the stalks by hand. This mutual help is called *ʿaunah* (assistance). When a number of people work together they often separate according to sex; singing and joking relieve the monotony of the task. Yet this is an obligation which is easily evaded, except between close kin. Members of peasant camps rarely help each other in harvesting, for this is the time at which they are most dispersed; each family reaps its plot of leased land, and this is perhaps the only task in which all its members participate equally.

Peasant camps are often largely identical with groups of kin, but even among peasants members of a camp disperse during the ploughing and harvesting seasons. Moreover, the association in camps is basically insecure and unstable because it is not tied to a permanent site. Among Bedouin, too, there is a certain amount of overlap between camps and agnatic associations of their members. The structure of most camps, however, is ever changing. On the one hand a Bedouin camp rarely includes all the members of an agnatic association, and on the other hand it will often include people of diverse origins. This is especially the case with chiefs' camps. Sometimes other Bedouin camps will be made up of families of various groups, although they never include men of peasant origin. The camp of Abu Rafīʿa, which retained its composition throughout the period surveyed, even while moving from one site to another, serves as an example.

In this camp there were six tents, three of which constituted the

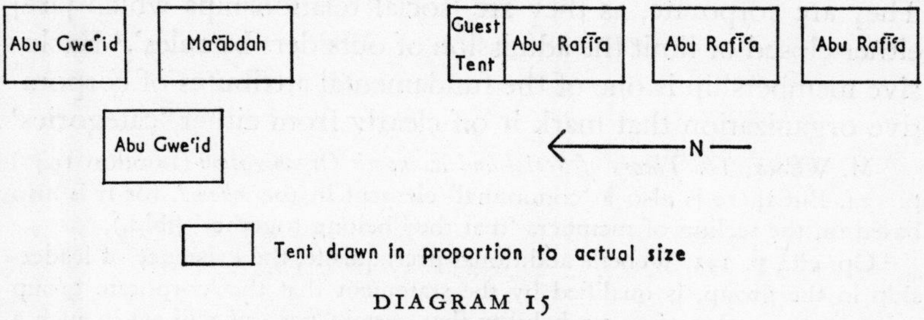

DIAGRAM 15
Composition of a mixed Bedouin camp

whole Abu Rafīʿa group. The guest tent of the camp was that of its leader, Sulimān Abu Rafīʿa. Next to it in line was his other tent, in which lived his second wife. The southernmost tent belonged to his brother. North of the *shiq* followed the tent of a Maʿābdah man who joined Abu Rafīʿa several years ago, after a quarrel with his brothers. The remaining two tents belonged to a man of Abu Gweʿid group. The one which stood in line was that in which he lived with his newly-wed wife, while in the other, which was out of line, he kept his repudiated wife and her children. Sometimes camps unite men who have joined in a common economic enterprise, and indeed the above-mentioned Abu Rafīʿa and Abu Gweʿid men had engaged one shepherd to care for their combined flock.

Bedouin camps, then, are not identical with political groupings, though membership of groups is one of the factors affecting their composition. Tents are moved easily, and membership of a camp entails no obligations beyond those stated, so that a person can join a camp with little pretext. Consequently, local associations of Bedouin are not identical with kin relations. Nor can such unstable associations as camps take on more permanent commitments on members' behalf, such as dealing with the often pernicious disputes, which may drag on for years.

Bedouin sections and co-liable groups are corporately organized associations. Before discussing these groups in detail, it may be useful to review some of the literature on corporate relationships and find out something about their inherent characteristics. In Max Weber's sociological scheme, sections and co-liable groups may probably be classed as 'corporate associations'. 'Associations' because he calls a social relationship associative 'if social action within it rests on a rationally motivated adjustment of interests'.[1] They are corporate, as they are 'social relationships which [are] either closed or limit the admission of outsiders by rules'.[2] Exclusive membership is one of the fundamental attributes of corporative organization that mark it off clearly from either 'categories'

[1] M. Weber, *The Theory of Social and Economic Organization* (London 1947) p. 124. But there is also a 'communal' element in the *khams*, for it is also based on the feeling of members 'that they belong together' (ibid.).

[2] Op. cit., p. 133. Weber's additional prerequisite, the existence of leadership in the group, is qualified by the statement that the 'corporate group exists so far as there is a probability that certain persons will act in such a way as to tend to carry out the order governing the group' (op. cit., p. 134).

of people that have no clearly defined boundary, such as a social class, or from kinship relations, which extend in an endless succession of overlapping networks. The various rules of admission referred to by Weber serve to define a group's membership in a precise fashion, at least in a formal sense.

Weber goes on to add a further dimension to corporateness: the group is committed to an order 'which is specifically directed to its enforcement'.[1] The group's rules of membership, that is, must direct it to certain types of activities.

All these basic components are included in Fortes' definition of descent groups: 'descent groups exist to unite persons for common social purposes and interests by identifying them exclusively and unequivocally with one another'.[2] On this definition, descent groups can be classified as a specific type of corporate group.

Anthropologists have stressed an additional aspect of corporateness: the equality of all members of a group. Fortes has stated this principle succinctly: 'Where the lineage is found as a corporate group all the members are to outsiders jurally equal'.[3] This formal equality is not only apparent to outsiders, it is also believed to apply to the group's internal constitution:[4] with regard to the ostensible interests pursued by the group, each member is viewed as equal in a formal, legal and ideological sense. This aspect of corporateness seems to have been accepted by anthropologists who were preoccupied with societies with relatively limited accumulations of power and property, and cannot be said to apply to the highly differentiated corporate groups typically discussed by Weber.[5]

And lastly, in Maine's discussion of the corporation, from the viewpoint of the historical lawyer, perpetuity emerges as 'the leading attribute of Corporations'.[6] The desire to continue a

[1] Op. cit., p. 134.

[2] M. Fortes, 'Descent, Filiation and Affinity; A Rejoinder to Dr Leach' (*Man* 1959) p. 206.

[3] M. Fortes, 'The Structure of Unilineal Descent Groups' (*AA* 1953) p. 26.

[4] E. E. Evans-Pritchard, *The Nuer* (Oxford 1940) p. 4: '[In each group] . . . the status of its members, when acting as such towards one another and to outsiders, is undifferentiated.'

[5] On the contrary, Weber emphasizes internal differentiation within corporate groups and posits the imposition of an order even in voluntary associations (op. cit., p. 136).

[6] H. Maine, *Ancient Law* (London 1906) p. 200.

political order and to regulate the transmission of property or rights apart from the individuals in whom they are vested, are assumed to have given rise to the corporation.

I now propose to examine, first, how far these various characteristics are reflected in Bedouin legal precepts and ideologies on sections and co-liable groups; and after that, to relate the activities of sections and co-liable groups to these ideological formulations.

Although Bedouin groups frequently have leaders, and there is always internal differentiation of statuses, the ideology of equality is maintained with specific reference to the group's express purposes. Thus members of a Bedouin section claim that they are prepared to fight for one another, and that they exact vengeance for one another; and members of a co-liable group assert that they will stand by any of their number who becomes involved in a dispute, and will contribute equally to blood-money. Actual cases diverge from this ideal, for the economic and political statuses of the men involved take their effect. Most cases are so complex that they seldom can be dealt with by the rules alone; they have repercussions on all the spheres of social life. It is here that discrimination is practised: the assistance rendered by members of the corporate group to a favoured individual often goes far beyond the minimum required by the rules, whereas another man might receive help within the limited aspects covered by the rules only.

A comparison between the following two cases can bring out this last point:

A member of Abu Gweʿid co-liable group, of Beni ʿAṭīah descent, whose section now comprises only two men, had in the course of an angry discussion struck a member of Abu Rbēʿah tribe in a tent of his group. For striking the other man he was to pay blood-money (*ḥaqq al-damm*, literally the price, or right, of blood), although actually no blood had been drawn; for the violation of the peace of the tent, the 'right of the tent' (*ḥaqq al-bēt*) was due. When the Abu Gweʿid negotiated the payments, their representatives tried to discuss the two claims separately, and eventually got the plaintiff to drop his claim for blood-money altogether. The culprit thus had to pay only the right of the tent, and this was whittled down to a mere IL. 300, but this amount he had to pay himself. An Abu Gweʿid man explained afterwards: 'Had the Abu Rbēʿah people claimed blood-money, the whole co-liable group would have had to pay, but as he demanded only the right of the tent, the offender alone has to face the bill.'

In a fight between two Abu Ṣulb groups,[1] the leader of one of the groups, the Awlād Saʿad, had slightly injured an opponent, and had also in the heat of battle entered the guest-tent of the other group and threatened to use his rifle. The elder of the Awlād Saʿad himself took part at the meeting which finally settled the dispute. In this case the parties agreed on a composite indemnity, the blood-money, the fine for violating the tent and medical expenses were all calculated together at IL. 1,500. The Awlād Saʿad shared the whole amount without a murmur.

It will be seen that both co-liable groups had fulfilled their obligations towards their members, and had settled blood-disputes for them. Yet the different way the groups dealt with the two cases shows that they took full account of the status of the persons concerned.

The obligations incumbent on individuals as members of an association are usually precisely and jurally defined. Thus the obligations of a Bedouin towards his section are phrased in terms of his ultimate responsibility for another member's blood, to the extent that he may be killed for blood spilt by another member, or may be required to exact vengeance for a murdered member. One of the terms connoting an avenger of blood is *qomāni*, derived from the same source as the term used for section, *qōm*. Similarly, a man knows that as a member of a co-liable group he will have to contribute his share towards the payment of blood-money, and that as a Ẓullām tribesman he has to defend the common territory against outsiders. The formal obligations are not the only ones expected from members, for once a group is established it can extend co-operation to many diverse fields. The jural obligations only specify the ultimate sacrifice a member might be expected to make, or conversely, the ultimate benefit he might derive from membership. A group that commits its members so heavily may, at one time or other, engage in almost any activity. Thus it is impossible to predict precisely in which spheres and ways people will collaborate within the framework of an association.

The obligation a member of a co-liable group most commonly fulfils, is to participate in payments of blood-money. One way of describing the participation of people in a co-liable group is to say

[1] This case is also discussed on p. 239

that they 'contribute the blood-penny' (*ḥaṭṭīn qirsh al-damm*), i.e. they share the payments. Payments and receipts are apportioned in equal shares among all the adult males of a group, without distinction, an order which reflects the formal equality of members. Members of large groups do not consider their contributions to blood-money an undue burden, and in fact payments may be relatively small. The collection of blood-money is a good way of mustering a group's manpower. Not that its members are unable to give a detailed account of their numbers, but such occasions serve to demonstrate their manpower in real, concrete terms. Smaller groups may find blood-money a heavy burden, and they are supposed to take care not to become involved in fights.

After a fight with the Abu Mṭēr of Abu Qrenāt tribe in 1962, in which one man sustained a fractured skull, the assessor of blood-money (*manshad*) made the Abu Gweʿid pay about IL. 1,200 in blood-money. The Abu Gweʿid counted 32 men,[1] and collected identical contributions from 30 of them. One man was 'so destitute that one could not ask him to pay', though others only slightly less poor paid their shares in full; another man was mortally ill in hospital. The other men paid IL. 43.5 each (a little over £5), and the small additional sum was to cover some incidental expenses incurred. The Abu Mṭēr divided the money in identical shares among their members, and the victim received no extra portion.

A corporate group must recruit members on a clear and precise principle, with reference to which all members can regard themselves as equals. There is a wide range of such criteria for determination of membership, the most prominent and widely employed among which are local contiguity and unilineal descent, real or putative. This idea was first advanced by Maine, in an oft-quoted passage:

> When with our modern ideas we contemplate the union of independent communities, we can suggest a hundred ways of carrying it out, the simplest of all being that the individuals comprised in the coalescing group shall . . . act together according to local propinquity.[2]

And also:

> It may be affirmed . . . of early commonwealths that their citizens

[1] There were, according to my count, 36 Abu Gweʿid men at that time. Unfortunately, I omitted to inquire about the difference of four men.

[2] H. Maine, op. cit., p. 138.

considered all the groups in which they claimed membership to be founded on common lineage.[1]

Most societies employ both criteria of membership, in various combinations, according to their needs. Thus among Bedouin, membership of the section and of the co-liable group is determined by the principle of descent, while membership of the *rubaʿ*, the tribe and the tribal group is obtained by permanently living on Ẓullām land. Recruitment to the political corporate groups by descent is the inevitable course in an ecological situation which forces the Bedouin to move about on the available pasture, and in which the peasants also remain unattached to the land, to the extent that even when living in common camps they still recruit members of their political associations on a basis of descent.

In the Negev the emphasized line of descent is through males. In familial relations this is connected with inheritance of land, cisterns and herds by males only. The principal heirs are a man's sons, among whom his property should be divided in equal parts, while his wife and daughters are not held entitled to inherit. Women retain only a little personal property, such as their ornaments, clothing and bedding, and perhaps one or two goats or sheep which they obtained as gifts during the deceased's lifetime. If a man dies without leaving sons, his property reverts to his father or his brothers and not to his widow or daughters.[2] Some widows, who seemingly have remained in control over their deceased husband's land and herds, do so only temporarily because they have adolescent sons who will take over the property in due course. A widow may choose to remain with her children and thus become dependent on her husband's agnates, who are obliged to provide her with the necessities of life. She is also free to return to her agnates, who also must provide for her or make arrangements for her to remarry. She is not compelled to marry any of her late husband's agnates, although there occur isolated cases of levirate. When she marries into another section she leaves her children behind, both male and female, and they then come under the tutelage of the husband's agnates, i.e. father, brother or patrilateral cousin, in that descending order.

Succession in membership of associations proceeds on lines similar to inheritance: both descend from father to son, to the

[1] Ibid., p. 137.

[2] See also ʿĀref, *Qaḍā*, p. 125.

exclusion of daughters.[1] While the rights of women are fully recognized in the domestic sphere, Bedouin are quite explicit that only men take part in political action in any form, and that only men become members of sections (of the *qōm* and the *khams*) in the political sense. All a man's sons are jurally equal in status without regard to their order of birth or their mother's status.

In this fashion, men who in some respects interact as kinsmen in numerous overlapping networks of kinship, are for political purposes assigned to one clearly defined social unit only. Members of these groups are still kin to one another; they constitute 'sections' cut out of the web of kinship. Recruitment of new members is also based on a specific type of blood kinship: people are automatically incorporated by being born into the agnatic group, and thus no initiation is needed. This fact does not necessarily make membership of a group compulsory and inescapable, and thus fundamentally different from membership of an association freely entered into. Nor does it prevent the occasional outsider from joining a co-liable group. If one must draw a distinction between a unilineal descent group and a freely entered corporate association, it lies in the method of recruitment only, which in the one is by birth and in the other by formal admission. For the rest, the structure of both is determined by, and dependent on, the interests pursued by members.

In Bedouin society, therefore, membership of a section and in a co-liable group is determined by the fact that a number of people are descended in the main line of one man. One might assume that this explains the fact that each section acknowledges a patronymic ancestor. There is more to it than that: the ancestor provides a common point of reference to which all the living members of the section stand in the same relationship. They are all equally removed from the ancestor, and on this criterion all of them become equal members. This becomes apparent when one looks at the kind of genealogy adduced for Bedouin and peasant co-liable groups. The Ṣarāiʿah genealogy in diagram 16 is typical of the larger Bedouin groups.

[1] This connection explains the wide discrepancy between Bedouin rules of inheritance and the Muslim legal code, based on the Koran, 4, 11; according to this, female agnates inherit, in principle, half of the shares of males at each degree of agnatic kinship. In the absence of agnatic heirs, other close kin inherit. See also Fyzee, op. cit., pp. 329 ff.

I call genealogies of this type 'structural', because they are abbreviated reflections of the internal political constitution of co-liable groups and of the relations between the sections. This is

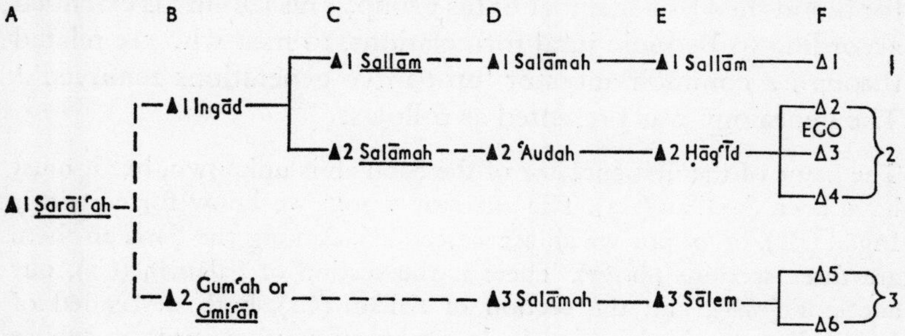

— — — Corporative gaps

Eponymous ancestors of the co-liable group and of sections have been underlined

Generation F shows only living elders

DIAGRAM 16

Structural genealogy of Ṣarāiʿah Bedouin co-liable group

recognized implicitly by Bedouin, and shows in the manner in which they recount the genealogies. When recounting them, Bedouin start from the ancestor common to the whole co-liable group and then descend through the sectional ancestor until they reach the living males. Each section is represented by a string of ancestors descending to the leading representative of the present generation. In the living generation the genealogy branches out to include brothers of the section's leaders, as the section's power is based on clusters of brothers. Cousins of the leading group of brothers are omitted, and so are insignificant small sections. A comparison between the structural genealogy in diagram 16, and the actual composition of the group (see diagram 18), shows how some of the living members have been left out, so as to present to the members of the section from which the informant was drawn a simplified picture of the political power structure of the co-liable group.[1]

The account of the Ṣarāiʿah genealogy was obtained from the

[1] See also diagram 7 for the detailed membership of the Salāmah section of Ṣarāiʿah group.

chief of the group, who is also the leader of section 2, the Salāmah. He was at first reluctant to provide the information, as it is usually only required if one wants to establish a man's personal liability for blood shed by a member of his group. This liability is extended according to Bedouin jural formulations, to men who are related through a common ancestor 'up to five generations removed'.[1] The genealogy was presented as follows:

The name of the first ancestor of the Ṣarāiʿah is unknown, but it must have been Ṣarāiʿah (A1). The ancestor whom we know for certain is Ingād (B1), of whom we all are descended. Among the Ṣarāiʿah there are three sections (*qwām*). There is the section of Salāmah (C2), our ancestor (*gidd*), and the section of Sallām (C1), both descended of Ingād. But the third section is descended of another ancestor, whose name is Gumʿah or Gmiʿān, I am not sure which. Still we all belong to one co-liable group (*khams*) which comprises many more than five generations.

From there he went on to recount the living representatives of each section, referring in fact only to the leaders and their brothers. When I asked him to give a full list of ancestors, he began by giving his father and father's father, but admitted that he had no definite information about the ancestors beyond that. Yet he was clear about one point: that the section's ancestor was not his father's father's father and that there was a gap of at least one or two generations between his father's father and the section's ancestor. He then attempted to fill in the gap, interpolating two names already found in the section, which these ancestors very likely bore, because men are frequently given their grandfather's name.

On page 189 are two versions of the structural genealogy of the Abu ʿArār peasant co-liable group, as expounded by two men belonging to different sections.

There is some disagreement between the genealogies given by the two Abu ʿArār men, but there are also points common to both. The first genealogy was recounted by Salmān (D2), the oldest Abu ʿArār man, who claims to have been born in 1874. According to him, the eponym ʿArār was a man who had been living with the Ḥuweṭāt Bedouin confederation in Northern Sinai many generations ago. Two of his descendants, two brothers, came via Khān Yūnis to live with the Ẓullām Bedouin in the Negev. He knew the

[1] What this implies will be discussed in the following chapter.

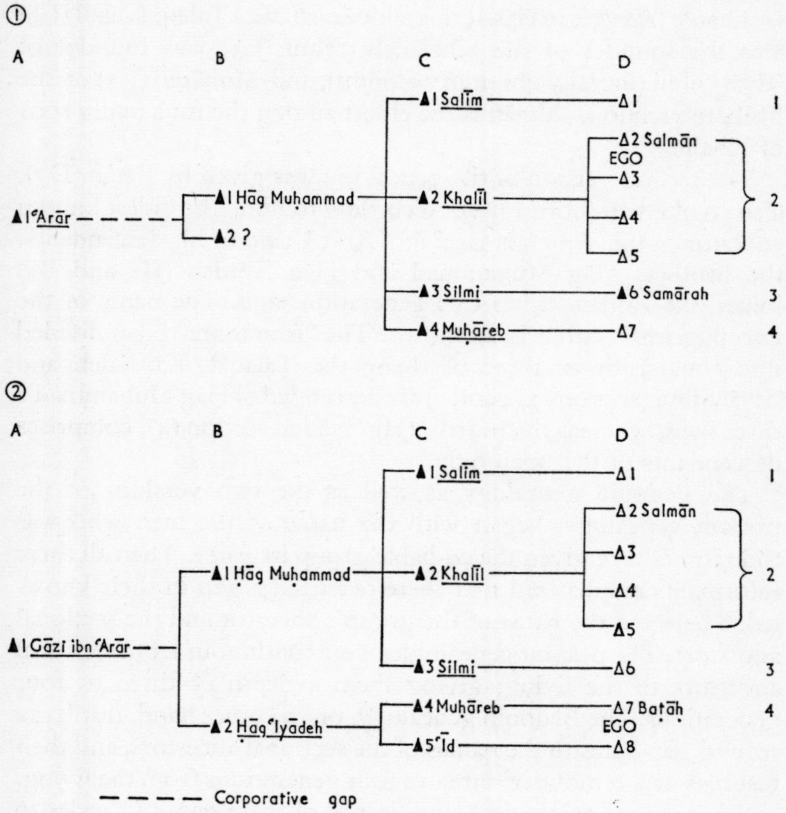

Names of eponyms of the co-liable groups and of sections have been underlined

Generation D shows only living elders

DIAGRAM 17

Structural genealogies of Abu ʿArār peasant co-liable group

name of only one of the two brothers, Ḥāg Muḥammad (B1), who begat four sons, each of whom founded one section. Salīm (C1) was the founder of the Ṭalaqāt section, and some say that his nickname (*nibdheh*; in classical Arabic *laqab*) was Ṭalāq; Khalīl (C2) was the founder of the Khalāileh; Silmi (C3) was founder of ʿEyāl Silmi (literally children of Silmi); and Muḥāreb (C4) of the Muḥāreb section. Salmān is the eldest among the four living sons of Khalīl.

The second version of the genealogy was given by Baṭāḥ (D7), also an old man (born 1884). According to him, 'the oldest known ancestor of the ʿArarāt is Gāzi ibn ʿArār.[1] Two of his descendants, the brothers Ḥāg Muḥammad and Ḥāg ʿIyādeh (B1 and B2) joined the Ẓullām tribes two generations ago. The name of the two pilgrims'[2] father is unknown. The ʿArarāt are today divided into four sections; three of them, the Ṭalaqāt, Khalāileh and ʿEyāl Silmi (sections 1, 2 and 3) are descended of Ḥāg Muḥammad's three sons, whereas the fourth, Ḥāg ʿIyādeh section (4), comprises descendants of that man only.'

The Bedouin genealogy as well as the two versions of the peasant genealogy, began with the name of the man who was thought to have given the co-liable group its name. Then all three informants emphasized that there occurred a gap in their knowledge between the name of the group's ancestor and the sectional ancestors. The peasant genealogies were continuous from sectional ancestors to the living, giving them a depth of three to four generations. The Bedouin genealogy, on the other hand, displays a second gap beneath the names of the sectional ancestors, and then resumes at a remove of three to four generations from the living.

What is the sociological significance of these gaps? In order to find out more about this problem, we must turn the accounts given by informants upside down, and start not from an eponym, but begin with the living. In this way one soon finds that the ancestors of a Bedouin section for three, four and, very rarely, five generations are actual deceased agnates of the living members of a

[1] This is probably an oblique reference to the Ibn Gāzi division of Ḥuweṭāt Bedouin, from whom the ʿArarāt sometimes claim descent.

[2] Muslims who have participated in the pilgrimage to Mecca are addressed as Ḥāg. Although the pilgrimage is one of the five pillars of Islam, very few Bedouin carry it out. In the Ẓullām area there are now only four old men who can claim to have completed the pilgrimage, of whom three are peasants and one a Bedouin.

section, who are able to trace kin relationships between one another through their ancestors. Then there occurs in Bedouin genealogies a gap, at the end of which stands the ancestor of the section. This ancestor is not a kinsman, for his precise relationship is untraced, and he stands therefore outside the section and at an equal distance from all members. With reference to this ancestor they are thus formally equals in rights and obligations, and with reference to him they also define membership of the section. The gap in the genealogy thus signifies the transition from kinship to corporate association, and may therefore be called a 'corporative gap'.

In Bedouin structural genealogies there occurs a second gap, between the sections' ancestors and the eponym of the whole co-liable group. For Bedouin groups are corporate at two levels: each section is corporately organized, but its members also participate corporately in the co-liable group.

In peasant groups, sections do not usually act as independent political units; as such they are to a large extent merged in the co-liable group. Thus they have no need to give sections a corporate identity, and, indeed, no gaps occur in the genealogy at the sections' point of separation. Yet we shall see later that at this point the names of ancestors who have lost significance are elided, and thus members of other sections are brought into a closer quasi-kin relation. The whole co-liable group considers itself as united by traced agnatic ties. Sections are connected by pervasive kin relationships, though these are cognatic ones. The genealogy thus culminates without a break in the two pilgrim brothers, at a depth of three to four generations. Only at this point does there occur a gap in the genealogy, and this denotes the transition from kin relationships to corporate relations. ʿArār, or Gāzi ibn ʿArār, the eponym of the Abu ʿArār, stands outside the range of kinship, and becomes a common point of reference to the men associating in the framework of the co-liable group.

The problem of gaps in genealogies is related to the 'areas of ambiguity' found by Peters[1] in the genealogies of Cyrenaican Bedouin. These genealogies showed no actual gaps at these points, which were recognizable as areas of ambiguity chiefly by the fact that here names of ancestors changed with great facility. Peters

[1] E. L. Peters 'The Proliferation of Segments in the Lineage of the Bedouin of Cyrenaica' (*JRAI* 1960).

shows that although the Cyrenaican 'Bedouin are expert genealogists', whenever they discussed names of ancestors 'at about the fifth ascending generation . . . arguments would flare up over the names to be included or excluded . . . with the result that for several people of the same segment there would be several versions of a genealogy which differed only at this one point.'[1] In fact, in the various samples of genealogies given by Peters, the living elders of segments and their deceased kinsmen were identical, and so was the corporate ancestor, and only the 'area of ambiguity' was filled in in various ways. I would then suggest that we are here dealing with something akin to a gap, except that it had been overlaid by names.

The 'areas of ambiguity' have been shown by Peters to absorb developments taking place in the living fabric of the political associations of Cyrenaican Bedouin. His analysis also fits the peasants in the Negev, who indeed accommodate at this point of their genealogies organizational changes or realignments. The number of sections in a group may decline or increase, in accordance with a constantly changing demographic situation, and names may be pushed back into, or retrieved from, the 'area of ambiguity' to fit emerging organizational patterns. That there are no 'corporative gaps' in our peasant genealogies at this point indicates that sections are not corporately organized, and the same may perhaps be true for an analogous level of organization of the Cyrenaican Bedouin. Only where the 'corporative gap' is open and undisguised, it clearly indicates a transition from kinship to corporate organization.

The analysis of 'corporative gaps' leads on to another point. Various authors view genealogies as 'conceptualizations of the existing lineage structure viewed as continuing through time and therefore projected backwards as pseudo-history'.[2] Now genealogies which show undisguised gaps obviously should lose all their value as 'conceptualizations of continuity', for they are themselves not continuous. Although it was seen that Bedouin have a handy method for filling up genealogical gaps, they felt no urge to use it until egged on by an inquisitive anthropologist. Apparently they did not put great store on the genealogy's continuity. Yet Bedouin

[1] *JRAI*, 1960, pp. 40–1.

[2] M. Fortes, 'The Structure of Unilineal Descent Groups' (*AA* 1953) p. 27, who is following Maine in this.

have a vital interest in the continued existence of their groups. This interest is not reflected in any particular trait of their genealogies. Continuity is rather an attribute of all ideologies of social organization, and these ideologies, by being firmly imprinted in men's minds and passed on from generation to generation, provide the connection through time.

Another criterion of corporate organization is the stated ultimate obligations of members. In Bedouin society the duties of members of a co-liable group are expressed in the laconic formula, 'they pursue and are pursued together' (*biṭardu wa-yanṭaridu maʿa baʿaḍ*).[1] This means, according to the Bedouin, that where one member of the group has been killed any other member can carry out vengeance by killing any member of the offender's group. Conversely, if one of their number should commit a homicide, they would all have to flee for their lives. In reality Bedouin draw a distinction between the agnates who are exposed to vengeance or have to exact it on one hand, and the co-liable group which shares in payment and receipt of blood-money. When discussing actual cases, Bedouin explain that vengeance is not exacted by any member of the co-liable group, but only by the victim's close kin, such as his father or brother, who are the 'owners of the blood' (*dammāwi*), and to whom the fulfilment of this duty becomes a matter of personal honour. All the vengeance killings that have come to my knowledge were executed by able-bodied members of the victim's section, though not necessarily the closest kinsman. Justice is considered to have been fully done only if the culprit himself is killed in revenge, though members of his section are also in some danger. If an avenger were to meet one of the latter, he might perhaps maltreat him, so that the close kin of the culprit prefer to keep out of his way until the affair is settled.

The only case in which I was able to observe the reaction to a murder at close range concerned Bedouin of Abu Rqaiq tribe. In June 1961 a Bedouin had been brutally murdered outside the reservation by two Arabs from Nazareth. The deceased's elder brother told me a few days later about the tragedy, and he added that his father had appointed him as the avenger: 'He told me to

[1] Musil, *The Manners and Customs of the Rwala Bedouins* op. cit., p. 489, renders a similar formula of the Rwala as 'bound to mutual protection, both aggressive and defensive'. See also Musil, *Arabia Petraea* (Vienna 1908) vol. 3, p. 361.

do the necessary'. He claimed that no-one but he could exact vengeance, for he was the victim's full-brother. His father had another grown-up son by another wife, but this half-brother was not under the heavy duty. 'Neither the head of my co-liable group nor any other member will do anything because it is the duty of the brother or of the son alone to take revenge,' he claimed.

The murderers had been arrested by the Police and were awaiting trial. That did not solve the avenger's problem, for his duty was to kill one of the murderer's close kin, though in this case not the culprits themselves, who would be safe behind prison bars for many years to come. As he was not acquainted with their families he was unable to specify further whom he was to slay. After much heartsearching, he eventually decided not to exact vengeance, knowing that he too would have ended up in prison.

In their formal accounts of killings and vengeance, Bedouin refer to the group which collectively carries out, and suffers, vengeance, as the *khams* (the fiver). This is also the term denoting the co-liable group, which can consist of several sections of kin. In some small groups, the section may be identical with the co-liable group, as is the case, for instance, of the Abu Msāʿad Bedouin group and Abu ʿĀbed peasant group. Members of a large co-liable group also consider themselves as a *khams* and they bear full collective responsibility for blood shed by any of its members, or for any loss they suffer. They insist that 'unless people secede from a group by a formal declaration, they continue as members with full obligations, even to the tenth generation'. This apparent ambiguity is evident in the following passages from ʿĀref.

Together with the killer, all the members of his *khams* flee. These are the descendants of the killer, those of his father, grandfather, grandfather's father and grandfather's grandfather.

A few lines further on, however, he states:

The dead man's family has a right to avenge the killing on any member of the killer's *khams*. This means, that anyone related to the killer even up to the tenth generation is considered as belonging to his *khams*, unless there has been a previous secession.[1]

These formalized statements of the responsibilities of the co-liable group clearly do not tally with one another, nor with actual

[1] ʿĀref, *Qaḍā*, p. 77.

behaviour. Bedouin realize this but do not see any contradiction in it. In real situations a victim's close agnates will avenge him, they say, but vengeance is still the responsibility of all members of the co-liable group, in the sense that failing a close agnate any other member would hold himself responsible. Co-liability for blood shed is, then, the ultimate responsibility of all members of a co-liable group.

Killings do not occur very often. During my fifteen months in the field, there occurred among the Ẓullām one murder and two other less serious blood disputes, while two more Bedouin from other parts of the Negev were killed. Thus it may be many years before a *khams* becomes involved in such a case. If the *khams* is still defined, and its workings described, in terms of killings and vengeance, this must be a formal paradigm of the activities which members would be expected to undertake. The best way to define them is to state the most onerous duty which might ever fall to a member's lot, in this case to kill or be killed for another member. Once the ultimate responsibility is made clear, the association can engage in any activity of a more limited scope, if required by members, without having to redefine its constitution. As the co-liable group's ultimate responsibility has been set so high, it becomes an all-encompassing association that can be called upon to serve a wide variety of interests.

The discussion of structural genealogies has shown that, with regard to recruitment of members, Bedouin view the co-liable group as an extension of the section. Now we have seen this to apply in another sphere: the ultimate responsibilities of the co-liable group are also viewed as an extension of those of a section.

Although the bases of corporate organization are stated in a formalized manner, they are still of great practical importance. They provide Bedouin with a framework for co-operation to serve some interests, in the same way that principles of kinship can be invoked for mutual assistance to serve others. When the actual activities of Bedouin sections are considered, the two methods of association cannot be seen in isolation, for members of a section act as kinsmen and as a corporate group at one and the same time; the same statement would be true for peasant co-liable groups. In some activities members emphasize their corporateness, and in others their kinship, but in all their co-operative efforts they constitute a group of kin.

While in the above discussion the Bedouin were seen to view their sections as corporations, they do not ignore the kinship aspects of sectional relationships. Bedouin describe their kin relationship to other agnates by counting ascending generations until they arrive at a common ancestor. Thus for a second patrilateral cousin a man would have to count up to the father's father's father. This procedure is adopted not only where personal relationships are being defined, but it is also supposed to be used for the definition of membership in a corporate association, as the following formalized account demonstrates:

When the avenger apprehends one of the killer's agnates, he requires him to clasp a stick in his outstretched hand, and to count the kinsmen from the murderer upwards and then again down to himself. With each name pronounced he opens one finger of his hand. If the stick drops from his hand before his name is reached, he is safe, if not, the avenger takes his life.[1]

This account seems to conflict with the ways for defining membership of a section described above. There the section's first ancestor, who sometimes gives it its patronym, was seen as point of departure for the definition of membership, and the number of generations intervening between him and the living was of no concern. If we reflect on the fact that a section is at one and the same time both a corporate group and a group of kin, the incongruities disappear: the sectional ancestor is the corporate rallying point, whereas the counting of kinship reflects the familial aspect of one and the same collection of persons. The avenger must know how close the kinship link is between the man he caught and the killer; it is not enough to know that he is a member of the same co-liable group.

There exists practically no area of life in which members of a section do not co-operate at one time or another. At first sight it seems as if each family is a separate economic unit, for land, herds and cisterns, one is told, are owned by individual men, who can freely dispose of their property and give no account to members of the section. In reality, members of the section retain residual and reversionary rights in land and cisterns, for when the owner intends to sell, they have first option on them. An embittered

[1] A similar version has been recorded by Musil, *Arabia Petraea*, vol. 3, p. 363.

bachelor of Abu Gweʿid Bedouin group complained that he could not call a dunam of land his own, because his father had sold it during the Mandatory period: it had gone partly to one father's brother's son and partly to another. He also complained that he did not even own animals. Now he cultivated, as sharecropper, 130 dunams of land belonging to a father's brother's son on the basis of a half share of the harvest,[1] thus having precious little grain left for himself. He lived by himself in a tent pitched next to his sister's, who was married to one of the father's brother's sons holding his land. On the face of it, this man was in a hopeless situation; but in fact he was fed by the other members of the section, he joined one man or another in his camp, he never needed to prepare food for himself, and his efforts to get other employment were erratic. After a few weeks of work he had usually had enough and returned to loaf about in the tribe. Yet I never heard a harsh word against him from the members of his section. A peasant once complained to a member of the section about the sad life our young man was leading, but obtained no response. The only thing the section would not do for him was to provide him with a bride. He would either have to collect the required amount himself in outside work, or else remain unmarried.

The contrast between individual ownership of land, cisterns and herds, and communal consumption of produce, is apparent everywhere, although it is more obvious among the wealthier Bedouin than among peasants. In this fashion property is shared with others but it can be exploited by the owner for the acquisition of prestige and leadership. A man of the Abu Gweʿid group had by hard work prepared a flood-irrigated vegetable plot. On this he had successfully sown cucurbits, mainly water melons and cucumbers. He insisted that he had never yet been able to sell the produce of his garden, as 'everything is given to the kinsmen or eaten at home'. By kinsmen he meant the members of his section, who at that time (it was the end of July) were all camping in the vicinity.

[1] This means that he obtained no special concession as an agnate. When the landowner supplies the land, implements and the draught animal, the sharecropper as a rule gets 50 per cent of the grain. If the owner has provided the seeds as well, he first subtracts the quantity supplied from the net harvest, and the grain is then measured out in equal shares.

Camels and asses are also freely borrowed among members of the section for threshing their grain by driving the animals round and round over it, or for riding. Members of a camp who were non-agnates were sometimes refused the loan of animals. Money is liberally loaned by the Bedouin to members of their section and by peasants to practically any member of the co-liable group, without charging interest or pressing for repayment. On one occasion I saw a man of the Abu Gāmeʿ peasant group, who had returned from two months' work outside the reservation, going from one man to the next in the guest tent of the group, repaying to each the varying amounts he had borrowed. Members of sections often co-operate in smuggling activities, the young men doing the dangerous work, while the older and wealthier men cover the commercial aspects.

In the economic sphere, co-operation and mutual aid are extended to individuals, not as members in the organizational framework of the section, but rather as from one kinsman to another. Food, access to cisterns, loans of money and animals, can be obtained from any kinsman, whether agnate or not. In practice, agnates are in a preferred position, for they are bound together by the heavy all-encompassing obligations of co-liability. Men who bear such great responsibility for one another must also be ready to help one another in smaller matters, and the co-operation with agnates becomes more binding and stringent than with kin who do not share mutual co-liable obligations. In occasional and minor matters a man can turn for aid and advice to any kinsman, but people who are in permanent need of help (such as men suffering physical disabilities) rely on their agnates, the members of their section. Blind, incapacitated and mentally deranged persons are maintained by their agnates, and so are childless widows, orphans and the aged. The closest agnate assumes responsibility for such persons, and very few would shirk this responsibility. Thus members of a section provide all-round social insurance for one another and for their families against sickness, hunger and death.

In order to be certain of assistance by other members of the section in time of need, men have at all times to keep relationships with them alert and active. Relations between members of a section are, therefore, not only very demanding, but also tense, frequently fraught with petty disagreement; and the closer the kinship the more trying these relations may become. This applies particularly to relations between brothers which, being egalitarian, are more competitive than others. Disputes among members of the section very rarely come out into the open. People resort mainly to grumbling, backbiting and ostentatiously evasive behaviour. Relations with kinsmen outside the section are more easygoing and less demanding.

Here are some examples of the things brothers used to grumble about. One man asked me to have his binoculars repaired. When a brother of his saw them, he complained to me that he had never been shown them by his brother. Another man of the same family refused to visit his brother because he had neglected to visit him some time ago. A third brother commented on this: 'Nothing serious is amiss, they still are on speaking terms.'

Another man told me:

> Last year my brother's camel ran wild and attacked my camel, which died a couple of days later. According to our custom, he should have given me his camel as compensation,[1] but I did not ask for it. Neither did he offer to compensate me. It is not good to raise problems among brothers.

Evidently the matter was still rankling in his mind, but he had to hold his peace. Relations among agnates are set in a clearly defined framework, which cannot be replaced by an alternative. There is no substitute for the section and therefore men are loth to risk an open dispute which may have unforseeable results.

The following case demonstrates what may happen to a Bedouin section when a dispute becomes publicly acrimonious. In 1956 a Maʿābdah man, whose father had died, received the marriage-payment for his sister, who had been given in marriage to a Bedouin of Abu Qrenāt tribe. When his four brothers demanded their equal share, he declared that he had spent it and that nothing was left for them. Furthermore, the young man had at the same time received a marriage-payment from another suitor, of the Abu Gweʿid group, and he also dissipated this. In the ensuing dispute the brothers disowned the culprit but could not have had him expelled by the rest of the co-liable group, and they still remained responsible for his future misdemeanours. There followed a series of mutual recriminations and denunciations until finally the

[1] This bears close resemblance to the biblical rule, *Exodus*, 21: 35–6.

section disbanded. The culprit went to live with a group of the adjacent Abu Qrenāt tribe, one brother with another group of Abu Gweʿid tribe, and a third crossed the frontier into Jordan in disgust. The two remaining brothers attached themselves to a larger section of their own group. Although formally they remained members of a large section, in practice they had all lost the benefits, such as the all-round social insurance, conveyed by membership.

Hitherto, all sections, irrespective of size, have been assumed to be equal, more or less. This is roughly true when one considers economic co-operation, vengeance and marriage arrangements and other matters which are primarily dealt with as between kinsmen. We shall now look at situations in which members of sections and co-liable groups are corporatively involved, namely in tribal politics. Here the size of a section and its internal structure become important. Bedouin usually reserve the term *qōm* (band of men) for large sections, that is, those which are included in the 'structural genealogies'. The Ṣarāiʿah Bedouin group's structural genealogy (diagram 16) enumerates only three sections. Compare this with the following diagram, which lists all the sections of close kin in the group, giving the number of adult men in each.

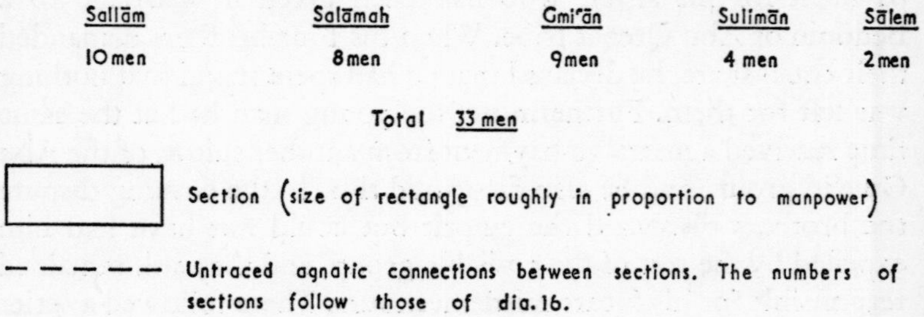

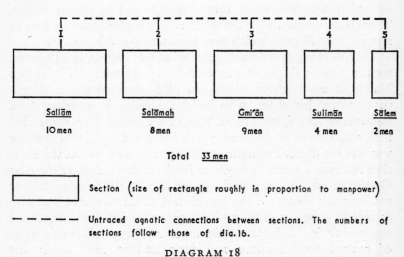

DIAGRAM 18

Sections and manpower of Ṣarāiʿah Bedouin group

In addition to the three large sections of the structural genealogy (1–3), two smaller ones are included here, which are half their size or less. The large sections are certainly the ones which make the political decisions, but the small ones cannot simply be dismissed as insignificant. They are not mechanically connected to one or the other of the large sections. They are free groups making their decisions with some independence. Each section has a clearly-defined membership and an acknowledged elder, and the leadership of the co-liable group culminates in one man, the headman of section 2. This clear-cut political organization allows the group, when necessary, to make decisions quickly and to initiate and co-ordinate activities. In an emergency the group can act quickly and with united determination. A murder, a rebellion of peasants, government interference in land ownership, would constitute such emergencies. It must be emphasized that we are dealing with a latent political organization, which does not necessarily affect other day-to-day affairs. The group does not react to these latter as a unit, and each section, large or small, takes its independent stand on any issue. As often as not the opinions of Salamāh section (2) and Gmiʿān section (3) will diverge, but again they will seek to avoid open disputes.

Among most peasants, it has been argued, the sections are less clear cut, and pervasive kinship ties fuse them in the co-liable group. In the Abu ʿArār group, however, sections are discernible as political units, but with a difference: here a number of close agnates band together to exert influence, so as to dominate in their sections. They do not exercise leadership, in the sense that they do not concentrate control in one hand, and they neither initiate decisions nor impose them on other members.

In contrast to the structural genealogy of the Abu ʿArār (diagram 17), diagram 19 has not been drawn up from the information given by a member of the section. Instead, it has been reconstructed from the fathers' and fathers' fathers' names of the individual members. The Khalāileh section comprises 17 adult men, who fall into two clusters. The larger cluster is based on four brothers and their descendants, 11 men in all. The other cluster consists of their first parallel patrilateral cousins, represented by two brothers and their sons, making a total of 6 men. The four brothers C1–C4, with the support of their seven sons, preponderate considerably over the smaller cluster of their section C5 and

C6, and D8–D11. But no less than five marriages firmly link the two clusters together. They reside together in summer camps and constitute the predominant section of the co-liable group. The

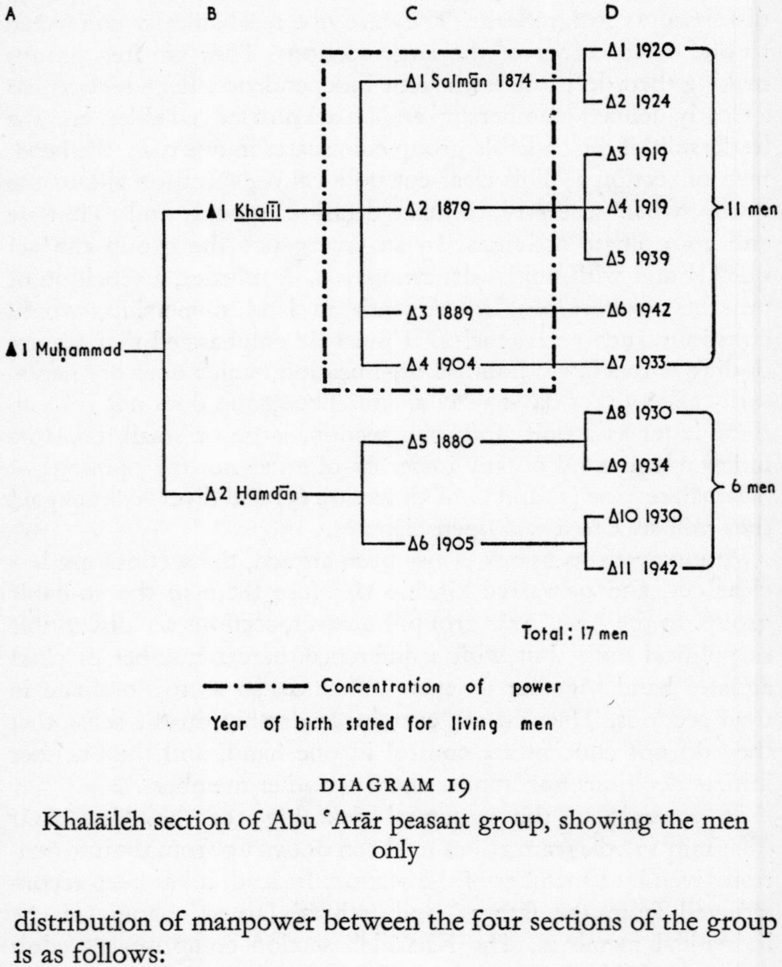

DIAGRAM 19

Khalāileh section of Abu ʿArār peasant group, showing the men only

distribution of manpower between the four sections of the group is as follows:

Khalāileh	17 men
Ṭalaqāt	10 men
ʿEyāl Silmi (*qōm* Samārah)	5 men
Qōm Ḥāg ʿIyādeh (*qōm* Muḥāreb)	7 men
Total manpower	39 men

Although this constellation makes the Khalāileh the predominant section of the co-liable group, they do not dominate it. Even where joint action of the co-liable group is indicated, the Khalāileh cannot translate their power potential into forceful activities, as it is not focused on a leader who could co-ordinate the members. On several occasions I inquired who were the leaders of the ʿArarāt, and obtained the standard reply that they had no leader. When pressed to name the most important man, they used to point either at Salmān (C1) who was not only one of the four influential Khalāileh brothers, but also the oldest living member of the group, or at Mṭāwaʿ (C4), the youngest and most active of the four brothers. These men were considered as spokesmen or representatives of the group, not as leaders. They did not initiate many activities on behalf of the members, but when they responded to a challenge from outside they were conspicuously active.

This political structure is reflected in the section's structural genealogy. A Bedouin section is a corporate unit, and has an ancestor common to all its members. In the Abu ʿArār peasant group a section is not much more than a group of close kin. The name Khalīl (B1) is not that of the ancestor common to all members of the section, but only that of the father of the four brothers (C1–C4). Khalīl is still in living memory of the section's older members, and they all recognize that he stands in a closer kin relationship to his own descendants than to those of his brothers. This means that the descendants of Ḥamdān (B2) are politically not viewed as full-fledged members of the section; they are more of an accretion around the stronger core of the section. Membership is unequal, and the section is not corporate. The name of Muḥammad (A1), the real common ancestor of the section, has become fused with that of Ḥāg Muḥammad. In this fashion the genealogy has been foreshortened and a closer kinship link with the other sections of the Abu ʿArār co-liable group has been simulated.

Another example will perhaps illustrate even more clearly this type of power structure and how it is expressed in the genealogical idiom.

The genealogy of the Ḥāg ʿIyādeh section of Abu ʿArār group has also been pieced together from the father's and father's father's names of the men. Assuming that most men can remember their grandfather's name, which is very likely, as kinship relations are traced through one's ascendants, then a genealogy reconstructed from these particulars may enable one to obtain a better picture of the power relations in a group. In the Ḥāg ʿIyādeh section there is one cluster of six closely related men, grouped around Baṭāḥ (C2), the oldest living member; the other branch of the section is represented by one man only (D1), who is tied by

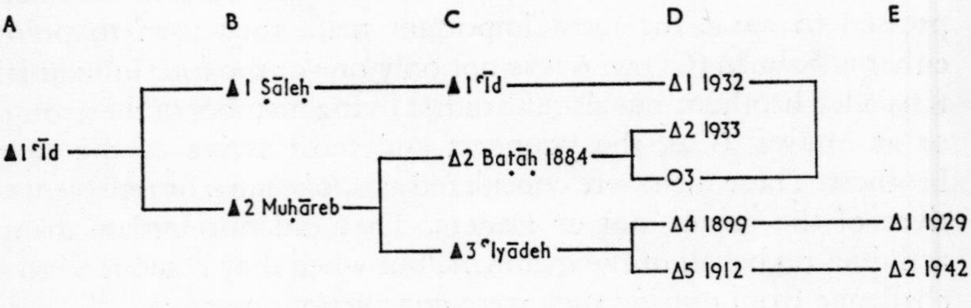

Year of birth stated for living men

DIAGRAM 20

Ḥāg ʿIyādeh section of Abu ʿArār peasant group, showing mainly adult men

marriage to a second patrilateral cousin (d3) into the main cluster. Part of the section resides in one line of tents in summer camps, and this includes D1, who also co-operates with C2 in farm work, though probably less as son-in-law than as an agnate and member of camp. The section traces its common kinship through ʿĪd (A1), the first ancestor connecting the two branches.

The structural genealogy (diagram 17, 2) supplied by the senior member of the section, Baṭāḥ (D7), shows that he recognized the bifurcation of the section, by giving two names of descendants of Ḥāg ʿIyādeh (Muḥāreb C4 and ʿĪd C5). He has attempted to resist the growing separation by his daughter's marriage. The name of ʿĪd has been dropped from the structural genealogy; it may be the two men named ʿĪd (diagram 20, A1 and his grandson C1) have been imperceptibly fused into one. Ḥāg ʿIyādeh, who is also the link connecting the section bearing his name with the other sections of the co-liable group, has thus been brought one generation closer to the living and one degree closer in kinship. Baṭāḥ was not, in this context, unduly concerned with the fact that he had discarded his own grandfather from the genealogy, though he had included his name in his personal particulars. When

I confronted him with the inconsistency he became first confused and then angry, and refused to volunteer any further information.

We can give some indication, however, how and why Baṭāḥ came to omit his grandfather ʿĪd from the genealogy. Bedouin fully realize that when they discuss the genealogical positions of persons not contemporaneous with themselves, their information becomes imprecise. 'I was not contemporaneous with him' (*mā laḥiqte*) is the standard excuse proffered by Bedouin whenever the details about ancestors more than two to three generations removed become inadequate. ʿĪd had been dead for many years, and Baṭāḥ remained the only member of the section who had known him alive. Thus it became possible for him to manipulate ʿĪd's position in the genealogy, or even to omit his name completely.

Baṭāḥ's section has a strong interest in maintaining its political ties with the other sections of the Abu ʿArār group. By making Ḥāg ʿIyādeh the father's father of Baṭāḥ, and thus turning members of the other sections into descendants of his grandfather's brothers, he simulates a kinship connection closer than that actually pertaining. The genealogical manipulation reflects the political interests of Baṭāḥ's section.

To a member of Khalīl's section, the Ḥāg ʿIyādeh section appears in a different light. To him the genealogical connections between the individual members of the Ḥāg ʿIyādeh section are of little relevance, and he is much more concerned with that section's contribution to the manpower of Abu ʿArār co-liable group. Therefore in Salmān's structural genealogy (diagram 17, 1), the Ḥāg ʿIyādeh section is accorded only one name, as it is only one section, while Salmān in turn gives details of his own section 2; and the section's ancestor is no longer Ḥāg ʿIyādeh, but Muḥāreb (section 4), whose direct descendants provide most of the section's manpower and constitute its core.[1]

The only occasion on which I was able to observe the Abu ʿArār acting as a co-liable group, was a situation in which they reacted to a provocation. One day in October 1961 news came to the ʿArarāt that a member of the tiny Zaghārnah Bedouin group of Abu Gweʿid tribe had attempted to assault a woman of the Ḥāg

[1] A similar situation prevails in the ʿEyāl Silmi (section 3, diagram 17), but not in the Ṭalaqāt section (4). We shall have occasion to discuss the latter in the following chapter.

ʿIyādeh section. One of the members of the Ṭalaqāt section, into which the woman was married, retaliated immediately by beating the young Bedouin. At the same time messengers were sent to all Abu ʿArār sections, whose men immediately rallied for the expected fight. Bedouin notables hurriedly stepped into the breach, 'put in their face', arranged a truce between the parties and thus averted a clash. The meeting-place of the ʿArarāt had been at the Khalāileh brothers' camp, but they were not mentioned as leaders.

The Abu ʿArār are not typical of all peasant groups. The Abu Ṣaʿalūk, for instance, display different characteristics.[1] The 22 men of this peasant group are distributed in six sections, each of which is descended from one of the six founders of the group—the fathers' fathers of the older living men, as they claim. The sections are neither named after their ancestor in the fashion of the Bedouin, nor after an ascendant representing the predominant cluster of men in a section as among the ʿArarāt. Instead, each section traces its kinship ties only through the grandfathers of the living males, and the agnatic connection between the ancestors is vaguely described as one of 'brothers and cousins'. The genealogy does not go back beyond these founders. Indeed, members of sections appear to interact mainly as kin, whereas from a political point of view sections are merged in the wider framework of the co-liable group, the only corporate political association of the Abu Ṣaʿalūk. Members insisted that the group had no leader, and they could not even name an outstanding individual who could act as spokesman on their behalf.

It must be very hard for a group which has no leadership of any kind to initiate joint action, or even to respond properly to a challenge coming from outside. In one-sectioned co-liable groups, and in the corporate sections of Bedouin co-liable groups, the older men exercise leadership by virtue of their position in the kinship structure: they are the fathers or father's brothers of the younger men. Counting the men of the older generation only, the Abu Ṣaʿalūk still have twelve men who are in the father's generation in relation to the able-bodied younger men, and these elders have neither resolved on handing over leadership to one of their number, nor can they point out any cluster of men who could become a nucleus for the group's political activities. The group

[1] The marriage patterns of this group have been discussed in detail in Chapter 5, which also includes an abbreviated genealogy (diagram 4).

can be roused into concerted action only by an exceedingly serious provocation.

In 1960 an Abu Ṣaʿalūk man was killed in an accident while staying with the ʿAṭaunah tribe. A tractor belonging to ʿAṭaunah men had been parked at the top of a slope. Suddenly it began to roll downhill, and gathering momentum crashed through the guest tent at the bottom, hitting the Abu Ṣaʿalūk man. He was immediately taken to hospital but after a short while died there. The ʿAṭaunah thereupon sought, in the customary manner, for a truce (*ʿaṭwah*), to allow the parties time to negotiate the amount of blood-money to be paid.[1] A Bedouin group, or even a peasant group like the Abu ʿArār, would have avidly grasped the opportunity to test the efficacy of their co-liable group, to rally and revitalize it through joint action, even if this only entailed alerting the fighting men and adopting threatening attitudes. The Abu Ṣaʿalūk did not act in this way. The father's brother of the dead man declared that he was not prepared to follow customary practice; instead he disclaimed any need for declaring a truce, and suggested putting the matter into the hands of a lawyer. He claimed he would be satisfied with whatever compensation the court awarded. At no stage in the proceedings was the co-liable group mobilized.

The varying internal structures of the three co-liable groups examined are not the result of chance, but of their particular positions relative to their environment. In Chapter 5 we examined how land ownership, or lack of land, affects the marriage patterns of Bedouin and peasants. There Bedouin and peasants were treated as two contrasting types, and we did not go deeper into the variations found in each sector. Thus while the Abu ʿArār had more land than the Abu Ṣaʿalūk, they clearly fell into the category of peasants, and this was also the case with their marriage patterns. While the proportion of marriage out of the group was higher for the Abu ʿArār than for the Abu Ṣaʿalūk, they made no political links or links for pasture in the hilly area. They enjoyed a firm foothold on the land, they were not constrained to marry as much as possible within their groups, and in this respect approached

[1] Bedouin customary law draws no formal distinction between an accidental killing and premeditated murder; the same (unspecified) amount of blood-money is thought to be due in both cases. The actual course of events differs greatly in both cases.

closer to the Bedouin pattern. With regard to political organization, however, the Abu ʿArār appeared to be very different from the Abu Ṣaʿalūk, and to represent a type lying halfway between peasants and Bedouin. Before an examination of the connection between the environmental positions of the three groups and their political structure is undertaken, it may be useful to glance at the relevant data, assembled in Table 15.

TABLE 15

Land ownership, marriage patterns and political structure in three large co-liable groups*

Group	Men over 18	*Land* Proportion of land held on lease (%)	*Marriage* Marriages recorded	Proportion of marriage in co-liable group (%)	Political structure
Ṣarāiʿah (Bedouin)	33	3	21	24	Corporate sections, corporate co-liable group, individual leaders
Abu ʿArār (peasants)	39	40	36	67	Influential clusters, corporate co-liable group, no leaders but spokesmen
Abu Ṣaʿalūk (peasants)	22	67	15	80	Non-political sections, corporate co-liable group, no representatives

* For detailed figures consult Appendices.

The political structure of each of the three co-liable groups is adapted to the part its position in the environment permits it to perform in the field of power. The Ṣarāiʿah Bedouin, and most of the other Bedouin groups, dispose over relatively large areas of arable land, part of which they lease to peasant sharecroppers. They organize politically so as to remain, jointly with other Bedouin, in control of the territory of the tribal group and its natural resources, and to retain their peasant sharecroppers in a state of economic and political dependence. Each section of the Ṣarāiʿah is a corporate unit, complete with its leader, which can formulate policies and initiate political action. It can also quickly co-ordinate its activities with other sections, when needed, in the framework of the co-liable group and in even wider associations.

The Abu ʿArār peasant group, and a few other large peasant groups owning a substantial proportion of their farm land, still depend on the Bedouin for the complement of their land, but not to a marked extent. They take little interest in herding and are not in a position to lease land to others. Therefore they have no need to combine with other groups with similar interests, and they initiate no political action against Bedouin, but they are able to defend themselves if challenged. The Abu Ṣaʿalūk and most other peasant groups are utterly dependent on the Bedouin landowners: in their case two-thirds of the farm land are obtained from Bedouin. They can be arbitrarily deprived of their livelihood by the Bedouin. They have no interests beyond the confines of the co-liable group, and thus their political organization is turned inward and it is passive. Members of the co-liable group assist one another in many ways as kinsmen, but are able to co-operate as a group only under extreme provocation.

It must be borne in mind also that under the present administration the relative position of the various groups with regard to land ownership can hardly change, that Ẓullām tribesmen have access only to farm land situated in their territory, and that they are at most times physically confined to that territory and to the natural resources available there. The land situation thus affects and delimits the political activity of groups.

In 1963 there occurred an extremely heavy drought, which forced many Bedouin to move temporarily out of the Negev. For a time a new ecological situation had been created, one of whose features contrasted sharply with the traditional situation: land ownership had, for the time being, become relatively unimportant. The following analysis of a herding-camp established by the Abu Gweʿid in that year shows how formal organizational patterns are adapted to particular circumstances and how they continue to affect the association of individuals. It also shows how various elements of the political and the kinship organization may combine.

The uninterrupted series of droughts in the Negev that began in 1957–8 culminated and ended in the terrible dry season of 1963. In that year the authorities did not actively assist the Bedouin in locating pastures in the farming areas north of the Negev. Owners of small flocks could still wander from one patch of pasture to another, and a few Bedouin even grazed their sheep in the backyards of Tel-Aviv's suburbs. Pasture for larger flocks became increasingly difficult to obtain, although Bedouin were prepared to pay the often exorbitant charges. Farmers and settlements became afraid to allow on their harvested land Bedouin herds which, for lack of alternative pasture, were likely to stay on even after the pasture had been exhausted. Hungry flocks often invaded orchards and gardens and caused considerable damage, and there arose frequent disputes with herdsmen. Bedouin tried to negotiate with villagers through individuals who had connections there and who could vouch for their disciplined behaviour. Quite often peasants of the Negev who had been employed in Jewish settlements mediated such arrangements.

The Abu Gweʿid chief and his brothers got permission to graze on stubble land belonging to a settlement in the Sorek valley, through the good services of Sulimān Qrenāwi, a peasant from Abu Rbēʿah tribe. This peasant was himself the owner of over a hundred head of sheep and the Abu Gweʿid men gladly entered into partnership with him to exploit the pasture. At the beginning of September 1963 the Abu Gweʿid herding-camp in the Sorek valley was composed as shown in diagram 21. The diagram includes all the men whose flocks were grazing on the leased pasture, except the peasant partner and several men whose few animals were attached to the flocks of their kinsmen; also included are all the men staying in the herding-camp at the time.

Four Abu Gweʿid brothers were present or were represented in the camp, including the tribal chief and his elder full-brother (B1–B4). In fact all the brothers who owned large flocks were there, whereas two others who owned only a few sheep each were careful not even to visit the camp: they feared they would be pressed to take turns as herdsmen. The Abu Gweʿid brothers constituted the core of the camp; they had initially entered into a partnership with the peasant Qrenāwi and they held themselves responsible for all members of the camp. The peasant partner never attended the camp, not even to inspect his flock. The Abu Gweʿid chief (B3) visited the herding camp at frequent intervals, but never stayed long because tribal business called him away. Therefore all administrative matters were settled by Muḥammad (B2), the chief's elder full-brother. He settled the water-accounts and apportioned the payments to members of the camp, and he received visitors in his tent. In his absence the guest-tent transferred to the eldest brother (B1).

There were altogether about 1,200 sheep and goats compressed

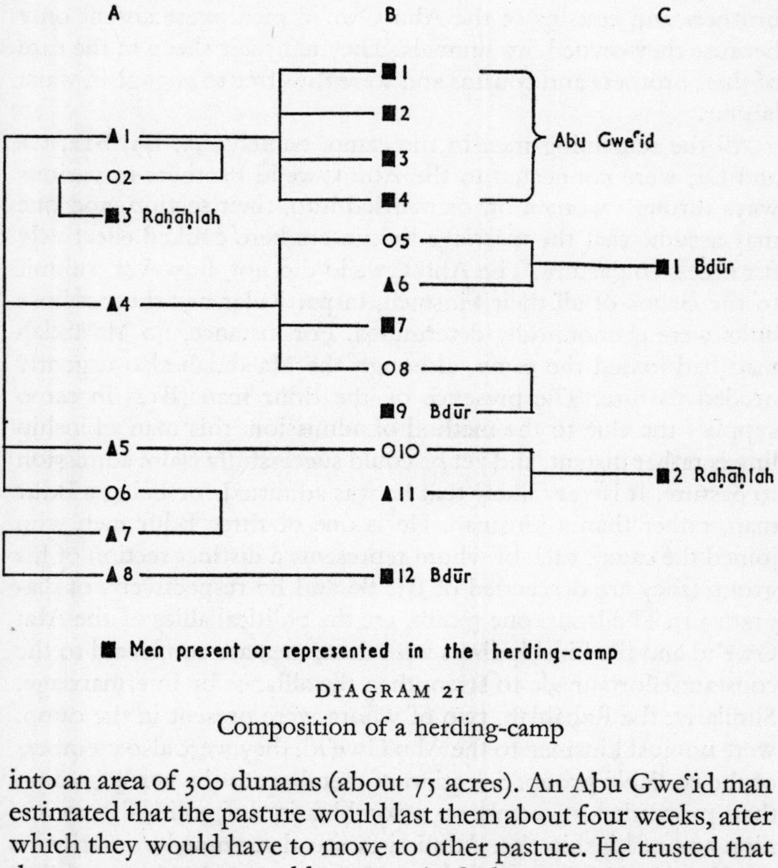

DIAGRAM 21

Composition of a herding-camp

into an area of 300 dunams (about 75 acres). An Abu Gweʿid man estimated that the pasture would last them about four weeks, after which they would have to move to other pasture. He trusted that the peasant partner would once again find pasture, but he had his doubts about that. If pasture was so scarce, why then did the Abu Gweʿid men share it so liberally with others? The answer is that the Abu Gweʿid men were obliged to accede to requests for pasture when they came from certain kinsmen.

The diagram shows that all the men in the camp (with the exception of the Qrenāwi man) were connected by kinship to the

Abu Gweʿid brothers. There was first a close agnate (B7), a first parallel cousin to the four brothers, who tended the chief's herd as well as his own animals. Although he was the only other member of the chief's section, he represented in the camp a whole category of men who might consider themselves entitled to a share in the pasture: the other members of the section. These men, the brothers and cousins of the Abu Gweʿid men, were absent only because they owned few animals. They left their sheep in the care of their brothers and cousins and were thus free to engage in wage labour.

All the remaining men in the camp, namely A3, B9, B12, C1 and C2, were connected to the Abu Gweʿid brothers in various ways through women of, or married into, their section, and one may assume that the marriage links were here evoked effectively for access to pasture. The Abu Gweʿid did not, however, submit to the claims of all their kinsmen, in particular not those whose links were economically determined. For instance, no Maʿābdah man had joined the camp, although the Maʿābdah also urgently needed pasture. The presence of the Bdūr man (B12) in camp supplies the clue to the method of admission: this man's kinship link is rather distant, and yet he could successfully claim admission to pasture. It is very likely that he was admitted for being a Bdūr man, rather than a kinsman. He is one of three Bdūr men who joined the camp, each of whom represents a distinct section of his group (they are descended of B5, B6 and B7 respectively, of diagram 14). The Bdūr, one recalls, are the political allies of the Abu Gweʿid and the kinship links with these men are connected to the constant efforts made to strengthen the alliance by intermarriage. Similarly, the Raḥāḥlah, two of whom were present in the camp, were not just kinsmen to the Abu Gweʿid, they were also members of the co-liable group. Selection of members to the herding-camp then proceeded, it seems, on a combination of political communion and of kinship ties. Admission was determined primarily by the closeness of the political association, and only in second line by kinship. Men who were both political associates and kinsmen could not be refused access to pasture.

In the situation described above, the economic links of the Abu Gweʿid gave way to their political associations, although economic links are made precisely for access to pasture. One must realize that here, however, we are not dealing with a sharing of pasture as ordinarily understood by Bedouin. The Abu Gweʿid were facing a critical situation which had forced them to move out of their tribal territory. At the time they had already been away from the Negev for six months. In these conditions the economic links of normal times, which facilitated the sharing of the traditional pasture grounds of the Ẓullām, became meaningless and inoperative. The grain harvest in the Negev had completely failed and the former sharecroppers of the Bedouin had found employment outside the Negev, and many of them were likely never to return to the tribes. The whole political organization was temporarily out of joint, and economic links for pasture could help the Abu Gweʿid neither in their quest for pasture nor in overcoming the uncertain prospects for the near future. They could hope to overcome their difficulties only if they all held together. And this they did along the lines of the already existing political frameworks of the section, the co-liable group and the *rubaʿ*.

CHAPTER 8

Recurrent Process in Sections and Co-liable Groups

WE shall now examine how demographic change, namely the reproduction and replacement of human beings, affects sections and co-liable groups. A section is in no way a perpetual social unit; founded as it is on kinship, its very existence is intimately bound up with the lives of its members. When one looks at a sufficiently wide cross-section of a population one finds at any time human beings at various stages of their lives. Similarly, a large enough sample of Bedouin society will include sections at various stages of their development. By arranging them in the proper sequence, one can reconstruct a complete cycle of development. Thus even a relatively short period of observation may permit insight into the long-term processes involved.[1]

Let us now examine the processes as they occur in a specific section. A section which has already been analysed for marriage patterns will be used as an example. It is the relatively large chief's section of Abu Gweʿid Bedouin co-liable group. Diagram 22 shows the state of the section in 1960; it gives only those details pertinent to our discussion. Hence most of the women have been omitted.[2]

In 1960 the section comprised 17 adult men, all of whom were descended in the male line of Ḥmēd (A1), who was chief of the Abu Gweʿid tribe until his death in 1917. The oldest living member was Sheikh Muḥēsin (B4), who became chief of the tribe at his father Ḥmēd's death. He was not only the sole surviving man of

[1] This is, of course, an application of the concept of 'structural time' developed by E. E. Evans-Pritchard in *The Nuer* (Oxford 1940) and by M. Fortes in 'Time and Social Structure: an Ashanti Case Study', *Social Structure: Essays presented to A. R. Radcliffe-Brown*, 1949. J. C. Mitchell in *The Yao Village* (Manchester 1956) has analysed the developmental cycle of a village in this manner.

[2] Diagram 8 sets out the full genealogical data for this section.

the ascendant generation, but also the begetter of one half of the living members, numbering in all seven sons and three grown-up grandsons. Muḥēsin was too old and feeble to lead the section any

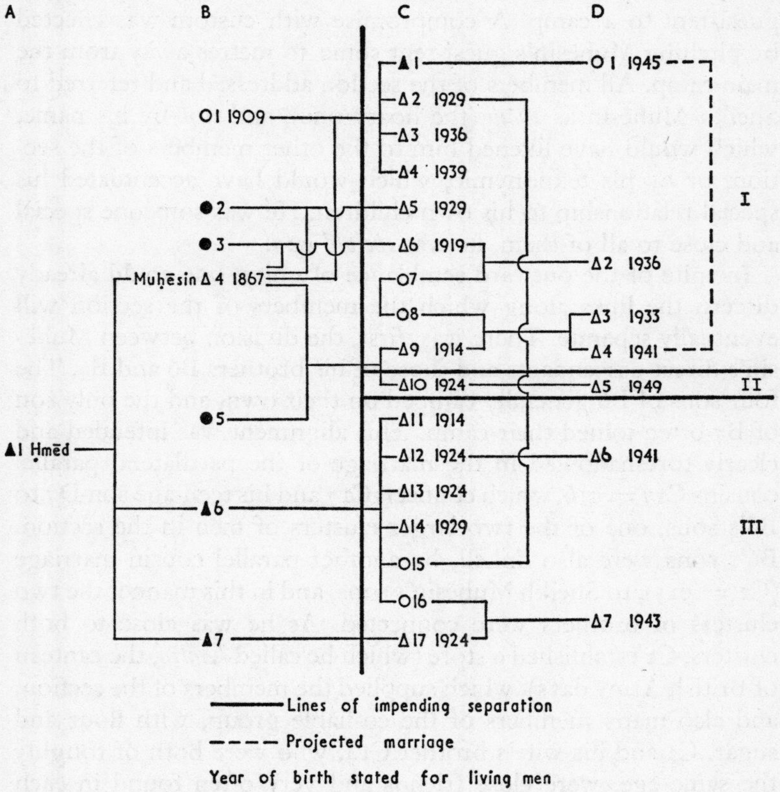

DIAGRAM 22

Chief's section of Abu Gweʿid Bedouin group, indicating lines of separation

more. The actual head now is his son Mḥemmed (C10), the present tribal chief.[1] But while old Sheikh Muḥēsin's influence on practical day-to-day affairs was negligible, he was the man who held together the section. For he was the only member of the section who stood in close kinship to all the others: they all came to visit him

[1] Another son of Muḥēsin, ʿAwād (C1), had become chief in 1947 and after his death in the following year Mḥemmed took over.

and in his tent met one another. It is significant that his youngest son ʿAbdallah (C4), with whom he lived, maintained a guest-tent for him even when staying in the chief's permanent camp at Ṣdēr, although custom decrees that there should only be one guest-tent to a camp. A compromise with custom was effected by pitching Muḥēsin's guest-tent some 50 metres away from the main camp. All members of the section addressed and referred to Sheikh Muḥēsin as *shāib* (the hoary one), and not by his name, which would have likened him to the other members of the section, or by his teknonymic, which would have accentuated his special relationship to his own children. He was someone special and close to all of them, he was *the old man*.

In spite of the outward semblance of unity, one could already discern the lines along which the members of the section will eventually separate. There was, first, the division between Muḥēsin's direct descendants and those of his brothers B6 and B7. The four sons of B6 generally camped on their own, and the only son of B7 often joined their camp. This alignment was intended and clearly foreshadowed in the marriage of the patrilateral parallel cousins C17 = c16, which connects C17 and his teen-age son D7 to B6's sons, one of the two larger clusters of men in the section. B6's sons were also linked, by another parallel cousin marriage (C2 = c15), to Sheikh Muḥēsin's sons, and in this manner the two clusters of brothers were connected. As he was close to both clusters, C2 established a store (which he called *kantīn*, the canteen of British Army days), which supplied the members of the section, and also many members of the co-liable group, with flour and sugar. C2 and his wife's brother C14, who were both of roughly the same age, were close friends and very often found in each other's company.

Among Sheikh Muḥēsin's sons there were also signs of an incipient separation into clusters. The seven living sons of Sheikh Muḥēsin (C2–C6, C9 and C10) were born of four mothers, and one expected differentiation to occur between these paternal half-brothers. Sheikh Muḥēsin had only one wife still living with him (b1), whose three sons were devoted to their mother. In a family quarrel they unhesitatingly took her side against their father. Yet the fact that they have one mother did not in itself set the three brothers apart from their other siblings. If they had constituted a sufficiently large contingent of men, this might have proved a ground for clustering apart. The fact that one of the three brothers (C3), was very ill and unable to marry, and that the children of the other two were still young, inhibited any tendency they might have had to form a cluster. Instead, they maintained very close relations with their paternal half-brothers, and especially with C9, the chief's elder full-brother. Their plan to marry C9's son (D4) to his father's brother's daughter (d1) intended to strengthen this alignment. Another brother (C6) is also hovering close to these men, for his wife (c7) is the sister of C9's wife (c8).

The case of another brother (C5) was again different. He bore a grudge against his father, and against everyone else it seems, because his mother (b2) had been repudiated. In 1961 he contracted a second marriage using his full-sister as an exchange bride for his new wife, without consulting his father or brothers. They were quite annoyed at this apparent disregard for the other members' interests, but after a few weeks of sulking they agreed to restore amicable relationships and slaughtered a kid to show their goodwill. The feast constituted an acknowledgment by the brothers that this man still remained a member of their section. Although he stayed for extended periods at the cisterns of his wife's father in the Hilly Area, and in spite of his sometimes sullen behaviour, it was inconceivable to anyone that he, a solitary individual, would wish to renounce the support of his brothers.

Not only were the six brothers attracted to each other to form a cluster because this gave them strength, but they were also brought together by the seventh brother's (C10) chieftaincy. As a tribal chief he is, as we have seen,[1] under pressure to enlarge his family, and in particular to beget many sons that they may come to form a separate cluster. The chief's separatist tendencies were felt, and resented by his brothers; but to the outside world they still presented a united front, for a separation can only become effective if the chief has many mature sons. This was some way off, for his eldest son (D5) was born in 1949. Here, then, separation certain to take place at some future date, was already wearing away a tie between full-brothers.

When I returned to the Negev in the summer of 1963, I learned that Sheikh Muḥēsin had died a few weeks before. Now his stabilizing influence was gone it was likely that separation would proceed at a faster pace, but even so the process would be drawn out.

[1] See Chaper 5.

Some indications of the direction it would take were, however, emerging.

Sheikh Muḥēsin was laid to rest in the cemetery at ʿArʿarah,[1] and after about ten weeks his youngest son and sole heir (C4) hired a mason to build a tomb over his grave.[2] When it was completed, the tribal chief's elder full-brother (C9) gave a feast at which all the members of the section present in the area took part. C9 had now become the elder, if not the leader, of the section: he had three mature sons, he owned a large herd and land, more than any other member of the section except the tribal chief, who was his junior in age. It thus fell to him to prepare the inscription on Sheikh Muḥēsin's tomb. It ran: 'In the name of God the Merciful the Compassionate; here lies Sheikh Muḥēsin Ḥmēd Abu Gweʿid.' In conversation C9's sons referred to him now as *shāib*, the old man, as if Muḥēsin's role of uniting the section had devolved upon him, but they were not emulated by others.

One of the incipient divisions in the section in 1960 had by 1963 come much more into the open: the tribal chief (C10) had become more isolated. He remained encamped at the usual place in Ṣdēr. The kinsmen who had formerly been almost regular members of his camp (C2, C3 and C14) had moved away and for the time being they had joined his full-brother's (C9) camp and guest-tent. Only the youngest brother (C4) still camped close to the chief, but considered reopening the separate guest-tent he had maintained for his father. Members of the section reasoned, in a somewhat circular fashion, that they did not attend at the chief's guest-tent because it was mostly deserted, and that they therefore preferred the guest-tent of his elder brother. It was true that the chief spent much of his time in town, yet he returned home nearly every evening. He had not quarrelled with any member of the section, and he continued to exchange visits with his brothers. He made no serious

[1] Sheikh Muḥēsin was buried at the wells of ʿArʿarah, because this was the cemetery nearest to his camp. The Ẓullām, peasants and Bedouin, bury their dead also in two other cemeteries situated near wells, at Bīr Mshāsh and Tel al-Milḥ, and one in the hilly area, at Mirqib. (See Plate VI).

[2] Only important Bedouin are accorded monumental tombs in the manner of Muslim city-dwellers. Most Bedouin are buried in shallow graves, and only two stones (*ʿimdān al-ḥaqq*, the two pillars of judgment) mark the position of the head (west) and of the feet (east) of the dead man. After a few years the site is obliterated, and the dead man forgotten. See also Musil, *The Manners and Customs of the Rwala Bedouins*, op. cit., pp. 670–1.

effort, however, to attract followers to his camp, for not only was his position as the section's leader in political and economic action assured by virtue of his being the tribal chief and the wealthiest member of the section, but also his eldest son had grown into a young man, his second son was now an adolescent, and there were also two younger sons. The chief's family had begun to emerge as a separate section (section II of diagram 22), and yet no one in the section had become aware of the change.

The relations between the other brothers had hardly been affected. The marriage between the patrilateral parallel cousins D4 = d1 had taken place; C4, who had to all intents and purposes been the girl's guardian, and had had other things in mind for her, consented to the match in deference to the wishes of the other members of the section. C5's relations with his brothers were still slightly formal and reserved, and each visit paid by one party to the other became a feast, at which goats were slaughtered in token of the desire to establish warmer relations.

The sections I and III (diagram 22) were now assembled in one camp, and the guest-tent of the chief's full-brother (C9) was their centre. The joint camp did not, however, indicate a reversal of the earlier trend to separate. The failure of crops in the Negev had forced many Bedouin to seek employment in the north, and they combined camps to provide for the families they left behind. Thus for the time being the two clusters of men had become dependent on one another. At the same time, however, there were signs that the two clusters had separated further: C2 had some months earlier closed his store as he could not make a profit. His younger and wealthier brother C4 had taken over, but he too complained about lack of custom. C4, unlike his brother, was no affine to B6's descendants, and therefore he could not expect them to purchase flour and sugar only from his store. In October of that year the men who had been away at work flocked back to the Negev, to prepare for the imminent rainy season. Soon they would be moving to their winter camping sites and the joint camp of clusters I and III would break up. One day the news was out: C11 had established a store of his own. This store would naturally compete with C4's, for each man would attract the people most closely related to himself, and the members of the section would be drawn in two directions.

In Abu Rbēʿah Bedouin group, the process of separation can

be observed at a later stage in the dominant core-group which bears the tribal name. Here the chief's family has become a full-fledged section. Sālem, the tribal chief at the turn of the century,[1] begat eight sons of three wives. One son, Khalīl, took over the chieftaincy when his father grew too feeble to carry the burden any longer. Khalīl died in 1927, and his father soon followed him to the grave. Khalīl left eight sons, who together with their descendants now constitute a separate section of the co-liable group, *qōm* Khalīl. Three of his sons have occupied the chieftaincy since. The present incumbent is one of them. All the other male descendants of Sālem, including those of a full-brother of Khalīl, make up another section, *qōm* Sālem.

A Bedouin section usually contains agnates up to the third degree of kinship, i.e. first patrilateral cousins. But the backbone of a section is mostly a group of brothers. Members of the fourth generation sooner or later break away, according to lines of separation which can usually be traced long before the actual separation is complete. Separation may be delayed, even for decades, by the political clustering of men, when clusters of brothers seek to increase their power by joining forces with first, and sometimes second, patrilateral parallel cousins. Such clusterings are often reinforced by marriage ties. We have noticed that some patrilateral parallel cousin marriages are arranged with this end in view, while others connect the larger clusters of the section. Second patrilateral cousins can apparently remain together in a section only if a member of the father's father's generation is alive and acts as a focus of common close kinship.

The possible effects of patrilateral parallel cousin marriage on the structure of a section can best be demonstrated in diagrammatic form. Diagram 23 shows, schematically, a section at two stages of its development. In the first stage, the section comprises kin up to the degree of first patrilateral cousin. A marriage between the first patrilateral parallel cousins, C4 and c3, ties up the two clusters of brothers in generation C, and may help to postpone their separation even after the death of the ascendants, B1 and B2. The second stage shows the same section a generation later. Should one of the brothers B1 and B2 be still alive, he may possibly persuade his

[1] See ʿĀref, *Taʿarīkh*, p. 195, for his part in the series of clashes between the Ẓullām and the peasants of Yattah in the Hebron mountains, in the years 1900–12.

children to arrange a marriage between the second patrilateral parallel cousins, D3 and d4, and thus renew a close kin connection between the two branches of the section which are gradually growing apart. The descendants of D3 would then be first matrilateral cousins to D5's children. But if the members of the ascending generation have died out, it is very likely that a marriage will be

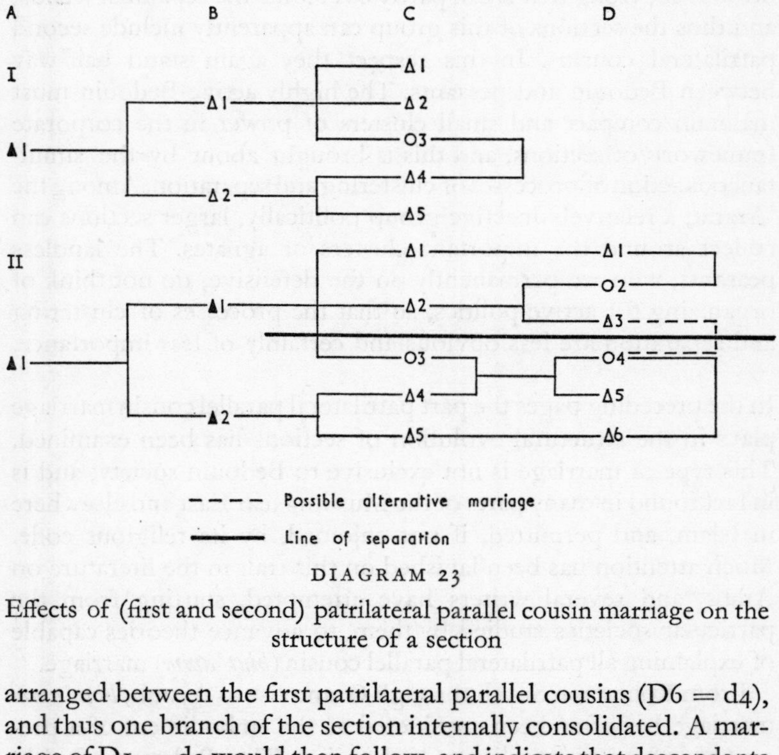

DIAGRAM 23

Effects of (first and second) patrilateral parallel cousin marriage on the structure of a section

arranged between the first patrilateral parallel cousins (D6 = d4), and thus one branch of the section internally consolidated. A marriage of D1 = d2 would then follow, and indicate that descendants of B1 had become a separate section.

In the process of separation, paternal half-brother differentation plays an insignificant part, though it affects the clustering together of men. For separation occurs only between the descendants of a group of brothers. It is unlikely that a father's mother would at that stage be able to unite her descendants against their tendencies to cluster and to separate. On the other hand, the chieftaincy tends to draw a chief away from his section, alienating him from his full-brothers and compelling him to establish a separate section.

The same processes of clustering and separation are at work in the peasant groups. In groups such as the Abu Ṣaʿalūk they are much less obvious, because agnates who grow apart are brought together again by marriages and affinity as a matter of course, and not as part of the efforts to create concentrations of power. Among the Abu ʿArār peasants the clustering is evident. The tendency to do so is so strong that it can partly overcome the separatist trends, and thus the sections of this group can apparently include second patrilateral cousins. In this respect they again stand half-way between Bedouin and peasants. The highly active Bedouin must maintain compact and small clusters of power in the corporate framework of sections, and this is brought about by the simultaneous action of processes of clustering and separation. Among the ʿArarāt, a relatively inactive group politically, larger sections can collect around the important clusters of agnates. The landless peasants, who are permanently on the defensive, do not think of organizing for active politics, so that the processes of clustering and separation are less obvious and certainly of less importance.

In the preceding pages the part patrilateral parallel cousin marriage plays in the structural evolution of sections has been examined. This type of marriage is not exclusive to Bedouin society, and is in fact found in many parts of the Muslim Near East and elsewhere in Islam, and permitted, if not enjoined, by its religious code. Much attention has been lavished on this trait in the literature on Arabs, and several writers have attempted, starting from the particular societies studied by them, to advance theories capable of explaining all patrilateral parallel cousin (*bint ʿamm*) marriage.

From Robertson Smith through Granqvist to Ayoub, *bint ʿamm* marriage has often been considered as the embodiment of a precept of endogamy peculiar to Arab society. Thus Robertson Smith, writing in 1885, thinks that 'the *ibn ʿamm* (father brother's son) . . . is literally a man of the same stock group'.[1] Granqvist concurs with Doughty and Wellhausen, whom she quotes, that in parallel cousin marriage 'not a particular marriage of kin is being enjoined . . . but rather endogamy'.[2] Ayoub's 'contention is that preferred

[1] W. Robertson Smith, *Kinship and Marriage in Early Arabia* (London 1903) p. 72.

[2] H. Granqvist, *Marriage Conditions in a Palestinian Village* (Helsingfors 1931–5) vol. 1, p. 78, quoting Wellhausen, *Die Ehe bei den Arabern*, p. 436. My translation.

patrilateral parallel cousin marriage . . . is better seen as but the most extreme expression of an overall pattern of preferred endogamy'.[1]

The fact that the terms for male and female patrilateral cousin are usually extended to include a wide range of kin, generally of speaker's own generation, is thought by these scholars to lend support to their view. In the Negev, the term *ibn ʿamm* (father's brother's son) is applied not only to the age-mates of one's own group, but also to matrilateral cousins in an allied group. The term *bint ʿamm* (father's brother's daughter) is used in a more limited fashion, and denotes chiefly a true female patrilateral parallel cousin, but may also be employed, by men and women, for a woman of approximately their own age born in the co-liable group. I have not heard men refer to, or address, their wives as *bint ʿamm*, as is the custom in some areas,[2] unless they were true kin. The way the parallel terms for male and female cousin are employed in the Negev appears to me to have no bearing on marriage, and therefore they cannot be 'an expression of preferred endogamy'. What they do express is the extension of the obligations of agnates from the members of the section to all members of the co-liable group, and in a way, even to the men of an allied group. For cousins are the most peripheral category of kin included in the section, and the obligations due among cousins set the standards for the co-operation among its members. Similarly a woman born in the group is usually termed a *bint ʿamm* because her marriage is made to serve the interests of both section and group.

I would deny that there is endogamy at all among the Bedouin of the Negev. 'Endogamy is the rule enjoining marriage within a specified social group,' is the definition in *Notes and Queries on Anthropology*.[3] There is no rule enjoining either marriage into a prescribed group, or out of one, in Bedouin society, except the limited incest prohibitions. Beyond that, there is an extremely wide range of permitted marriage. This wide range must be accepted as a fact which has sociological repercussions on societies professing

[1] M. R. Ayoub 'Parallel Cousin Marriage and Endogamy' (1959) p. 266.

[2] See for instance Jaussen's sweeping statement (op. cit., p. 45): 'L'Arabe appelle sa femme "*bint ʿammy*"'. In the Negev, men usually address their wives by their name, and refer to them as *al-ʿōrah* ('the woman', here not in a derogatory sense of 'shame') or, to a mother of children, *ahl al-bēt* (family).

[3] *Notes and Queries on Anthropology*, p. 116. See also Radcliffe-Brown's 'Introduction' to *African Systems of Kinship and Marriage*, p. 68.

Islam, but does not require explanation in the context of a study of a specific community or area. A historical study of Islamic origins would have to show how these rules of marriage came to be part of the religious code, but for our purposes they can be considered as extraneous to the society studied. It may be argued that some Islamic precepts, such as the rules of inheritance giving women half a man's share, are ignored in parts of Islam, including the Negev, and that therefore all kinds of unlawful marriage practices might persist in different areas. It should be borne in mind that in this context we are not dealing with a set of restrictive rules, but instead the code itself has here thrown open the gate of marriage, and it has, among other things, permitted marriage between cousins, ranging from the first onwards. Given this, it is not surprising to find that these possibilities are exploited by Muslims for a wide variety of interests. There is no evidence of overwhelming first parallel cousin marriage and we shall see that there are situations in which marriages of other kinds are preferred to father's brother's daughter marriage. The same is, of course, true for adherents of other religions permitting marriage between categories of close kin: where group interests can be furthered by marriage among such relatives, pressure will often be brought to bear on persons to contract them.

As the association of agnates is a focus for varied interests, a greater desire to make marriages among agnates may well develop. Hence the emphasis on patrilateral parallel cousin marriage in some circumstances. It would be a mistake, however, to assume that this is the only kind of cousin marriage practised among the Bedouin.

Table 16 compares the incidence of first patrilateral parallel cousin marriage among Arabs in various rural areas in Israel and adjacent countries. There are as yet no data on urban communities or on other Bedouin.

The table shows very clearly that the rate of father's brother's daughter marriage varies only slightly from place to place. The only exception are the Christians of Ṭurʿān village. Rosenfeld[1] states that one quarter of the Christians are Greek Orthodox, to whom marriage between first cousins is forbidden, but unfortu-

[1] Op. cit., p. 53. The legal prohibition extends, in fact, even to third cousins. See F. J. Bliss, *The Religions of Modern Syria and Palestine* (Edinburgh 1912) p. 146.

TABLE 16

Marriage between first patrilateral parallel cousins in various Arab rural societies (by men)*

Areas	*Negev Bedouin*	*Arṭas*[1]	*Kafr Qāsem*[2]	*Ṭurʿān*[3] *Muslims*	*Ṭurʿān*[3] *Christians*	*Druze village*[4]	*Juba Shiʿites*[5]	*Totals*†
All marriages	214	264	417	578	211	254	229	1,956
Bint ʿamm marriages	25	35	61	76	13	23	32	252
As percentage	11·7	13·3	12·6	13·1	6·1	9·1	14·0	12·9

* Sources:

1. Arṭas (Etam), near Bethlehem. H. Granqvist, *Marriage Conditions in a Palestinian Village* (Helsingfors 1931–5) vol. 1, p. 81.
2. Kafr Qāsem, in Central Israel. A. Cohen, *Arab Border-Villages in Israel* (Manchester 1965) p. 111.
3. Ṭurʿān, Lower Galilee. H. Rosenfeld, 'An Analysis of Marriage and Marriage Statistics for a Moslem and Christian Arab Village, *IAE*, XLVIII (1957)' pp. 35, 44.
4. Druze village, in Syria. M. R. Ayoub, 'Parallel Cousin Marriage and Endogamy', *SWJA*, XV (1959) p. 267.
5. 'Aspects of Status and Rank among Muslims in a Lebanese Village', by E. L. Peters, in *Mediterranean Countrymen*, ed. J. Pitt-Rivers (The Hague 1963) and unpublished figures.

† Totals exclude Ṭurʿān Christians.

nately does not provide separate marriage figures for them. One may assume that the Greek Orthodox have depressed the rate of *bint ʿamm* marriage, though this does not necessarily account for the whole difference rate of the other Christians. For all other denominations appearing in the table, first cousins are the closest permitted marriage partners. If the figures are similar for the different communities, then, this may indicate that the rates of *bint ʿamm* marriage are affected by demographic factors, namely that there seem to be limits to the 'possibilities of one's marrying a first cousin, no matter how large the clan, for it requires a number of brothers whose children will be reasonably near the same age'.[1] Within a given population there will always be only a limited number of cousins of the right age, not counting additional factors tending further to reduce the chances of arranging matches between them, such as physical disabilities, quarrels between the families, and perhaps even more important, competing interests. The rates of *bint ʿamm* marriage do not therefore show a maximal

[1] Rosenfeld, op. cit., p. 36.

exploitation of such marriages, but are made up of a combination of demographic and sociological factors. The variations in the rate of *bint ʿamm* marriage in the societies concerned, ranging from a maximum of 14 per cent in the Lebanese village of Juba to a minimum of 9·1 per cent in a Druze village, may be partly due to demographic factors. An expanding population will produce more cousins than a stationary or declining population. Higher standards of living, better nutrition, improved medical care, will lower child mortality, so that in due course more cousins will become available for matching. In any given number of marriages then, a higher percentage of cousin marriages might become possible, and while assuming the sociological factors affecting cousin marriage to have remained constant, its rate might rise considerably. In Israel a process of this kind was begun in the 1930's, when the country's economy first showed signs of all-round development, and may have come to fruition in the 1950's. The increased rate of cousin marriage under Israeli rule, reported by Rosenfeld and Cohen,[1] may be due in part to a changing demographic structure of the Arab population and not only to political factors, as claimed.[2] The

[1] H. Rosenfeld, op. cit., p. 40: '. . . . the increase of cousin marriage, especially for the present 18 to 39 year old generation, may point to a need for the internal solidarity of the kin in the non-kin oriented State, in which, as yet, the former have not become integrated'. A. Cohen, op. cit., p. 121, considers that the increase in *hamūlah* marriage is a partial manifestation of 'the revival of the *hamūlah* as a political unit', and that because of the first cousin's priority over more distant members this results in a higher rate of this type of marriage.

[2] Government of Palestine, *A Survey of Palestine* (Jerusalem 1946) vol. 2, pp. 705, 707, provides the basic data for a rough and ready calculation of this kind. The estimated total number of children borne by a Muslim woman in Palestine was in

1927–9 6·1; 1930–2 6·4; 1942–3 8·1

Of each 1,000 Muslim children the following numbers were likely to survive to the age of 15. In

1926–7 561; 1930–2 613; 1942–4 722

(The published table gives separate figures for males and females).

The number of children borne by a woman multiplied by the survival rate at the age of 15 gives us a rough idea about the number of marriageable children available in a Muslim family in Palestine (and Israel) at various times. (One must, of course, also add 15 years to the dates):

About 1942 3·4; about 1946 3·9; about 1958 5·8

This means, amongst other things, that in the relatively short period covered

differential general rates of cousin marriage cannot by themselves provide conclusive evidence.

In order to eliminate possible effects of demographic variations or change, one must calculate more specific rates of cousin marriage: to compare the number of cousins who married each other to the number of possible cousin marriages.[1] This has been done for a sample of the Negev Bedouin in the following manner. Using all the genealogical material I possessed, I tried to match all married males to any married father's brother's daughter who might be considered a suitable partner. The analysis of actual *bint ʿamm* marriages has shown that the approximate limitations were as follows. The woman should not be more than ten years younger or over five years older than her male cousin, neither of them should be mentally or physically incapacitated, nor should their parents have quarrelled. Differences in economic status proved to constitute no barrier to marriage, so there was no need to match the cousins in this respect. Obviously, an intimate acquaintance with the persons concerned might have shown additional insuperable obstacles to marriage and perhaps further reduced the number of possible matches. Table 17 sums up the result of the analysis of the 219 marriages of peasants and Bedouin about which I had the necessary details. Full results of the analysis are set out in Appendix 5.

TABLE 17

Marriage within the Section among peasants and Bedouin (by males)

Sector	*Possible Fa Br Da marriages*	*Actual Fa Br Da marriages*	*Specific rate of Fa Br Da marriages (%)*	*Other marriages in Section*
Peasants	25	15	60	8
Bedouin	17	10	59	1
Total	42	25	60	9

by our figures, a mere 16 years (1942–58), a man's choice of marriageable cousins had increased by approximately 70 per cent.

[1] This procedure has been suggested by E. L. Peters.

The number of cases is too small to be conclusive, but it suggests that there is very little difference between peasants and Bedouin in the overall rate of first cousin marriage.[1] It also shows that three-fifths of all possible cousin marriages do actually take place, a very high proportion considering the many possible objections and obstacles to any proposed marriage of this kind. The fact that some possibilities of *bint ʿamm* marriage remain unexploited suggests that there is no compulsion to arrange such marriages. The oft-repeated saying that a man has a right to his father's brother's daughter 'even when she sits astride a camel',[2] taking her to her bridegroom's tent, shows that a member of the section is thought to have prior claim to its women, but implies that it will not always insist on keeping them and may deploy them in marriage elsewhere. A man can do little to obtain his father's brother's daughter unless he is supported by his section. When a man of the Abu Qwēdar peasant group (Abu Rqaiq tribe) claimed his cousin's hand, her father demanded the exorbitant bride-wealth of IL. 12,000, over four times the average payment, and as the section did not support the suitor he had to relinquish his claim.

Once it has been established that *bint ʿamm* marriage is not obligatory but is voluntarily arranged among members of the section, the path has been cleared for an investigation into the interests that can be served by such marriages.[3] When looking closer at the various *bint ʿamm* marriages, one finds that they are employed dif-

[1] If calculated as a proportion of all marriages, the Bedouin rate of *bint ʿamm* marriage is 8·1 per cent, and the peasants' is about twice as high, 16·6 per cent. It appears that these figures mainly reflect a difference in demographic structure of the two sectors.

[2] *Ibn al-ʿamm, wa-lau min al-gamal biṭīḥha.* Similarly Musil, *The Manners and Customs*, op. cit., p. 137: 'Only the father brother's son can tie or unbind her.'

[3] The 'functions' of *bint ʿamm* marriage have been discussed by F. Barth, 'Father's Brother's Daughter Marriage in Kurdistan' (1954), p. 171: 'A pattern of father's brother's daughter marriage plays a prominent role in solidifying the minimal lineage as a corporate group in factional struggle.' This may be so, but the analysis of Bedouin society shows that this type of marriage does a number of other things besides, and also that it should be viewed in conjunction with the overall pattern of marriage. Rosenfeld, op. cit., p. 37: 'Close cousin marriage, and parallel cousin marriage especially, is the preferred marriage, primarily as it affords protection from property being taken out of the extended family and out of the lineage.' Rosenfeld's explanation cannot well apply in a society which gives daughters no share in the paternal inheritance, except in the special case of brotherless women.

ferently by Bedouin and peasants, in large and in small groups, and that in some cases sections deliberately refrained from contracting possible matches.

In the first section of this chapter it was shown how cousin marriage was used in a large section of the Bedouin group, the Abu Gweʿid, to enhance the clustering of men, and to score the lines along which they would in future branch out into separate sections. This group contracted five out of six possible patrilateral parallel cousin marriages, so it appears that their contribution to the political structuring must have been considered of critical importance. Similarly in Ṣarāīʿah core-group, the only suitable pair of parallel cousins have been married to each other. It will be recalled that these two core-groups live on the Plain, and lease land to a considerable number of attached peasant sharecroppers. They have to be on the alert and prepared to nip insurrection in the bud, and therefore are organized in small, distinct clusters of men. Whenever an emergency arises they can immediately mobilize for action and also link up in a predetermined manner with other similar clusters. This rigid order is similar to the organization of a military unit, in which sections of men combine into platoons, and in which the effectiveness of the whole depends on the way in which the smallest unit functions. Marriage among cousins, we have seen, helps consolidate the small clusters and to connect several clusters.

The third core-group of Abu Gweʿid tribe, the Maʿābdah of the Hilly Area, shows a different pattern: there only two out of seven possible cousin marriages have taken place. The Maʿābdah own little good farm land which they could profitably lease out, and are thus not encumbered with peasant sharecroppers. They do not need to pay constant attention to insubordination, and can indulge in a more spacious order, in which the section constitutes a sufficiently well-defined fighting group. The large sections do not employ patrilateral cousin marriage to accentuate the differentiation into clusters. It is highly significant how the alternative marriages of the five women who did not marry their father's brother's sons were arranged: while one of the women was assigned to an economic marriage link, all the remaining four were married into other sections. There are seven sections in the group, and linking them with each other required a considerable investment of marriages. Evidently this interlinking of one's section with other sections was considered so important that it took precedence over marriage in the section.

Men of the smaller one-sectioned Bedouin groups prefer to marry outside their groups, even where patrilateral parallel cousins are available. They need not be constantly prepared to deploy their power, and must rather rely on political alliance with core-groups to protect their interests *vis-à-vis* their sharecroppers. Therefore they do not form into clusters, and seek to strengthen their relations with a more powerful group. The group's marriages follow the dictates of these interests as can be seen in the case of the Abu Rafīʿa, of Abu Qrenāt tribe, illustrated in diagram 24.

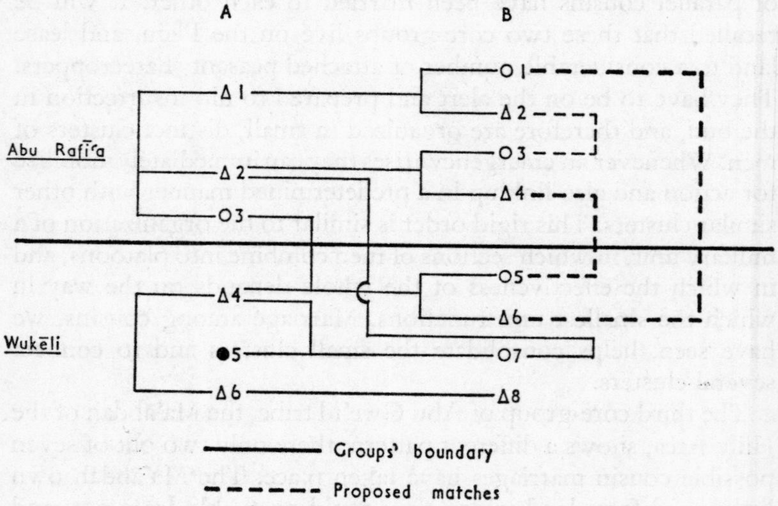

DIAGRAM 24

Marriage designs of Abu Rafīʿa Bedouin group

The Abu Rafīʿa group consists of three men, the two brothers Muḥammad (A1) and Sulimān (A2) and the latter's grown-up son Ibrāhīm (B4). When Ibrāhīm wished to get married in 1961, his father (A2) would not have his brother's daughter (b1), although she was nubile. Instead, he wanted Ibrāhīm to marry the daughter (b5) of his sister (a3), who had been married by exchange into the relatively large Wukēli group of Abu Rqaiq tribe. In exchange he planned to give his brother's daughter (b1) to his sister's son (B6), so as to continue and strengthen the relationship with the

Wukēli group. When the turn of his brother's young son (B2) to marry came in a few years' time, 'Sulimān would attend to his needs', I was told.

As it happened, Sulimān's designs clashed with those of the intended bride's section. The Wukēli are a larger group, where it becomes important for men to hold together in clusters and to exploit *bint ʿamm* marriage for this end. The bride's father's brother (A6) claimed her for his son (B8). The bride's father preferred to arrange the exchange with Sulimān (A2) to giving his daughter to his brother who would not be able to return a woman who could marry his son (B6). Therefore, he agreed with Sulimān that they should persuade his brother (A6) to forego his claim and to compensate him with a gift of money. The negotiations dragged wearily on for many months, and when I left the field the end was not yet in sight. Later I learned that Sulimān lost the race, and did not obtain the Wukēli girl for his son.

All Bedouin groups, it seems, desire a wide range of marriage links, but have to put preferential emphasis on one or the other kind of connection. The two large landowning core-groups had to make the most of their possibilities of patrilateral parallel cousin marriage, while the Maʿābdah preferred to strengthen the ties between the independent sections of the group. The small Bedouin group considers it most important to foster an alliance with a larger group. Matches between first patrilateral parallel cousins are, in the latter two groups, considered as less important.

The Abu ʿArār group, it will be recalled, stands halfway between Bedouin and landless peasants, politically. It has developed sections comprising a wider range of kin, including second patrilateral parallel cousins.[1] In this context, marriage between both first and second patrilateral parallel cousins falls within the section, and both kinds are employed for purposes of clustering. The remaining cousins are then usually directed to other sections of the group, to restore close kinship between them. In Abu ʿArār group nine marriages have been arranged within the sections; six of these are marriages between first patrilateral parallel cousins, and the remaining three between second patrilateral parallel cousins. Among the latter category there is one exchange marriage in the Khalāileh section, which could have been arranged between first cousins, but the section preferred to use it for binding together

[1] See diagrams 19 and 20.

its two clusters. This accounts for seven out of the eleven possible matches between first patrilateral parallel cousins; in three cases the women were linked to other sections of their own group, and in one case only was a woman given in exchange marriage out of the group in preference to marrying her father's brother's son. Clearly, marriage in this group also is subordinated to the interests of the members, and there is no sign that *bint ʿamm* marriage is preferred in its own right.

The sections of a large landless peasant group, like the Abu Ṣaʿalūk, subordinate themselves politically to the more inclusive co-liable group, and accordingly we should expect them to give their women to other sections of the group even where father's brother's sons are available. Yet three out of five possible *bint ʿamm* marriages have taken place. On closer scrutiny it appears that in all three cases the women have no brothers, and their marriage into other sections would thus not have constituted primary links for their agnates. In these circumstances, their father's brother's sons married them. But the two remaining women married, in fact, into other sections of the co-liable group. My record shows no marriage between second patrilateral parallel cousins for the living members of the group, while there are marriages between first and second cousins of other types. The latter renew connections between the sections, whereas the former would fall within the section.

In small peasant groups, and those comprising only one section, the frequency of patrilateral parallel cousin marriage is very high, as far as can be ascertained. In Abu ʿĀbed group (diagram 5), all three possible cousin marriages have been contracted. Among the Abu Shalẓam, a small group of Egyptian peasants, two marriages of second patrilateral parallel cousins were concluded, and these were the only close cousin marriages possible. In large peasant groups, in short, members tend to marry cognates or non-kin, while in small peasant groups there is a tendency to marry the *bint ʿamm* or another agnate. But in both kinds of group the reason for the marriage pattern is similar. In Chapter 5 it was shown that peasants marry within their groups in order to hold them together by means of kinship. This pattern of marriage is set while the group is small, so that no demands by outsiders for women of the group are established. In the smaller groups this pattern results in marriage of close kin. In larger groups, efforts are made to bring closer more distant sections and therefore marriage among close agnates decreases.

We have seen that the interests of several types of groups result in different patterns of patrilateral parallel cousin marriage, and that even where groups pursue a similar interest, difference in size alone can affect it. Clearly, then, *bint ʿamm* marriage cannot be treated as an isolated trait of Bedouin society, but must be seen in conjunction with the overall patterns of marriage.

All the interests served by marriages within the section are political, in the widest sense of the word, for they are concerned with the manner in which men combine in order to exert their joint power. Under close observation such a wide range of qualitatively different political interest appears, expressed in a variety of political structures, that one hesitates to subsume all of them under one term. Can a clearly-defined, active organization, such as the Ṣarāiʿah core-group's, be classed together with a loosely structured, leaderless and passive one, such as the Abu Ṣaʿalūk's? I believe it can and should be, for the different interests and structures are so many ways in which people adapt themselves to their particular position in a society in which resources are distributed unevenly. Each group occupies a specific position in regard to access to resources, manpower and relations with the outside world, and these differences are reflected in its political structure. These adaptations are not only mirrored in the political structure, but also have repercussions in other spheres of social organization, such as patterns of marriages, camps and ideological concepts. These ramifications may give a political structure a limited amount of stability, but it is essential to view each political structure as an adaptation to a contemporary situation, and to see that men can mould and remould their political organization to their requirements, within the limitations of their environment. Only thus can one understand the variety of political structures found within the narrow compass of one Bedouin tribe.

A section develops and branches out by slow degrees. There are no dramatic breaks or even formal intimations of separation. Men first become aware of a separation after it is well-nigh complete: when some men cease to consult their more distant agnates with regard to their marriage arrangements. Thus a section can imperceptibly branch out without members being aware of any fundamental change, as they go on living with the same people and continue to consider them their agnates. It is true that the interests of the separated sections may diverge, and they may even clash, but this does not annul their formal co-liability. In the relatively tranquil conditions of the Negev, the illusion that co-liability of the section and the co-liable group are identical can thus be maintained. Earlier it was seen that groups can co-operate in such weighty matters as blood-affairs only if they maintain close day-to-day relations between members. In some of the multi-sectioned co-liable groups the interests of sections may diverge, and they may drift apart in spite of the good relations between members. But members' belief in their co-liability may continue unshaken as long as it is not put to the test of reality.

An account was given me by the chief of the Abu Gweʿid on the manner in which groups branch out or split. It runs as follows:

> After five generations a family (*ʿēleh*, in literary language *ʿā'ilah*, here in the sense of section) can divide up by an announcement (*tuqsum bi-daʿwah*). Before that it cannot, nay is forbidden, to leave. It can also secede after four generations, but in that case the seceding section has to pay the main group a one-year old camel, which is called 'camel of the ancestor's death' (*bʿīr wafā al-gidd*). On the other hand one does not have to secede even after the passage of five generations. Thus our family (*ʿēleh*, here in the sense of co-liable group) exists already over ten generations, and all members pay the price of blood together.

This account shows how Bedouin conceive of the growth of a section into a co-liable group. Both groups are thought to fulfil identical tasks in blood disputes, and the same term is employed for both. The difference between section and co-liable group is seen to lie in that a group of four or five generations' depth can split only with difficulty, whereas a group comprising five or more generations is expected to split under certain conditions. In other words, agnates to the degree of second cousin hold together, and constitute a group with a common ancestor. When kinship becomes more distant, the section can branch out into several sections, but one of the new sections may decide to become a new co-liable group. The phrase 'ancestor's death' implies that it is not considered proper behaviour to split a group of close agnates. Where 'five'[1] or more generations have elapsed, i.e. where no

[1] It will be recalled that an ancestor removed to the fifth generation and

agnatic kinship can be traced between the sections making up the co-liable group, there a split may occur. It is not inevitable, for unless a group becomes too large and unwieldy, or a blood dispute shakes its foundations, it can continue to expand to include an indefinite number of generations. Bedouin theory, then, does not explicitly recognize separation of sections but explains how groups can split when they have become too large.

To what extent does Bedouin theory coincide with what actually happens? It will be our task now to examine this question. In some groups there occurs a development which may, at first sight, be thought to indicate an intermediate stage between separation and fission. This is the assumption by sections of a group of a separate patronym. Thus the Salīm section of the Abu ʿArār peasant group (section 1, diagram 17) has adopted the name of Ṭalaqāt and shed that of Abu ʿArār. Members gave this name when registered by the authorities. The name Ṭalāq appears nowhere on their genealogy, but one member of the section hazarded a guess that it was a nickname given to their ancestor Salīm. In contrast to the other sections of the ʿArarāt which derive their names from the father of the most influential cluster of men in each, the name Ṭalaqāt is that of an ancestor whose kinship position is unknown, who is thus common to, and equidistant from, all the section's members. It indicates corporate organization, which among peasants is generally found only in the framework of the co-liable group.

The trend of the Ṭalaqāt to differentiate themselves from the remaining Abu ʿArār may be due to a combination of two factors. Firstly, they are powerful: as one of the members put it, they 'now have over twenty men'. In fact, the section at present comprises only ten adult men as compared with the seventeen of the largest section of the group, and the larger number was only obtained by counting all males, including babes in their mother's arms. The implication is that the section was even now quite powerful, and that it would fully develop its considerable power potential in coming years. Thus the section had the principal prerequisite for becoming more independent of the rest of the group: a large number of males. The other factor was a murder which had

---

beyond has, in Bedouin genealogies, usually significance as an eponym, and not as a deceased kinsman.

remained unsolved and left a residue of dissatisfaction among the Ṭalaqāt. In 1950 Lāfi, a man of seniority of the Ṭalaqāt, surprised camel thieves in his camp at Buḥērah. The thieves shot and killed him and fled with their booty. The Abu ʿArār suspected Tarabīn al-Ṣāneʿ tribesmen of the robbery, and their chief, the late Muḥammad al-Ṣāneʿ, of having fired the fatal shot. The chief categorically denied the accusation. The ʿArarāt did not believe him but their elders preferred a peaceful settlement, so they agreed that the Tarabīn chief clear himself by swearing a solemn oath. When he had complied with this, there remained, according to custom, nothing for the ʿArarāt but to hold their peace; and to add insult to injury, they also forfeited the blood-price. The murder has remained unsolved to this day. The Ṭalaqāt felt that their interest had not been safeguarded by the co-liable group, that had they been on their own they would have acted more manfully and also extracted blood-payment from the Tarabīn al-Ṣāneʿ.

That the assumption of a separate patronym does not necessarily lead to fission is shown by the Abu Gweʿid. Several generations ago, according to hearsay evidence, there was only a Raḥāḥlah group, and Raḥāl was 'the ancestor of all'. Then a man called Gweʿid,[1] 'who lived at least five generations ago', and his descendants, separated from the Raḥāḥlah. Their section increased until it became larger than the Raḥāḥlah. The Abu Gweʿid and Raḥāḥlah have remained members of one co-liable group to this day, and pay blood-money together (*ḥaṭṭīn qirsh al-damm*). Indeed, the Abu Gweʿid have become more numerous than the mother group and comprise 20 out of the 36 adult men in the group. The difference may seem absolutely small, but proportionately it is large (one-quarter more).

What this represents is not a stage in an inexorable process of fission, but a specific political alignment in a group, brought about by the distribution of power between sections. In the cases of both the Abu ʿArār and Abu Gweʿid, new patronyms were assumed by large sections whose interests were not fully satisfied by co-operation with the rest of the co-liable group. Being large, they could push separation a degree further and engage in separate political activity, while still continuing to enjoy the advantages of membership in the co-liable group. Obviously when this happens the corporate identity of the co-liable group is

[1] Some members of the group give the names as Raḥāil and Gaʿad.

strained, and there is always a risk that this might lead to fission. Therefore small sections will not venture to detach themselves. Neither will a number of small sections be able to coalesce as a sub-unit in a wider co-liable group as a rule. They can align in various ways in political affairs but cannot create a separate corporate identity *vis-à-vis* other sections of the group. Members of a single large section, on the other hand, also share in the obligations of close kinship, and thus can differentiate themselves from the other sections. Large sections are also better able to shoulder the risks attending a greater degree of separation. This does not imply that they wish to forgo the advantages of political co-operation in a large co-liable group, and they will do their utmost to avoid a complete break. The separation of the Abu Gweʿid from the Raḥāḥlah took place at least three generations ago,[1] and still the two constitute one co-liable group and have recently contributed jointly to the payment of blood-price.

In 1960 a man of Ṣarāiʿah Bedouin group, of Salāmah section,[2] maltreated his wife, who later died of the injuries sustained. The dead woman's father, who had married the culprit's sister in exchange, claimed her blood, and some Bedouin speculated on whether the Gmiʿān section would not take the opportunity to split the co-liable group by making difficulties about paying their contribution to blood-money. The Gmiʿān section had been developing different interests from the Salāmah section, for instance it had specialized in camel-breeding and had fewer share-croppers than the dominant Salāmah section. The Salāmah section was apprehensive of a split if the co-liability of the group was put to the test. Finally the dispute was settled amicably by allowing the dead woman's father to retain his wife without paying bride-wealth. In this manner the Salāmah section circumvented the need to collect blood-money and the risk of a subsequent split. A member of the section told me afterwards that the woman's father had 'agreed to forgive and took no blood-price (*diyah*) for the death of his daughter. He is a good man, and also wealthy, so he does not need the money.' Here again the wish to keep the co-liable

[1] Jaussen, op. cit., p. 410, lists the Abu Gweʿid as one of the divisions of the Ẓullām, so that the separation must have occurred before his time, the turn of the century. Unfortunately, Musil's more detailed list, in *Arabia Petraea*, vol. 3, pp. 38–41, of 1898, omits the Abu Gweʿid tribe altogether.

[2] See diagram 16.

group together is evident. As it turned out, the Gmiʿān section had no intention to secede and continued to take part in the Ṣarāiʿah's political manœuvres *vis-à-vis* the Abu Gweʿid.

Among the landless peasants, such as the Abu Ṣaʿalūk, there occurred no cases of separate patronymic names within the co-liable group. We have already learned that in these groups sections do not act as political units apart from the co-liable group. The sections are too much interlaced by kinship ties to set themselves apart easily.

Bedouin realize that when sections of a group have grown apart, a serious blood-dispute may precipitate fission, and the Ṣarāiʿah case has shown that they act accordingly. The following account of secession, by a Bedouin, brings out this point:

> When a man is killed, all the culprit's section must flee, but whoever does not wish to share in the blood-price together with the rest of the section gives the dead man's agnates a camel called 'camel of sleep' (*bʿīr al-nōm*),[1] and then does not flee. He can sleep securely in his tent. This rule applies only to men who are separated from the murderer by four or five generations [i.e. second patrilateral cousins and more distant kinsmen]. They still have to contribute their share of the blood-price. After doing such a thing, these men cannot remain in the family [here in the sense of co-liable group], as they deserted it at a critical moment.

Needless to say, there are no authenticated cases of payment of the 'sleeping camel', for today avengers are not allowed to retaliate, and the culprit's agnates do not flee. Notables intervene immediately, seek a truce from the avengers, and initiate negotiations between the parties. Still, vengeance killings have occurred when negotiations ceased, but only the culprit in person has been attacked.

Secessions occur from time to time,[2] and proceed according to customary protocol. The split is publicly proclaimed in the guest-tents of several notables. Both parties are represented and make the announcement in a prescribed formula:

[1] According to ʿĀref, *Qaḍā*, pp. 78–9, members of the sixth and seventh generation pay the 'camel of sleep'. Other accounts are again different. See Jaussen, op. cit., p. 160; G. W. Murray, *Sons of Ishmael* (London 1935) p. 204.

[2] There have been no recent secessions in Abu Gweʿid tribe, but I obtained information on two secessions in the Qderāt tribal group, in the Hawāshlah and Abu Ṣulb Bedouin groups.

We have seceded (*ṯlaʿna*). You shall not bring for me [a contribution to blood-price], nor shall you bring me [ask me to contribute]. I shall bring [share responsibility] neither for your stolen property nor for your slain (*mā bagīb mālak al-mashlūl u-ghulāmāk al-maqtūl*).

Two 'guarantors' (*kafīl*) are appointed to bear witness to the secession. This is a clear and complete renunciation not only of co-liability but also of other forms of co-operation, and henceforth the two groups go their separate political ways.

The Abu Ṣulb Bedouin of the Qderāt tribal group had split during the last years of British rule. In 1950 most of the members of one group, the Awlād Saʿad (literally children of Saʿad) registered with Abu Rqaiq tribe, to which the Abu Ṣulb had originally been affiliated,[1] while most of the other group, the Awlād ʿĪd, registered with al-Aʿsam, another Qderāt tribe (see diagram 25). During the 1961 parliamentary elections a quarrel broke out between men of the two groups, and in the ensuing scuffle one of the Awlād ʿĪd men received a superficial cut. Whenever blood is shed, compensation must be paid. The representative of the Awlād Saʿad met the other group a month later to settle the blood-price. According to customary procedure the elder of the Awlād ʿĪd at first demanded a very large indemnity and then agreed to omit varying amounts in honour of God, the Prophet, notables, the mediators and other guests. No-one hinted at the co-liability, or 'agnation', that had formally existed between the two groups as a ground for reducing the amount. The split was irrevocable, and to recall a previous condition of unity now broken would have exacerbated matters.

A split does not always develop as a result of growth and over-expansion of the co-liable group. A very serious blood dispute can also be the direct cause of a split. In the case of the Maʿābdah referred to above,[2] a man's crimes broke up his section, but the co-liable group did not become involved and persisted. Among the Abu Ṣulb, the appalling misfortunes of one member caused a further rift of the Awlād Saʿad.

Gadūʿ Abu Ṣulb (D1) was 'haunted by bad luck', as one man put it. Time and again he became involved in bloodshed. In a brawl with the Hawāshlah group in 1951, he broke a man's hand.

[1] Musil, *Arabia Petraea*, vol. 3, p. 38, lists the Abu Ṣulb under the Ḥrēzāt, today's Abu Rqaiq tribe.

[2] See p. 199.

After the dispute had been settled the other sections of the Awlād Saʿad would have no more of him. The Salāmah section (B1) had emigrated to Sinai, although it had not formally seceded. Mrēziq and Sulimān sections (B2 and B3) formed a separate co-liable group, while the culprit's close kin, the Salmān section (B4), now had separate and sole liability.

Two years later Gadūʿ accidentally shot a woman of the Fregāt

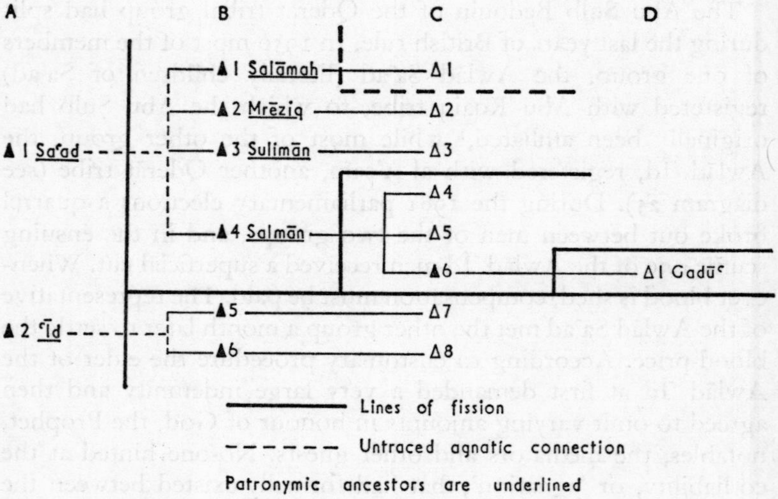

DIAGRAM 25

Splits in the co-liable group: Abu Ṣulb Bedouin

group, who later died of her wounds; in consequence of which the Awlād Salmān also expelled him. They 'exposed him to the sun', as Bedouin put it (*shammasūhu*). After the formal expulsion they could not be held responsible for any further misdeeds of Gadūʿ. In 1957, while employed as a watchman, he was attacked by an Abu Gabr man (peasants of Hazail tribe) and shot him in self-defence. The Abu Gabr obtained no blood payment for their victim, while Gadūʿ served three years in prison and in 1961 was back among the Bedouin. He was directed by the Administration to remain in Ẓullām territory, so as not to expose himself to the Abu Gabr's vengeance. At about that time the Abu Gabr group began to suspect that Gadūʿ's agnates were still maintaining relations with him, and that therefore their announcements of expulsion had been deceptive.

The Abu Ṣulb group had first split because it had grown too large. Presumably the split came out into the open during a blood dispute, but I have no data on this. The second split in Awlād Ḥamad group, which we are now considering, occurred because the members felt unable to share responsibility for a confirmed mischief-maker any longer, but as Gadūʿ had not offended against his agnates they remained loyal to him. Thirdly, he was later formally expelled by his agnates from their co-liable group because they could not afford any further payments of blood-money for his accidents. Their obligations as kinsmen were not affected. Abu Ṣulb group, then, illustrates three types of secession, each qualitatively different from the other.

Members of a co-liable group are only rarely called upon to co-operate in blood disputes. Most of their joint activities take place in day-to-day situations, and they cannot but become aware of divergences in their interests. Yet fission usually takes place only after the group has been involved in payment of blood-money. Here the Bedouin account of secession provides a clue. According to what they say, it is not a refusal to contribute to the blood-price which provokes a split, for it is assumed that the seceders have paid their share. Rather, secession is brought on by a reluctance of part of the group to contribute to payments. This reluctance destroys something which is of crucial importance to the continued existence of the association: the moral conviction of members of its usefulness and efficacy. The 'desertion' for which part of the group has to leave is due not to a failure in fulfilling formal obligations, but to a breakdown in moral commitment.

Although blood disputes occur only infrequently, they constitute the 'ultimate obligation' of members of a co-liable group, one of the ideological cornerstones of their corporate association. The ideology of the corporate association is not just a simplified explanation of its constitution, a reflection of relationships on the ground. It also provides the thread of continuity, which allows men to combine in the same convenient framework for a series of actions, and for a variety of activities. Whenever men engage in an activity within this framework, there is the underlying assumption that the collaboration is possible because they must also co-operate in blood disputes. Failure to collaborate in everyday activities does not constitute a direct assault on the corporation, as it does not question its ideological basis. Therefore, although it undermines the corporate organization, it does not bring on a crisis, particularly as most activities entail the co-operation of only part of the members. The crucial test of a co-liable group occurs therefore in a blood dispute, when all members have to fulfil their ultimate obligations of co-liability. Reluctance to comply with these obligations shows members that their interests have diverged to such an extent that the ideological basis of co-operation has crumbled, and that therefore a realignment must take place.

Fission is quite another matter in a land-hungry peasant group, like the Abu Ṣaʿalūk. Such a group bears the seeds of destruction in itself, as it were, because it cannot properly execute its ultimate obligations to defend and avenge its members' lives. Yet up to a point the intricate interlacing kinship and its attendant obligations hold the group together and enable it to present a corporate front to the outside. But kinship ties cannot ramify indefinitely; sooner or later a stage is reached when it becomes impossible for each member to span the whole group with his kinship ties. A split in the group does not usually occasion a major disturbance, nor does it have to follow in the wake of a blood dispute, and members of the divided groups can continue friendly relations and intermarry. Thus among the Qlāʿīah peasants living in Ẓullām territory, the Ḥawāmdeh group left the Zabārqah about 15 years ago 'because of a minor dispute in the family', to become a separate co-liable group. 'We seceded because we had grown big enough,' explained a member of the group. Several years later the ʿAwābdeh followed suit. Neither group ceased to collaborate harmoniously with the other Qlāʿīah groups in the political field.

APPENDIX 1

Employment of Bedouin outside the Reservation (1960–2)

		days
I. 1.	About 400 Bedouin were employed during the greater part of the year on Jewish farms, except when cultivating their land and changing from summer to winter camps. Thus they spent about 9 months on outside employment (a labour month is calculated at 25 days). 400 men working 225 days each:	90,000
2.	During four months of the citrus season (January to April) an average of 600 Bedouin were employed, including most of the men working outside the reservation for the best part of the year. 200 men working 100 days each:	20,000
3.	During two months of the cotton season (September to October) an average of 600 Bedouin were employed, including most of the men working outside the reservation for the best part of the year. 200 men working 50 days each:	10,000
	Total working days:	120,000
II.	The total of labour days accumulated by Bedouin in the course of a year, divided by the 300 days of a labour year, gives the average number of Bedouin engaged on outside work during a year:	400 *men*
III.	The male Bedouin working population (men between the ages of 14–45) in 1960 is estimated at about 3,100. The proportion of men engaged on work outside the reservation at a time is then approximately:	13 %

It should be noted that this is an approximate calculation, based on informed estimates.

APPENDIX 2

Land cultivated by Bedouin tribes (1958–9)

Tribe (confederational affiliation in brackets)		*Persons (12.1958)*	*Area cultivated (in dunams)*	*Arable held in lease (in dunams)*
1. Living on own land				
Abu Rbēʿah	(Tiāha)	1,984	70,514	9,500*
Abu Qrenāt	,,	1,356	51,629	3,250*
Abu Gweʿid	,,	1,067	36,680	3,000*
al-Aʿsam	,,	904	29,139	—
al-Asad	,,	256	1,918	250
	All	5,567	189,880	16,000
2. Owning some land, supplemented by leased land				
Abu Rqaiq	(Tiāha)	2,800	89,254	12,675
Hazail	,,	1,874	21,441	23,264
	All	4,674	110,695	35,939
3. Living on leased land				
Qderāt al-Ṣāneʿ	(Tiāha)	1,059	23,645	28,000
ʿAṭaunah†	,,	525	8,680	11,500
al-ʿOqbi	,,	512	7,835	7,000
Afēnish	,,	304	4,670	5,600
Abu ʿAbdūn	,,	166	1,989	2,600
Abu al-Qiʿān	,,	197	6,475	12,000
Abu Blāl	(Tarabīn)	298	3,569	5,000
Nigmāt al-Ṣāneʿ	,,	203	4,425	8,000
Abu Sriḥān	,,	110	1,580	3,200
Abu ʿAmrah	,,	78	1,216	2,215
Masʿudīn	(ʿAzāzmah)	1,031	28,531	12,540‡
	All	4,483	92,615	97,655
Total		14,724	393,190	149,594

* This area was held by the tribe's chief without formal lease.

† The chief's family still own about 1,000 dunams in the reservation.

‡ The tribe cultivated part of an additional area leased as pasture; therefore the cultivated area exceeds the arable area leased.

APPENDIX 3

Averages of land cultivated and animals owned by Bedouin and peasant groups in Abu Gweʿid tribe

Group	*Adult males (over 18)*	*Average area cultivated, including land leased out of Group (in dunams)*	*Proportion of land held on lease from source outside the Group (%)*	*Average number of: Camels*	*Sheep*
Peasants:					
Abu Ṣaʿalūk	22	164	67	½	5
Abu Mṭēr	20	141	56	½	9
Abu ʿArār	18	182	40	½	9
Abu Gāmeʿ	18	85	65	½	3
Katnāni	7	235	52	½	4
Abu ʿĀbed	7	179	100	½	3
Abu Kush	7	161	47	1	13
Abu Ghnēm	6	125	80	½	2
Abu Shalẓam	5	156	87	½	3
Bedouin:					
Abu Gweʿid	36	179	9	1½	17
Ṣarāiʿah	33	228	3	2	10
Maʿābdah*	31	118	3	1	5
Far'aunah	19	85	9	1	7
Bdūr	16	100	34	1+	9
Abu Msāʿad	8	294	—	¼	1
Abu Wādi	7	150	—	2	16
Zaghārnah	5	80	—	1	1
Zbēdi	5	114	61	½	3

* Including the Far 'aunah and Abu Wādi groups, who are also listed separately.

APPENDIX 4

Marriages of males in peasant and Bedouin co-liable groups (N = 219)

Group	*Within group* FaBrD	*Within group* Others	*Within group* All	*Out of Group* In Rubaʿ	*Out of Group* Out of Rubaʿ	*Out of Group* All	*Total*	*As percentages* In group	*As percentages* Out of group
Peasants:									
Abu ʿArār	6	18	24	—	—	12	36	67	33
Abu Ṣaʿalūk	3	9	12	—	—	3	15	80	20
Abu Ġāmeʿ	3	6	9	—	—	15	24	38	62
Abu ʿĀbed	3	1	4	—	—	5	9	44	56
Abu Shalẓam	—	2	2	—	—	4	6	33	67
Totals	15	36	51	—	—	39	90	57	43
Bedouin:									
Abu Gweʿid	5	6	11	5	21	26	37	30	70
Maʿābdah*	2	9	11	2	20	22	33	33	67
Ṣarāiʿah	1	4	5	4	12	16	21	24	76
Abu Msāʿad	—	—	—	1	5	6	6	—	100
Bdūr	—	1	1	6	8	14	15	7	93
Abu Dghēm	1	1	2	4	2	6	8	25	75
Abu Wādi	1	—	1	2	3	5	6	17	83
Zbēdi	—	—	—	—	3	3	3	—	100
Totals	10	21	31	24	74	98	129	24	76

* Excluding Abu Wādi.

APPENDIX 5

Marriage in the Section (by males)

Group	*Father's brother's daughter marriage* Possible	*Actual*	*%*	*Other marriages in section*
Peasants:				
Abu ʿArār	11	6		3
Abu Ṣaʿalūk	5	3		—
Abu Gāmeʿ	6	3		2
Abu ʿĀbed	3	3		1
Abu Shalzam	—	—		2
All	25	15	60	8
Bedouin:				
Abu Gweʿid	6	5		—
Maʿābdah*	7	2		—
Ṣarāiʿah	1	1		—
Abu Msāʿad	—	—		—
Bdūr	—	—		—
Abu Dghēm	2	1		1
Abu Wādi	1	1		—
Zbēdi				—
All	17	10	59	1
Total	42	25	60	9

* Excluding Abu Wādi.

Bibliography

The following list includes books and articles cited in the text, as well as a number of other books bearing on the Negev or Bedouin. The literature on Bedouin is very extensive, but only a small proportion of it deals with the Negev Bedouin. Fuller bibliographies are to be found in Graf, Granqvist, Henninger and Patai.

Periodicals are cited by abbreviated titles, as listed on p. ix. Daily newspapers quoted in the text are:

Haarets *Haarets Daily Newspaper*, Tel-Aviv (published in Hebrew).
Maariv *Maariv*. Evening paper, Tel-Aviv (published in Hebrew).

ʿĀREF, ʿĀREF AL-. *Al-qaḍā bain al-badu* (Bedouin justice) (= *Qaḍā*), Jerusalem 1933.

—— *Taʿarīkh Bīr al-Sabaʿ wa-qabāilha* (History of Beersheba and its Tribes) (= *Taʿarīkh*), Jerusalem 1934.

ASHBEL, D. *Aklim Erets-Israel le-ezoreha* (Regional climatology of Israel), Jerusalem, 1951.

ASHKENAZI, T. *Tribus semi-nomades de la Palestine du Nord*, Paris 1938.

AVRAMSKI, S. *Parashah be-toldot ha-Negev* (A chapter in the history of the Negev), *ʿIyunim*, vol. XI, Jerusalem 1953.

AYALON, D. & SHINAR, P. *Milon ʿArvi-ʿIvri* (Arab-Hebrew Dictionary), Jerusalem 1947.

AYOUB, M. R. 'Parallel Cousin Marriage and Endogamy', *SWJA*, XV, 1959, pp. 266–75.

BARTH, F. 'Father's Brother's Daughter Marriage in Kurdistan', *SWJA*, X, 1954, pp. 164–71.

—— *Nomads of South Persia: The Basseri Tribe of the Khumseh Confederacy*, Oslo 1961.

BEFU, H. & PLOTNICOV, L. 'Types of Corporate Unilineal Descent Groups', *AA*, LXIV, 1962, pp. 313–27.

BEN ASSA, B. J. 'Vital Statistics concerning Tuberculosis among Bedouin Tribes in Southern Israel', *IMJ*, XIX, 1960, pp. 69–73.

BEN-ELKANAH, S. *ʿArab al-Tiāha* (The Tiāha Bedouin, unpublished manuscript, 1961.

BLISS, F. J. *The Religions of Modern Syria and Palestine*, Edinburgh 1912.

BURCKHARDT, J. L. *Notes on the Bedouins and Wahābys*, London 1830.

COHEN, A. *Arab Border-Villages in Israel*, Manchester 1965.

CONDER, C. R. *Tent Work in Palestine*, London 1887.

DOUGHTY, C. M. *Travels in Arabia Deserta*, London 1921.

EPSTEIN (ELAT), E. *Ha-beduim ḥayyehem u-minhagehem* (*The Bedouin, their life and customs*), Tel Aviv 1933.

EVANS-PRITCHARD, E. E. *The Nuer: A Description of the Modes of Livelihood and Political Institutions of a Nilotic People*, Oxford 1940.

—— *The Sanusi of Cyrenaica*, Oxford 1949.

FINN, J. *Stirring Times or Records from Jerusalem Consular Chronicles of 1853–1856*, 2 vols., London 1878.

FORTES, M. *The Dynamics of Clanship Among the Tallensi*, Oxford 1945.

—— *The Web of Kinship Among the Tallensi*, Oxford, 1949.

—— 'Time and Social Structure: An Ashanti Case Study', *Social Structure: Essays Presented to A. R. Radcliffe-Brown*, Oxford 1949.

—— 'The Structure of Unilineal Descent Groups', *AA*, LV, 1953, pp. 17–51.

—— 'Descent, Filiation and Affinity: A Rejoinder to Dr Leach', *Man*, LIX, 1959, pp. 193–7, 206–12.

FYZEE, A. A. A. *Outlines of Muhammadan Law*, 2nd ed., Oxford 1955.

GENNEP, A. VAN. *The Rites of Passage*, London 1960.

GLUCKMAN, M. 'The Village Headman in British Central Africa', *Order and Rebellion in Tribal Africa*, New York 1963.

GLUECK, N. *Rivers in the Desert*, London 1959.

GOITEIN, S. D. & BEN SHEMESH, A. *Ha-mishpat ha-muslimi bi-Medinat Israel* (Muslim law in Israel), Jerusalem 1957.

GRÄF, E. *Das Rechtswesen der heutigen Beduinen*, Walldorf-Hessen 1952.

GRANOTT, A. *The Land System in Palestine*, London 1952.

GRANQVIST, H. *Marriage Conditions in a Palestinian Village*, 2 vols. Helsingfors 1931–5.

HENNINGER, J. 'Die Familie bei den heutigen Beduinen Arabiens und seiner Randgebiete', *IAE*, XLII, 1943.

HEYD, U. *Ottoman Documents on Palestine 1552–1615*, Oxford 1960.

ISRAEL (Army). *Beduei ha-Negev bi-Medinat Israel* (The Negev Bedouin in the State of Israel). Tel-Aviv 1954.

—— (Central Bureau of Statistics). *Statistical Abstract of Israel*. Jerusalem, published annually. Vol. 9 (1957–8) to vol. 15 (1964).

—— *Government Yearbook*. Jerusalem 1962.

—— (Meteorological Service). *Climatological Norms. Part I: Rainfall*, 2nd ed., Tel-Aviv 1958.

—— (Ministry of Foreign Affairs). *The Arabs of Israel*, Jerusalem 1961.

JARVIS, C. S. *Yesterday and Today in Sinai*, Edinburgh 1933.

JAUSSEN, A. *Coutumes des Arabes au pays de Moab*, Paris 1908.

KENNETT, A. *Bedouin Justice*, Cambridge 1925.

LÉVI-STRAUSS, C. *Les structures élémentaires de la parenté*, Paris 1949.

LEWIS, I. M. *A Pastoral Democracy: A Study of Pastoralism and Politics among the Northern Somali*, Oxford 1961.

MAINE, H. *Ancient Law*, London 1906. (Published 1861).

MALINOWSKI, B. *A Scientific Theory of Culture and Other Essays*, Chapel Hill, N. Carolina, 1944.

—— *Magic, Science and Religion and Other Essays*, Boston 1949.

MARX, E. 'Beduei ha-Negev' (Bedouin of the Negev), *New East*, VII, 1956, pp. 89–98.

—— 'Ha-mivneh ha-ḥevrati shel Beduei ha-Negev' (The social structure of the Negev Bedouin). *New East*, VIII, 1957, pp. 1–18.

—— 'Dfusei nisu'in shel Beduei ha-Negev' (Marriage patterns of the Negev Bedouin), *New East*, XIII, 1963, pp. 395–409.

MITCHELL, J. C. *The Yao Village*, Manchester 1956.

MONTAGNE, R. *La civilisation du désert*, Paris 1947.

MURDOCK, G. P. *Social Structure*, New York 1949.

MURPHY, R. F. & KASDAN, L. 'The Structure of Parallel Cousin Marriage', *AA*, LXI, 1959, pp. 17–29.

MURRAY, G. W. *Sons of Ishmael: A Study of the Egyptian Bedouin*, London 1935.

MUSIL, A. *Arabia Petraea*, 3 vols., Vienna 1908

—— *The Manners and Customs of the Rwala Bedouins*, New York 1928.

NIEBUHR, C. *Travels through Arabia and other Countries in the East*, 2 vols., Perth 1799.

Notes and Queries on Anthropology, 6th ed., London 1954.

OPPENHEIM, M. VON. *Die Beduinen*, Leipzig 1939–52. 3 vols. To be continued.

PALESTINE. *General Bulletin of Monthly Statistics*. 'Survey of Social and Economic Conditions in Arab Villages, 1944', X (1945–6), parts published from July 1945 to March 1946.

—— *Report on Immigration, Land Settlement and Development*, by J. H. Simpson, H.M.S.O., Cmd. 3686. London 1930.

—— *A Survey of Palestine*, Jerusalem 1946. 2 vols. & supplement.

PALMER, E. H. *The Desert of the Exodus*, 2 vols., Cambridge 1871.

PATAI, R. 'Cousin-Right in Middle Eastern Marriage', *SWJA*, XI, 1955, pp. 371–90.

PEAKE, F. G. *A History of Jordan and its Tribes*, Coral Gables, Florida 1958.

PETERS, E. L. 'The Proliferation of Segments in the Lineage of the Bedouin of Cyrenaica', *JRAI*, XC, 1960, pp. 29–53.

—— 'Aspects of Rank and Status Among Muslims in a Lebanese Village', *Mediterranean Countrymen*, ed. by J. Pitt-Rivers, Hague 1963.

RADCLIFFE-BROWN, A. R. & FORDE, D. (eds.) *African Systems of Kinship and Marriage*, Oxford 1950.

RANDOLPH, R. R. *Elements in the Social Structure of the Qdiiraat Bedouin*, Houston, Texas 1963.

RASWAN, C. R. *The Black Tents of Arabia*, London 1936.

RAVIKOVITCH, S. 'The Aeolian Soils of the Northern Negev', Israel, Research Council. *Desert Research: Proceedings, International Symposium . . . 1952*. Jerusalem 1953.

ROBINSON, E. *Biblical Researches in Palestine: A Journal of Travels in the Years 1838 and 1852*. 3rd ed., 3 vols. London 1867.

ROSENFELD, H. 'An Analysis of Marriage and Marriage Statistics for a Moslem and Christian Arab Village', *IAE*, XLVIII, 1957, pp. 32–62.

RUPPIN, A. *Syrien als Wirtschaftsgebiet*, Berlin 1917.

SACHAU, E. *Reise in Syrien und Mesopotamien*, Leipzig 1883.

SCHAPERA, I. *Migrant Labour and Tribal Life*, Oxford 1945.

SCHIFF, Z. 'The Pros and Cons of the Military Government', *New Outlook*, v, 1962, no. 3, pp. 64–71.

SHIMONI, Y. *ʿArvei Erets-Israel* (The Arabs of Palestine), Tel-Aviv 1947.

SHUQAIR, Naʿūm. *Ta'arīkh Sīnā al-qadīm wal-ḥadīth wa-gighrāfīathā* (History and Geography of ancient and modern Sinai), Cairo 1916.

SMITH, W. ROBERTSON. *Kinship and Marriage in Early Arabia*, ed. by S. A. Cook, London 1903.

TRISTRAM, H. B. *The Land of Israel*, London 1866.

VOLNEY, C. F. *Voyage en Égypte et en Syrie pendant les années 1783, 1784 et 1785*. 2 vols. Paris 1825.

WEBER, M. *The Theory of Social and Economic Organization*, London 1947.

Index